Mode 2

T·E·A·C·H·E·R'S B·O·O·K

Paul Radley · Chris Millerchip

Nelson

Thomas Nelson and Sons Ltd
Nelson House Mayfield Road
Walton-on-Thames Surrey
KT12 5PL UK

51 York Place
Edinburgh
EH1 3JD UK

Thomas Nelson (Hong Kong) Ltd
Toppan Building 10/F
22a Westlands Road
Quarry Bay Hong Kong

© Collins ELT 1989

First published by Collins ELT 1989
Reprinted in 1991
ISBN 0-00-370452-1

This edition first published by Thomas Nelson and Sons Ltd 1993

ISBN 0-17-556703-4
NPN 9 8 7 6 5 4 3 2

Printed in Hong Kong

Other components of this course are:
Student's Book,
Workbook,
Cassettes.

Acknowledgements

The authors would like to thank the following people for their help in the
preparation of this book:

Friends and colleagues at Bell College, Saffron Walden, for their advice
and encouragement.

Jania Barrell of Bell Language Institute, London, for her assistance with
the recorded materials.

Gail Langley, Jan Keane and David Bull for their advice and suggestions.

The publishers would like to thank the following for agreeing to participate
in recorded interviews:

Jim Leach (26); Sir Richard Attenborough (43); Fionnoula Coulson (59);
David Job (74); Michelle Quacoe (91); Denis Lyons (106).

CONTENTS

INTRODUCTION

Mode 2 is the second part of a three-part course specifically designed for secondary schools. It is a challenging course, and the presentation and use of the communicative approach is highly motivating. The twin objectives of *Mode* are (1) to enable students to communicate effectively in English in situations relevant to their lives, and (2) to provide students with a thorough grounding in the main structures of English and their most common uses.

Mode 2 continues the two-level approach begun in *Mode 1*, which provides a practical answer to the problems arising in mixed ability classes. There is, however, as one would expect, more emphasis on learner independence, on skills development and on vocabulary development.

The components

Student's Book
Teacher's Book
Workbook
Cassettes (3)

The full colour **Student's Book** presents new language in a variety of situations relevant to young adults. In addition, all the language is practised and developed in contexts familiar to students.

Mode 2 contains numerous texts and dialogues for language presentation and a wealth of authentic reading texts taken for the most part from English newspapers and periodicals. Unscripted recorded material appears at regular intervals.

The 35 units are arranged in blocks of five, each block followed by a section devoted to revision and grammar. The first and third units in each block present and practise new language, the second and fourth units provide skills practice based on topical reading and listening material, and every fifth unit concentrates on a different aspect of writing.

The **Teacher's Book** contains page-by-page teaching notes, transcripts of the cassettes and keys to all Student's Book and Workbook exercises. The notes are presented clearly and, where possible, all the information relevant to a particular lesson is accessible at a glance. The Teacher's Book deals with the various exercises and materials in the order in which they are to be taught, providing notes detailing teaching procedures. Throughout, these procedures are intended as suggestions and are by no means the only ways of teaching target language.

The **Workbook** is far more than just a homework book. It does contain reinforcement exercises, of course, but there are, in addition, a large number of more motivating exercises. These include authentic reading passages linked to the themes of the Student's Book, additional reading texts which provide a background to British culture and vocabulary development exercises. A Grammar Summary is found after each block of five units in the Workbook.

The **Cassettes** contain all the listening material for *Mode 2*, in the order in which it appears in the Student's Book. The tapescripts are numbered consecutively throughout the course. The recordings offer a broad range of styles and become more demanding as the course progresses. Cassette 1 is approximately 90 minutes long, Cassettes 2 and 3 about 60 minutes. Complete transcripts appear in the Teacher's Book, except where a complete version appears in the Student's Book. Language repetition sections are recorded twice, the second time with pauses allowing students to repeat the phrases. These are indicated in the teaching notes by the presenter's words *Now listen and repeat*.

The syllabus

The three-year syllabus is based on the Council of Europe's Threshold specification. The progression is steep but thorough, it being assumed that the majority of learners already have some knowledge of English. Their passive knowledge is exploited by the course, which draws on a wide vocabulary right from the start. They are not expected to be able to produce any language themselves, however, without a presentation and controlled practice session. Structures and functions are presented, practised and developed in interesting and varied contexts relevant to the target age group.

The grammatical framework of the language is not neglected; as well as Grammar Focus sections in the Student's Book, which train students to analyse grammatical rules and patterns for themselves, the Workbook includes Grammar Summaries for reviewing and consolidating the language introduced in each block of five units. The extent to which these are treated as reference pages for students or brought into classroom time for class study is a matter for the teacher.

Skills work is systematically developed in the skills units and a complete Glossary is included at the back of the Workbook.

Timing

Since different exercises take different lengths of time in different classes, it would be foolish to specify how long each unit should take. However, as a very rough guide, teachers can reckon on each block of five units taking between ten and twelve hours. The seven blocks can then be covered in about eighty hours.

It is generally the case that skills pages take longer than presentation pages; however, teachers should be wary of hurrying a presentation lesson or letting a skills lesson go on too long. In timing their lessons, teachers should bear in mind that all Workbook activities are intended for home study, and that Supplementary Exercises are optional. In addition, the Revision Focus and Grammar Focus sections may be completed at home or left to a later date for revision, e.g. at the end of the year.

Methodology

Mode is a communicative English course with a structural framework. The materials and activities are student-orientated within the practical constraints of the classroom. Each new function, structure and lexical area is developed and practised within the realm of students' own experiences or expectations.

Mode 1 dealt in a practical way with the problem of mixed-ability classes. *Mode 2* continues this two-level approach, containing a section of Supplementary Exercises integrated into the main course. These can be used to occupy advanced students in class time while slower students are dealing with the basic material. Alternatively, they can be used as extension material where the teacher feels the class would benefit from further practice. These exercises are designed to stretch students' understanding of the target language while not introducing any new structures or functions.

The new-language units (the first and third of each block of five) break down into three sections as they did in *Mode 1*. Each section follows the same methodology of *presentation and focus – practice – development*. The presentation material, chosen for its potential interest to students, usually contains a topic-based text designed to stimulate discussion and motivate students. This is followed by Language Focus (including oral drilling) to isolate the relevant structure or function. The practice and development sections are also set within the students' own experiences, and provide realistic situations for speaking, writing, listening and reading.

Authentic reading and listening materials are used in the skills lessons to help students develop the skill of dealing with 'real' English. The tasks are carefully chosen to guide and train students to read and listen for specific information or overall gist.

The writing programme addresses a variety of kinds of writing and provides students with a comprehensive guide to the skills they require at this level.

A regular Vocabulary Development section in the skills units is aimed at making students aware of how to increase their vocabulary and how to organise their learning.

Mode provides students who plan to continue their studies to a higher level with a solid and thorough grounding in the language.

Classroom management

Integration of exercises

Relevant Workbook activities and Supplementary Exercises are indicated in the Student's Book by numbered symbols; red triangles for the Supplementary Exercises and grey tabs at the bottom of the right-hand page for the Workbook exercises. The Workbook activities are intended for individual work at home, although sometimes classroom preparation is advised. Supplementary Exercises, as has already been explained, are primarily designed to occupy faster students. However, as students begin to assume greater responsibility for their own learning, they should be given the choice of whether to stay with the main exercise or go on to the more demanding Supplementary Exercise.

Vocabulary presentation

Vocabulary is introduced through both the Student's Book and Workbook in *Mode 2*. Especially valuable is a regular Vocabulary Development section found in the second unit of each block of five. As students progress with learning the language, they need to build up and expand their active vocabulary. Each Vocabulary Development section illustrates a different way of recording and learning new vocabulary. Students should find these sections useful, especially if they continue to use the ideas systematically.

Pair work and group work

In trying to make activities resemble real life communication, pair work and group work are a vital part of the course. The fact that the teacher then is no longer the focus of attention means that students are less inhibited, they have more chance to speak and the teacher has the opportunity to monitor all students' progress. Students also tend to become more responsible for each other's learing, helping rather than intimidating other students. Classrooms are not always set out in the best way to facilitate pair work and group work, but it is usually possible with a minimal amount of reorganisation of the seating arrangements to make the activities possible. Even asking alternative rows of students simply to turn round and talk to the student behind is one way of dealing with the problem.

Students who have been encouraged to work in pairs or groups in the first year should now be ready to respond to the increasing demand on them to express their personal views on the topics and arguments which appear in *Mode 2*, and to be less teacher-dependent.

Classroom language

It should be possible to use English almost exclusively in the classroom at this stage but there are still times when a quick explanation in the mother tongue or translation can be beneficial and time-saving.

These guidelines may help you:

- Use the mother tongue if an activity is in danger of coming to a stop or when students are becoming confused or discouraged.
- Translate single items of vocabulary where deduction methods fail or where not understanding a key word is impeding an activity. Have the purpose of the activity at the front of your mind: Is it a vocabulary exercise or is communication the objective?
- Where an activity has complicated instructions, get students to read the instructions to themselves and then to explain either in English or in their own language what they have to do.

Using the cassettes

Mode 2 contains both scripted, controlled dialogues and natural, unscripted conversations. For the unscripted conversations, the speakers at the recording sessions were given a subject and various points to cover and then asked to improvise. These recordings are therefore complete with the *ums* and *ers*, mistakes and repetitions, which make up any natural conversation. Students need to become less dependent on listening to set dialogues and more confident about their ability to cope with everyday language of English-speaking people. The intention is to give them this confidence by carefully controlling the kind of activity that students are expected to carry out while they are listening.

These comments are intended to help you to enable students to approach listenings with confidence and success:

- Explain the purpose and importance of the listening activities to the students. Point out that in their own language they do not even try to grasp everything that is said, but listen out for relevant facts. This is what we are training them to do in English.
- Always introduce them first to the subject they are going to listen to. It is very difficult to follow a conversation or broadcast without knowing what it is about. It takes time to realise what is going on. Students are not able to do this *and* carry out a task expected of them.
- Make sure students are relaxed and ready to listen, and that they understand what they are expected to do while they listen. Each time they listen, they are only required to do a limited task. Tell them not to try to do more than this.

Teaching procedures

Presentation of new language

Target structures and functions are presented through dialogues and semi-authentic articles ranging in subject matter from planning a party and Maradona to UFOs and starvation in Africa.

Detailed presentation procedures are outlined in the teaching notes. Students are introduced to the material by looking at the pictures and heading and identifying the situation and characters. Set up an initial discussion by providing key words of vocabulary and guiding students in the right direction. This introduction should only take a matter of minutes.

Students will still need reassurance about their ability to handle the text with confidence. Remind them that on a first reading or listening they should aim to get the general meaning but not to get bogged down in details and then lose the thread. As students accept this procedure, they become more relaxed about approaching presentations and therefore more receptive. This approach prepares them for when they are confronted with an English-speaking situation outside the classroom.

Standard comprehension exercises follow the presentation. These are designed to consolidate students' grasp of the situation and characters as well as their understanding of the language. In addition, there is usually a supplementary exercise for more-advanced students while the other students are dealing with the basic exercise. The Supplementary Exercises do not repeat the ground covered in the main exercises and so both can be attempted by students. Leave the class check of the comprehension exercises until everyone has completed them.

Always give students plenty of opportunity to ask questions about the presentation text, whether on points of language, vocabulary items or plot.

Language Focus section

Each presentation passage is followed by a Language Focus section. Here the new structure or function is isolated and drilled on cassette. It is best to use the cassette for drilling so that the model does not vary.

Always give students a chance to ask questions about the structure or function and its use. Avoid giving a full-scale grammatical analysis of the structure at this point. Grammar notes, which you may want to use as the basis for your explanation once the section has been completed, are included in the Workbook (but not in the teaching notes). They provide useful reference for students.

The Language Focus section usually includes a second exercise based on the target language. Where this is the case, checking of the exercise can be done with the cassette, and the tapescript is in two parts: firstly, a language drill and secondly, a listening task.

Language practice

The activity following the Language Focus section provides guided practice of the target structure or function in a realistic context. Detailed teacher's notes on the teaching procedure accompany each activity. By now, students should be becoming familiar with the new language. If not, you may need to extend language practice by, for example, providing new substitution tables on the board, or by going back to the presentation section and reminding students of the new language in its original context.

Language development

The final part of each new-language section is a development phase, where students use the target structure or function in a freer activity, set in a relevant context. Detailed notes on procedure are given in the teaching notes.

This latter stage is the most student-centred one, where the teacher's role is to set up the activity and let the students get on with it. The teacher should circulate discreetly, making notes of anything which may need to be raised with the class after the activity. Discourage students from turning to you to resolve the slightest problem, such as an item of vocabulary, but do act as a monitor to solve any disputes if necessary. Make it clear to students that they are on their own and that you won't be there to help them outside the classroom.

Skills work

The other units in each block of five units are skills development lessons, concentrating on reading and listening (second and fourth units), and writing (fifth unit).

The reading texts in the second unit all contain authentic, unmodified texts dealing with a wide range of topics from nuclear power to apartheid. Each reading section starts with a warm-up session to lead the students into the subject and get them thinking about it. The text is followed by vocabulary exercises and activities involving the students in discussion about subjects which are often quite controversial. It is hoped that students will be sufficiently motivated to take a very active part in these lessons. Each reading skills lesson finishes with an authentic listening section. These unscripted conversations are linked with the readings and are usually with people closely involved with the subject covered in the readings.

Every fourth unit has an episode of the serial *Moondown*, a fictional story of two young journalists' involvement with the unlawful dumping of nuclear waste from a nuclear power station. Each episode consists of two parts; the first part is a text which is also recorded on cassette, while the second part is only on cassette. Students are thus prevented from reading too far ahead. The readings are followed by vocabulary exercises and comprehension activities.

The fifth unit of each block is a specific skills section. These units cover aspects of writing such as formal and informal letter writing, summary writing and composition writing. Each unit contains a sample of the kind of writing in question, notes on what is required for that type, and a section of guided writing practice.

Revision Focus

These lessons consist of a series of exercises, including role plays and listening activities, which consolidate students' knowledge of the target structures and functions introduced in the preceding block of five units. Each Revision Focus section includes a pronunciation exercise. Detailed notes on teaching procedure are given in the teaching notes.

Grammar Focus

These sections provide formal grammatical work based on the structures and functions introduced in the preceding block of five units. Students are encouraged throughout to reflect on the rules governing English and to try to work them out from carefully chosen exponents. This will give them a deeper understanding of what they are learning than will simply being told what the rules are.

Refer students to the relevant Grammar Summary in the Workbook when they have completed a Grammar Focus section. The Grammar Summaries are intended to be a simple reference covering the main features of the structures presented in *Mode 2* rather than to act as a complete grammar. Encourage students who are interested to buy a comprehensive grammar book.

Pronunciation

Correct pronunciation is an essential part of language speaking. Work on pronunciation regularly during the year, devoting a few minutes at the beginning of each or every other lesson to a particular lexical area or structure. Concentrate on pronunciation when checking through students' answers to vocabulary preparation exercises in the Workbook. If you and your students are familiar with phonetic script, encourage them to use the phonetic transcription of new words in their dictionaries to help them work out how words are said. Encourage them to listen to authentic English whenever they can, directing them to international radio broadcasts, films and undubbed television programmes.

Pronunciation exercises are included in each Revision Focus section. These concentrate on some problems commonly faced by learners of English. They are not intended to provide a comprehensive pronunciation programme, however, but to raise students' awareness of particular points of English pronunciation.

Using the Workbook

The Workbook is an integral part of the course, providing not only homework, a grammar reference and a glossary, but also authentic reading texts to extend the reading done in the skills lessons, and passages on British life and institutions.

Using a dictionary

Workbook 2 contains a glossary of all the important new words introduced in *Mode 2*, referenced to where each word first occurs in the Student's Book. However, this is no substitute for a dictionary. Dictionaries are an invaluable language learning aid and well worth students' investment if they are not freely available in the school library. Students should be able to use a monolingual dictionary and be given the necessary help in order to be able to use it. Teachers should guide students in deciding which dictionary to buy.

PLAN

Unit	Focus	Title	Structures	Functions	Skills
1	Language revision	Fame	Present and past of be Simple present and simple past Present continuous	Exchanging personal information Talking about occupations Describing people	All skills
		Old friends	Simple present Present continuous Simple past Tag questions	Exchanging personal information Talking about what's happening now Talking about the past	All skills
2	Skills	Nice not easy Vocabulary Development Keeping a vocabulary book			Reading Listening
3	Language revision	Plans for Saturday	going to for future Present continuous for future can/can't let's have got to	Talking about future plans Talking about permission Making suggestions Talking about obligation	All skills
		Thief steals £20,000 from finance company	Simple present Simple past Past continuous Prepositions The time	Talking about daily routine Talking about the past Talking about continued past action Describing where things are Talking about the time	All skills
4	Skills	Moondown: Episode 1			Reading Listening
5	Skills	Informal Letters			Writing
Units 1–5			Revision Focus	Pronunciation (e)	Grammar Focus
6	Language	Where's the bank?	Imperatives will future	Giving directions	All skills
		Looking at photographs	too/enough with adjectives Indirect statements Modifiers – a bit, very	Expressing opinions Agreeing and disagreeing	All skills
7	Skills	The power seekers Vocabulary Development Noun–adjective links			Reading Listening
8	Language	Break away!	Present perfect Simple past	Talking about experiences	All skills
		Who can cycle faster?	Comparative adverbs	Comparing abilities	All skills
9	Skills	Moondown: Episode 2			Reading Listening
10	Skills	Formal Letters (1)			Writing
Units 6–10			Revision Focus	Pronunciation (a)	Grammar Focus
11	Language	Spending habits in Britain	Qualifiers – little, much, few, many, a lot of, plenty of Countable and uncountable nouns	Talking about quantity	All skills
		John Nutting: motorcycle journalist	Present perfect with for and since	Talking about experiences	All skills
12	Skills	Angry lesson on freedom Vocabulary Development Prefixes			Reading Listening
13	Language	War on Want	shall for offers	Making offers	All skills
		The good language student	Modal verbs – must, should, have to, mustn't, shouldn't, don't have to, needn't	Expressing obligation	All skills
14	Skills	Moondown: Episode 3			Reading Listening
15	Skills	Narrating			Writing
Units 11–15			Revision Focus	Pronunciation (u)	Grammar Focus
16	Language	Guide to the galaxy	Long numbers	Talking about statistics	All skills
		I used to live in Italy	used to didn't use to did you use to?	Describing previous habits and situations	All skills

Unit	Focus	Title	Structures	Functions	Skills
17	*Skills*	*Message in a bottle* *Vocabulary Development* *Synonyms and antonyms*			*Reading* *Listening*
18	*Language*	*Fed up!* *The history of hi-fi*	too much/many not enough *Countable and uncountable nouns* *Present and past passive*	*Complaining* *Talking about processes*	*All skills* *All skills*
19	*Skills*	*Moondown: Episode 4*			*Reading* *Listening*
20	*Skills*	*Summaries*			*Writing*
		Units 16–20 *Revision Focus* *Pronunciation (stress)* *Grammar Focus*			
21	*Language*	*You've got to do something* *Madonna*	(much) too + *adjective* Would you mind …? Do you think you could …? Could you …? *Relative clauses*	*Complaining* *Making polite requests* *Talking about people, places, things*	*All skills* *All skills*
22	*Skills*	*The dirty old man of Europe* *Vocabulary Development* *Adjective–adverb link*			*Reading* *Listening*
23	*Language*	*Close encounters* *Where shall we go?*	*Modal verbs* – must, may, might, can't *First conditional*	*Expressing certainty/ uncertainty* *Talking about future possibilities (1)*	*All skills* *All skills*
24	*Skills*	*Moondown: Episode 5*			*Reading* *Listening*
25	*Skills*	*Reports*			*Writing*
		Units 21–25 *Revision Focus* *Pronunciation (e)* *Grammar Focus*			
26	*Language*	*What happened to you?* *Leave this to me!*	*Past perfect* *Reported speech (present)*	*Talking about an earlier past* *Reporting what people say*	*All skills* *All skills*
27	*Skills*	*Fair play for women's football* *Vocabulary Development* *Using a monolingual dictionary*			*Reading* *Listening*
28	*Language*	*The Royal Family* *First aid*	*Reported speech (past)* *Second conditional*	*Reporting what people said* *Talking about future possibilities (2)*	*All skills* *All skills*
29	*Skills*	*Moondown: Episode 6*			*Reading* *Listening*
30	*Skills*	*Formal Letters (2)*			*Writing*
		Units 26–30 *Revision Focus* *Pronunciation (ou)* *Grammar Focus*			
31	*Language*	*Diego Armando Maradona* *Plans for the end-of-term party*	*Present perfect continuous with for and* since *verb + object + infinitive* (want, let, make)	*Talking about unfinished activities* *Talking about what you want, are allowed, have to do*	*All skills* *All skills*
32	*Skills*	*Playing with fire in the north frontier* *Vocabulary Development* *Lexical sets*			*Reading* *Listening*
33	*Language* *Language revision*	*I wish I looked like Tom Cruise* *Mistaken identity*	wish + *past tense* *Tenses*	*Wishing*	*All skills* *All skills*
34	*Skills*	*Moondown: Episode 7*			*Reading* *Listening*
35	*Skills*	*Compositions*			*Writing*
		Units 31–35 *Revision Focus* *Pronunciation (r)* *Grammar Focus*			

UNIT 1 *page 6*

Revision structures
Present and past of *be*
Simple present and simple past
Present continuous

Revision functions
Exchanging personal information
Talking about occupations
Describing people

Fame

● Students look at the pictures and the four charts, and using the bank of information they complete the charts. They should do this individually.

UNIT 1 *page 7*

1 Language Focus

● Students complete the questions in their books, working in pairs or small groups.
● Play the cassette and tell them to check their work as they listen. Go over the answers.
● Get students to listen to each question and repeat it in a chorus drill and then individually. The intonation in all of these questions should fall. Check also that students do not omit *'s* in *what's* and *where's*.

PRESENTER   Tapescript 1. Unit 1. Listen.
1   What's her name?
    What's his name?
2   When was she born?
    When was he born?
3   Where's she from?
    Where's he from?
4   Where does she live?
    Where does he live?
5   What does she do?
    What does he do?
6   What is she doing now?
    What is he doing now?
7   Why is she famous?
    Why is he famous?

Now listen and repeat

2 Information check

● In pairs, students can now ask and answer questions in order to check their answers to the chart exercise. Certain information will be obvious to them. Other points may remain unclear.
● Play the cassette as students check their answers. Then check the answers with the whole class.

Key
Top left
Name: *Steffi Graf*
Year of birth: *1970*
Nationality: *German*
Country of residence: *Germany*

Profession: *tennis player*
At the moment: *training to remain number one in the world*
Famous because: *won the Wimbledon championship for the first time in 1988*

Top right
Name: *Said Aouita*
Year of birth: *1960*
Nationality: *Moroccan*
Country of residence: *Italy*
Profession: *athlete*
At the moment: *training for the Olympics*
Famous because: *set the World 5000 metres record (1987)*

Bottom left
Name: *Madonna*
Year of birth: *1959*
Nationality: *American*
Country of residence: *America*
Profession: *pop singer/actress*
At the moment: *making a new record*
Famous because: *first ten records were number one hits*

Bottom right
Name: *Bob Geldof*
Year of birth: *1952*
Nationality: *Irish*
Country of residence: *England*
Profession: *rock singer*
At the moment: *making TV programmes about the Third World*
Famous because: *organised the Live-Aid concert*

PRESENTER   Tapescript 2. Unit 1. Listen.
This man's name is Bob Geldof and he's from Ireland but he lives in England now. He was born in 1952 and he first became famous when he performed with the band the Boomtown Rats and later when he organised the enormously successful Live-Aid concert, when famous rock stars gave a free concert in aid of people starving in the Third World. At the moment he's continuing his work for the Third World by making TV programmes about how aid money is spent.

And the next person is very famous indeed, in fact she's one of the most famous pop singers in the world. Her name's Madonna Louise Ciccone, otherwise known as Madonna, and she was born in 1959 in America, although her parents came from Italy. One of the reasons she is famous, is that her first ten records were all number one hits. She's also an actress and has appeared in several films including *Desperately Seeking Susan* and *Shanghai Surprise*. Madonna lives in America and at the moment she's making a new record there.

And this girl is a famous tennis player from Germany, where she lives with her family. She was born in 1970 and she's famous because she won the Wimbledon championship for the first time in 1988 at the age of seventeen. At the moment she's training for next year's Wimbledon. She wants to remain the number one player in the world. Her name is Steffi Graf.

This man set the world record for the 5000 metres in Rome just before the World Athletics Championships in 1987 and was the first man to go below 13 minutes. He lives in Italy but he is from Morocco and his name is Said Aouita, one of the most successful track athletes of all time. He was born in 1960 and at the moment he's training for the next Olympics, where he will probably take part in both the 1500 metres and the 5000 metres.

3 Famous people

1 Think of a famous person and find out information about him or her (it is important to choose someone your students have a chance of guessing!) or use the information below.

- Students ask you questions to find out the person's name. They may only ask questions to which you give *Yes* or *No* answers. (This game focuses on Yes/No questions with *be* and other verbs.)
- Students have a maximum of 10 questions. Mark on the board the number of questions asked so that students are careful in choosing questions. When they have asked 10 questions without guessing the name of the person, you have won and you reveal the person's identity.
- Continue the game for as long as you want, either by giving the Teacher's Book to a student to use the information below, or by allowing students to think of their own characters and playing the game in pairs or small groups.

Information

Name: Carl Lewis
Year of birth: 1961
Nationality: American
Country of residence: America
Profession: Athlete
Description: Tall, short black hair, brown eyes

Name: Nastassia Kinski
Year of birth: 1960
Nationality: American
Country of residence: America
Profession: Actress
Description: Medium height, fair hair, blue eyes

Name: Steffi Graf
Year of birth: 1970
Nationality: German
Country of residence: Germany
Profession: Tennis player
Description: Tall, fair hair, blue eyes

Name: Sting (real name Gordon Sumner)
Year of birth: 1951
Nationality: English
Country of residence: England
Profession: Rock musician/ actor
Description: Tall, fair hair, blue eyes

Name: Diego Maradona
Year of birth: 1960
Nationality: Argentinian
Country of residence: Italy (at present)
Profession: Footballer
Description: Short, short black hair, brown eyes

2 Students look at the picture and read the paragraph about Sylvester Stallone.

- Ask students in class about Stallone using the headings already looked at and write these on the board, i.e. *Name, Year of birth, Nationality, Country of residence, Profession, Famous because.*
- Students then choose a famous person (from the game or from their own knowledge) and write down the personal details under each heading. Students should work in pairs.
- They write a paragraph about their famous person using all the information and working alone. When they have finished, encourage them to exchange papers and make comments about each other's work.
- Circulate and help as necessary. Finally, ask a few students to read out their paragraphs.

WB 1.1
Key
Guess the occupations.

1 teacher	2 dentist	3 journalist
4 bus driver	5 shop assistant	6 secretary

Say where these people work.

1 bank	2 factory	3 hospital
4 restaurant	4 bookshop	6 office

WB 1.2
Key
Mary and John *are* English. Mary *is* eighteen years old and she *is* at school in Bristol. John *is* twenty-three 'I*'m* a teacher at a school in Bath,' says John. 'Our parents *are* teachers too, but we *are* at different schools. Mary *is* glad we *aren't* at her school!' 'It's very difficult when members of your family *are* teachers,' she says.

WB 1.3
Key

Isaac Newton	04.01.1643	Marie Curie	07.11.1867
Neil Armstrong	05.08.1930	Ronald Reagan	06.02.1911
Edmund Hillary	20.07.1919	Albert Einstein	14.03.1879
Napoleon Bonaparte	15.08.1769	Elvis Presley	08.01.1935

WB 1.4 and WB 1.5
Student's own answers.

WB 1.6
Key
1 My friend has got a *small black* dog.
2 It was a *hot sunny* day.
3 My sister's got *beautiful long black* hair.
4 We've bought a *big red Italian* car.
5 I made some *delicious strawberry* icecream.
6 I felt much better after a *nice hot* bath.
7 I've got a *comfortable black leather* armchair in my bedroom.
8 She was wearing a |*dirty old* pair of| jeans.
  |pair of *dirty old*|

UNIT 1 *page 8*

> **Revision structures**
> Simple present
> Present continuous
> Simple past
> Tag questions
>
> **Revision functions**
> Exchanging personal information
> Talking about what's happening now
> Talking about the past

In year 2 students have to listen to a dialogue without having the text in front of them. In this unit they are asked to find out some specific information by making notes about three people.

Old friends

- Students cover the bottom half of the page to conceal the dialogue script, and look at the note-sheets.
- Tell students they are going to write notes about the three people and elicit possible answers for some of the spaces. Emphasise, if necessary, that full sentences are not needed.
- Play the cassette once without students writing anything. Then let them discuss possible answers in pairs.
- Play the cassette a second time with students writing and checking. Allow them time to confer before playing the tape a third time or letting them read the dialogue.

 3   See Student's Book for tapescript 3.

Key

	ROBERT	KATE	SANDRA
School	● Junior school Stevenage	● Junior school Stevenage	✕
Family	● Brother, David ● David lives in London ● David is a journalist	● Lives in Leeds ● Father policeman	✕
University subjects	● French and Italian	● Chemical engineering	● Biology
Address	✕	✕	● 26, New Road
Phone	✕	✕	● 68492
Physical description	✕	✕	● Tall, slim, blue eyes

UNIT 1 *page 9*

4 Language Focus

- Students listen to the cassette and follow the exchanges in their books.
- Tell them to pay particular attention to the intonation of the exchanges which they can mark in their books, if they wish.
- Students listen and repeat, and then practise the exchanges, in the usual way: T–S, S–T, S–S, then simultaneously in pairs.

 4

PRESENTER	Tapescript 4. Unit 1. Listen.
GIRL	You live in Leeds, don't you?
BOY	Yes, that's right.
GIRL	Where did you go to school?
BOY	I went to school in London.
GIRL	What are you doing now?
BOY	I'm studying at the university.
GIRL	You haven't got any brothers or sisters, have you?
BOY	Yes, I've got a brother.
GIRL	What's he like?
BOY	He's tall and slim and he's got brown eyes.
PRESENTER	Now listen and repeat.

5 Questionnaire

- Most of the students in the class will already know each other. Explain that they are going to try to remember details about each other. If there are new students in the group, they can guess the answers and verify them afterwards.
- Explain the meanings of any of the categories in the left-hand column that students have difficulty with.
- Make sure they fill in the information before they speak to each other.
- Take the first sentence and practise the intonation of it with the students. Remind them to pay particular attention to this.
- Students read out their sentences to their partners correcting the information where necessary.

6 Find your partner

- Put students into groups of six or four (with yourself completing the last group if there is an odd number).
- Allocate a character secretly to each student and ask them to read and memorise their personal details card. They must not read anyone else's personal details, (you may wish to photocopy the cards and hand them out to each student individually).
- In pairs, students ask and answer questions about each other and note how many things they have in common, and what those things are.
- Students then talk to other members of their group, trying to find a partner with whom they have three things in common.
- The correct partners are:
  Tony and Sarah (*18, swimming, football*)
  James and Kate (*17, biology, two sisters*)
  Peter and Julie (*18, biology, reading*)
- Make sure students ask proper questions and do not simply show each other their cards.
- Afterwards, during feedback, highlight any problems you heard, e.g. intonation.

WB 1.7
Key
I don't like fish and chips.
They haven't got a new car.
She isn't going to a football match on Saturday.
We didn't see that film last week.
We weren't at school yesterday.
I'm not visiting my aunt this afternoon.
I can't ski very well.
It wasn't raining yesterday.
She won't be here at 2 o'clock.

WB 1.8
Key
Prince Philip is Queen Elizabeth's *husband*. He is William and Henry's *grandfather*. Diana is Charles's *wife* and William and Henry's *mother*. William is Zara's *cousin*. Anne is Queen Elizabeth's *daughter* and William and Henry's *aunt*. Zara is Queen Elizabeth's *granddaughter*. Edward is Charles's *brother* and William and Henry's *uncle*.

WB 1.9
Key
Michael got up at half past seven. He didn't go swimming. He got to school at nine o'clock. He didn't have much homework and he played football in the evening. He was at home at eight o'clock, had dinner, and watched television before he went to bed at ten o'clock.

WB 1.10
Key
1 I'll see you *at* ten o'clock *on* (or *next*) Saturday morning.
2 I'm going on holiday *next* week.
3 You'll have to hurry. The train leaves *in* five minutes.
4 I stayed with my family *last* (or *at*) Christmas.
5 She's arriving *at* eight o'clock *in* the evening.
6 They usually go to the cinema *on* Sundays.
7 The film starts *at* five o'clock *in* the afternoon.
8 He last saw his mother *in* 1987.
9 Her birthday is *on* March 21st.
10 They usually go to the mountains *in* winter.
11 I'll come *in* a minute.
12 You can't do two things *at* the same time.

UNIT 2 *page 10*

Nice not easy

1 *Skills Focus: Reading*

1 Students do not read the text before they discuss the questions.

● They can work individually, in pairs or in groups, or you can discuss the questions with the whole class or use a combination of these approaches. For questions 3–5, pool the students' ideas; there are no fixed answers to this exercise.

2 Explain the play on words in the title. Students may conclude quite rightly that her experience was a negative one. However, do not correct them if they think anything else as they will discover for themselves.

3 This exercise is designed to raise questions in the students' minds about the content of the text. It will also help with vocabulary.

● Students tick the jobs which they think it would be fair for an au pair to have to do. When they have finished, they compare and discuss their answers.

● Students read the article and cross those jobs Alison actually had to do. Finish with a class discussion on any differences.

Key

✕ wash the children	✕ vacuum or wash the floors
✕ dress the children	✕ take out and feed the dog
– prepare the dinner	✕ wash up the breakfast things
✕ prepare the lunch	– prepare the children for bed
✕ prepare the children for school	– make breakfast
– do the gardening	✕ make the beds
✕ set the table	✕ polish ornaments and wood
– do the shopping	✕ clean the toilets and bathrooms

4 Students first find the words or phrases in the text. This will help them deduce the meaning of the words from context. If necessary, do this part of the exercise with the whole class to ensure that students follow the correct procedure.

● Students match the words or phrases with their definitions on the right and check their answers in pairs before you go over the correct answers.

Key

drop everything	suddenly stop doing what you are doing
abroad	in a foreign country
land	arrive in an aeroplane
mould	type
stipulated	stated, said
housework	cooking, cleaning, etc.
involve	consist of
chores	boring or unpleasant jobs
mounted	increased
day off	free day
fee	sum of money
visa	legal residence permit

5 There are now two comprehension exercises. The first, after the vocabulary exercise, should be attempted by all students.

Key

1 True 2 False 3 True 4 False 5 True 6 False 7 True

Supplementary Exercise 1 *(SB page 118)*
This comprehension exercise is quite demanding and could be set for homework after students have had the chance to read the article again. Alternatively, you could give it to more-able students when they have finished the first exercise.

Key

1 They want to improve their language skills, find out about other cultures or become more independent.

2 The contract stipulated that she would care for the children and do *light* housework, but she discovered that she was responsible for most of the housework.

3 She could not eat without the woman's permission, she had no key, she had only one free evening and she had to come home before 10 p.m.

4 No, she found a better family later.

5 Because they can meet other au pairs and attend a language course.

6 Yes, they can.

UNIT 2 *page 11*

2 *Skills Focus: Listening*

1 Before they listen, make sure that students have read and understood all the questions. Explain any difficulties.
● Play the cassette once, or at most twice, and check the answers.

Key
√ How many au pairs do you employ?
How many employees have you got at this agency?
√ How old are your au pairs?
√ Where do they usually come from?
Do you have any au pairs from the United States?
√ Do you ever employ men or boys as au pairs?
√ What sort of qualities do you look for in a good au pair?
√ Do you ever have any problems with your au pairs?
How many au pairs leave before the end of their contract?
√ How long do they usually stay?
√ What sort of conditions do you offer your au pairs?

2 Students look at and try to remember/guess answers to the questions above.
● Play the cassette again, pausing to check the answers.

Supplementary Exercise 2 *(SB page 118)*
● This is slightly more demanding in that it requires students to make more-precise notes about the woman's answers. If you think that your class will have difficulty with the listening, do not attempt this exercise. Refer to the tapescript for the answers.
● As a follow-up, there is a role play in which students close their books and act out the dialogue between Paul and the woman at the au pair agency.

 **5**

PRESENTER	Tapescript 5. Unit 2. Listen.
PAUL	Tell me, how many au pairs do you employ?
WOMAN	When we're busy in the summer, usually fifteen a week.
PAUL	Mmm . . . What about this time of year?
WOMAN	Usually about one a day . . . this time of year.
PAUL	Uhuh . . . and where do they come from?
WOMAN	Only Western European countries, such as France, Italy, Germany, Sweden, etc.
PAUL	Mmm . . . and erm, do you ever employ men, or boys as au pairs?
WOMAN	We do, but we don't have much call for them.
PAUL	Mmm . . . right . . . and er . . . what are the age limits, how old are your au pairs?
WOMAN	Minimum age is 17, maximum age is 27.
PAUL	Right . . . now tell me what sort of qualities do you look for in a good au pair?
WOMAN	A good au pair should understand English, be able to speak a little English, come with good character references from teachers and neighbours, have a good family background, be willing to do some of the housework . . .
PAUL	Uhuh . . .
WOMAN	Help with the children . . . live as part of the family, but also able to maintain some privacy.
PAUL	Yes . . . I see . . . and do you ever have any problems with your au pairs?
WOMAN	Sometimes we do . . . the family usually expect too much of the au pair . . . and they don't very often practise their English if there is a problem . . .
PAUL	Mmm . . . And how long do they usually stay?
WOMAN	Between six months and a year.
PAUL	Uhuh . . . right, er, finally, um . . . what sort of conditions do you offer your au pairs?
WOMAN	The pocket money is £25 a week. They work five hours a day, six

	days a week . . .
PAUL	Uhuh . . . any evenings at all?
WOMAN	With baby-sitting, three to four evenings a week . . .
PAUL	I see . . .
WOMAN	They attend school and they get free board and lodgings.
PAUL	OK, thank you very much.

3 For the final activity, put students in groups and let them discuss the two questions about the agency.
● Allow a maximum of five minutes for this exercise and ask representatives of each group to report their conclusions to the rest of the class.

3 *Vocabulary Development*

● This section is aimed at helping students learn more efficiently by making them more responsible for their learning.
● Try to give your students freedom of choice about the kind of vocabulary books which are best for them. Spend time talking with them about their choices and give advice if they ask for it. You could take into class examples of each kind of vocabulary book to show them.
● It is worth spending time on this now so that your students feel that their input is important and that they should spend time regularly keeping these books up to date.
● It shouldn't need too much checking from you but it would be a good idea after a couple of weeks to take the books in and check that the students are working efficiently. After that use your discretion about how and when to check.

WB 2
Key
Suggested paragraph
A girl who works as an au pair can work five hours a day and six days a week. She must look after the children and help with light housework. She should have her own room. It is necessary to be able to speak some English. The family will not pay for the journey to England and will not give an au pair girl money to study in England and buy clothes. Girls under 17 years of age can't be au pairs. Girls coming from EEC countries have to have a passport or identity card in order to come into the country. If an au pair has any problems when she is in England, she can go to the Citizens Advice Bureau.

UNIT 3 *page 12*

Revision structures
going to for future
Present continuous for future
can/can't
let's
have got to

Revision functions
Talking about future plans
Talking about permission
Making suggestions
Talking about obligation

Plans for Saturday

1 Students cover the dialogue, look at the photos and talk about the people, telling you what they can about them.
- Students guess what sort of things the people might be planning to do on Saturday.
- Write the three headings on the board and tell students to close their books.
- Tell students to write notes (not sentences) for each heading and play the cassette.

Key
1   Robert's plans:
    going to buy birthday present for Pete
    lunch with Kate
    going to cinema
    going to club
2   Kate's plans:
    going to town
    lunch with Robert
    going to cinema
    going to club
3   Sandra's got to:
    go to the dentist
    go to grandmother's for lunch
    stay at home in evening and talk to Nigel

2 When students have finished, let them compare their answers, look at the dialogue and listen to the cassette again to check.

⏴ 6 ⏵   See Student's Book for tapescript 6.

UNIT 3 *page 13*

1 Language Focus

Students listen to the exchanges and follow them in their books. They then listen and repeat. Give them time to practise: T–S, S–T and S–S.

 7

PRESENTER	Tapescript 7. Unit 3. Listen.
KATE	So, what are you doing on Saturday, Robert?
ROBERT	I'm going to buy a birthday present.
KATE	Let's meet for lunch.
KATE	We're having lunch in town on Saturday.
SANDRA	I can't go to the club.
SANDRA	I've got to go to the dentist.
PRESENTER	Now listen and repeat.

2 Roleplay

1 Divide the class into groups of three (if a group of two is needed, omit character C for that group).
● Before they begin, look at the dialogue again and highlight the questions that Kate and Robert asked. Tell them you want them to ask similar questions.
● Go round the groups while they are doing the role play, monitoring their progress without interfering in the activity. Deal with any points of difficulty in a feedback session afterwards.
2 The writing activity may be done in class or for homework.

3 Questionnaire

1 Go through the questionnaire by getting some students to read the questions out loud. Explain any vocabulary.
● Look at the possible answers. Tell them to write the appropriate answer in the column *YOU*.
● Then they ask another student the questions and fill in the answers in the second column. Make sure all pairs are asking and answering and not just copying from each other.
2 For the writing exercise, remind students of the linkers *both . . . and . . .*, and *but*.
● To shorten the time this exercise will take, tell students to choose two questions to which their answers are the same and two where they differ. Ask them to write only about these.
● As a lengthier exercise, you may like to prepare a class survey of the answers. Students will need vocabulary such as: *everybody*, *some people*, *a few people*, *nobody*.

WB 3.1
Key
1 '*How far* is London from Manchester?' 'About 100 miles.'
2 '*Where*'s Cathy?' 'She's at school.'
3 '*Whose* book is this?' 'It's mine.'
4 '*How long* does that film last?' 'About two hours.'
5 '*How much* does it cost?' '£5.'
6 '*What* time is it?' 'It's 2 o'clock.'
7 '*When* did you go to the dentist's?' 'Yesterday.'
8 '*Why* didn't you phone me?' 'Because I lost your number.'
9 '*How* do you travel to school?' 'By bicycle.'

WB 3.2
Students' own answers.

WB 3.3
Key
1 This is John's book, *isn't it?*
2 You've got a bike, *haven't you?*
3 They're going to the cinema, *aren't they?*
4 It's Friday tomorrow, *isn't it?*
5 David speaks French, *doesn't he?*
6 She can come to the swimming pool, *can't she?*
7 He's got to go to the dentist, *hasn't he?*
8 They like reading, *don't they?*
9 Susan went to France, *didn't she?*
10 Paul was in London yesterday, *wasn't he?*

UNIT 3 *page 14*

Revision structures
Simple present
Simple past
Past continuous
Prepositions
The time

Revision functions
Talking about daily routine
Talking about the past
Talking about continued past action
Describing where things are
Talking about the time

Here, students have the chance to practise the use of the tenses in a realistic communicative context. *Identify the thief* concentrates on the time, prepositions, simple present and simple past. The past continuous comes up in the game, *Alibis*.

Thief steals £20,000 from finance company

- From the headline, elicit what the article is about.
- Students read the article and check their guesses. Give help with any difficulties they have before telling them to do the *true* or *false* exercise.

Key
1 False   2 False   3 True   4 False   5 False

4 Language Focus

This section gives students examples of the questions they need to ask in 5, *Identify the thief.*
- Students listen to the cassette, following the questions in their books.
- They listen and repeat, and then practise in the usual way: T–S, S–T, S–S, then simultaneously in pairs. When they are asking the questions confidently, go on to 5.

PRESENTER   Tapescript 8. Unit 3. Listen.
What does Betty do at the company?
What time does Delia start work?
What time does Frank have lunch?
What time does Eric finish work?
Where's Colin's office?
Has Alice got the keys to the safe?
What was Eric doing from 12 o'clock to 1 o'clock?

Now listen and repeat.

UNIT 3 *page 15*

5 Identify the thief

- Divide the class into threes.
- Tell each Student A, B and C to read the relevant paragraph and fill in their chart with all the information that they can and complete the office plan by putting the names they have in the relevant offices. They must be very careful to put in all the information they have.
- Point out that all the information in the paragraphs is true.
- They then ask each other questions to fill in all the other information in the chart and on the plan. Tell them to use the questions they practised in Language Focus but tell them that these are not the only questions that they can ask. They should ask questions in turn.
- When they have all finished you may supply the solution if they haven't managed to.
- If students have difficulty with this exercise, go through the chart and office plan with the whole class.

Key

- You may need to give the following hints:
  - a The theft did not occur before 12.00.
  - b Only one person stole the money.

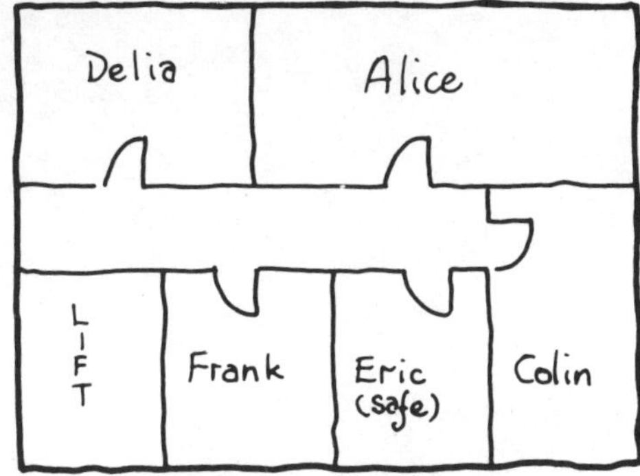

Solution
Colin is the thief – he had keys to the safe and between 12.10 and 12.20 he was the only person in the office apart from Alice, who was on the phone to her sister and had the door to her office closed. Colin could see who came and went as his office had a clear view of the corridor.

Name	Alice	Colin	Frank	Betty	Delia	Eric
Job	Director	Accountant	Post boy	Alice's secretary	Advertising manager	Sales manager
Work timetable Starts work: Has lunch: Finishes work:	9.00 1.00– 5.00	9.00 1.00–2.00 5.00	9.15 12.00–1.00 5.15	9.15 1.00–2.00 5.15	8.45 12.00– 4.45	8.45 (9.05) 12.00–1.00 4.45
Position of office:	Opposite Eric Next to Delia	Next to Eric	Between Eric and lift	Alice's office	Opposite lift Next to Alice	Next to Colin Next to Frank Opposite Alice
Keys to safe:	√	√	×	√	×	√
Other relevant information:	Phoned sister, door closed 12.00–12.20 Discovered theft at 12.30		Had lunch with Eric	Went out 12.10–12.20 for paper	Saw Betty go out at 12.10 Lunch in pub	20 mins late for work Had lunch with Frank Safe in Eric's office

6 Alibis

- Students read the rules of the game. Check their understanding by asking one student to explain the rules to the rest of the class in his or her own words.
- An alternative procedure to the one in the book, and which works well with more advanced students, is to divide the investigators into two groups and have them interrogate the two suspects at the same time. They then exchange information at the end of the interrogation and find any discrepancies. This version is slightly more difficult.
- It is important with either version that the two suspects are not permitted to communicate before the two interrogations are complete!
- If you wish to help the interrogators, you can give them an idea of things that typically students do not think of when they prepare their alibi, e.g.:
  - clothes they were wearing.
  - which floor the flat they visited was on.
  - who paid for meals, tickets, etc.
  - how much bills, tickets, etc. were.
  - what the weather was like.

WB 3.4
Key

Where do you live?
Have you got any brothers or sisters?
Hold old is she?
Can you play football? (or any game other than tennis)
Which class are you in?
What's your favourite subject?
Do you like English? (or other subject, or other activity, etc.)
What are you doing this evening?

WB 3.5
Student's own answers.

WB 3.6
Key

Joe Cocker *is* one of the most famous white blues singers in the world. He *comes* from Sheffield in England, but he *lives* in the USA now. He *started* singing when he was 18 years old, while he *was working* as a gas-fitter. His first important record *was Mad Dogs and Englishmen*, which he *recorded* in 1970. For a number of years Joe Cocker didn't *make* many appearances in public because he *had* an alcohol problem but last year he *made* a very successful tour of Europe. He *won* an Oscar for his song for the film *An Officer and a Gentleman* and another of his records, *You can leave your hat on*, from the film *9½ Weeks, became* very popular all over the world.

Moondown: Episode 1

Skills Focus: Reading and Listening

Moondown is a serialised story in seven episodes about two young people who work for a small local newspaper, the *Westfield Gazette* in Westfield, a town on the east coast of England. Near the town there is a nuclear power station called Moondown. Cathy and Pete, the two young people, get caught up in a scandal regarding the dumping of nuclear waste in the sea.

Each episode consists of a listen-and-read section and this is followed by a listening part not accompanied by text. The idea is to provide stimulating listening practice and it also prevents students from reading too far ahead in the story!

1 Students look at the three questions at the beginning of the episode.
● Tell students to read the whole episode quickly, including the newspaper article, but not to stop to try to work out the meaning of every word.
● Discuss the answers to the questions with the whole class.
● They now read the episode again while they listen to it on cassette.

Key
1 Thriller.
2 Cathy Edwards is a reporter and Pete Chisman is a photographer. They work for the *Westfield Gazette*.
3 Moondown is a nuclear power station on the coast near Westfield.

 9 See Student's Book for tapescript 9.

UNIT 4 *page 17*

2 This concentrates on vocabulary in the newspaper article which is more difficult than the rest, which should not present too many problems.

- Students look through the newspaper article and find the words. They write the line number of each word in the gap provided.
- Students then try to fit the same words into the new context of the sentences below.
- They should now have a clearer idea of the meaning of the words. If they still do not understand the words, they can check with another student or look them up in a monolingual dictionary.

Key

scare *1*
increase *11*   waste *20*   main *22*   below *30*
dumping *19–20*   power station *8–9*   fear *16 (feared 24)*   off *20*
danger *31*   matter *34*   poor *7*

1 scare   2 dumping   3 increase   4 below
5 main   6 power station   7 waste   8 off
9 danger   10 matter   11 poor   12 fear

3 Exercise 3 gives a series of comprehension questions on the episode for the students to answer. They can refer back to the text while they are doing this exercise.

Key

1 The *Westfield Gazette*.
2 Friday (afternoon).
3 Cathy's office at the *Westfield Gazette*.
4 Reading a newspaper article.
5 No, he isn't at first.
6 An increase in cancer cases in a village in northern Spain.
7 Because Pete isn't interested in the article.
8 Yes, he is.
9 Both are on the coast, both are fishing villages and they both have a nuclear power station nearby.

4 Students attempt to do this first without referring to the text.

Key

1 False   2 True   3 True   4 True   5 False   6 True   7 False
8 False

Supplementary Exercise 3 *(SB page 118)*
- This exercise can be given as an alternative to the previous two exercises or as an extra exercise for more-able students. These extra exercises should always be used when and how you think best.

Key
Westfield:
It's a small town on the East Anglian coast of England.
There's a nuclear power station near the town.
It's main industry is fishing.

El Garbo:
It's a fishing village on the north coast of Spain.
Fishing and tourism.
There has been a 40 per cent increase in cancer cases in the last ten years.
The power station opened fifteen years ago. They dump nuclear waste in the sea.

Cathy Edwards:
She's a reporter for the *Westfield Gazette*.
She finishes work at five o'clock.
She seems to have a strong character ...

Pete Chisman:
He's a photographer for the *Westfield Gazette*.
He seems to have a weaker character than Cathy ...

5 There is now the listening part of Episode 1 without a text for the students to follow. Tell students to read the multiple choice statements before they listen to the cassette.
- Play the cassette allowing students a chance to do the exercise adequately. Students discuss their answers before listening again.

Key
1 b   2 b   3 a   4 a   5 c   6 a   7 a   8 b

Supplementary Exercise 4 *(SB page 118)*
- Tell students to listen to the dialogue again and then try to complete the paragraph. Play the tape a second time so they can check their answers.
- A number of answers are possible, provided the meaning accords with the cassette.

Key
Cathy *phones* Pete because she has something *important* to show him. She arranges to *meet* him at the *Promenade Cafe* at *eight o'clock*. She has received *a letter* about *Moondown*. She doesn't know *the name* of the person who *wrote the letter* but she believes it is *genuine*. Pete is not really *convinced*. He thinks *the person* who wrote it saw the *article* in the *National Guardian*. *Cathy* is going to *speak* to the *editor*.

PRESENTER	Tapescript 10. Unit 4. Listen.
NARRATOR	Cathy phones Pete on Saturday morning. She's very excited ...
PETE	67543. Pete Chisman speaking.
CATHY	Hi, Pete, this is Cathy. The most amazing thing has happened. You won't believe it!
PETE	What do you mean: 'the most amazing thing'?
CATHY	I can't tell you on the phone. When can we meet?
PETE	I don't know. What's the time now?
CATHY	It's half past seven.
PETE	Half past seven! You must be mad, Cathy! It's Saturday morning!
CATHY	I know, Pete, but this is very important.
PETE	Oh, all right. I'll see you at the Promenade Cafe in half an hour.
CATHY	Thanks, Pete you won't regret it.
NARRATOR	Half an hour later ...
PETE	Well, what is it, then? What's so important that you ring me up at half past seven on a Saturday morning?
CATHY	Well, I was in bed and someone rang the doorbell. It woke me up. When I opened the door, there was no one there. But then I found this letter ...
PETE	A letter?
CATHY	That's right.
PETE	What's it about?
CATHY	Here! Read it for yourself ...
PETE	All right then. 'Dear Ms Edwards, You don't know me and I can't reveal my identity because it's too dangerous. I have evidence that security at Moondown power station is not adequate and that the town of Westfield is in serious danger from radioactive pollution from the power station. Please publish this letter in your newspaper or write an article about Moondown. We are all in terrible danger! Yours sincerely, A friend.' Mmm ... very dramatic! Is that all?
CATHY	What do you mean: 'Is that all?' Isn't it enough?
PETE	Oh, Cathy, it's probably some idiot who read that article in the *National Guardian* yesterday. Don't take it too seriously!
CATHY	Well, I'm not so sure. I'm going to talk to the editor about it on Monday morning ...

WB 4
Students' own answers.

UNIT 5 *page 18*

Skills Focus: Writing

Informal Letters

Encourage students to use these writing skills units as reference pages. They are in fact self-explanatory but students will need clarification at first.

● Discuss the illustrated letter in class. Ask students what they notice about it.
● Point out that the layout of an informal letter in English is probably different from what they are used to:
  a They write their own address in the top right-hand corner (without their name).
  b The house number in England comes before the street or road name.
  c There is usually a post code.
  d There are three ways of writing the date.
  e *Dear X,* is the standard way of beginning all letters.
  f The first word of the body of the letter begins with a capital.
  g Either paragraphs can be indented, or a line left blank when a new paragraph starts (but not a mixture).
  h In an informal letter, shortened forms like *I'm, it's, we're,* etc. can be used.
  i *Love,* is a friendly way of ending a letter.
● Read through the alternatives for beginning a letter. Ask students to suggest others if possible. Do the same for general news and for ending the letter.
● Read through the letter with them. Help them with any vocabulary they may find difficult. This will be useful when they are writing their letters.
● Tell them to write a similar letter to a friend using the guidelines provided. Students should organise their ideas first, making notes before writing the letter.

WB 5
Students' own answers.

REVISION FOCUS *page 19*

A Revision Focus section appears after every five units. It contains exercises which cover structures, functions and vocabulary areas studied in the preceding five units. Some vocabulary exercises require students to write sentences illustrating the meaning of words by their context. In addition, there are pronunciation exercises with accompanying tapescript.

There are various ways of approaching Revision Focus: you may wish to allow students to review the units, giving them specific homework time, or you may wish to test them by giving the exercises without warning. Alternatively, these exercises could be left for a month or more and given to help recap the material.

More detailed comments and answer keys are given where appropriate.

REVISION FOCUS
Units 1–5

1 *Days of the week*

● Answers depend on the year.

2 *Food and drink*

Key
ACROSS: CAKE, PEAR, MEAT, BREAD, LEMON, WATER.
DOWN: APPLES, COFFEE, EGG, COKE, POTATO, BEER, MILK, TEA, SWEET.

3 *Furniture*

Key

1 bed	5 bookcase	9 calculator
2 table	6 clock	10 mirror
3 lamp	7 television	
4 fridge	8 cupboard/wardrobe	

● When students have completed this quiz, they may like to make up their own questions about items of furniture.

4 *Clothes*

Key
scarf   hat   dress   coat   trousers   jacket   skirt
T-shirt   sweatshirt   jeans   belt   gloves   shirt
sandals   boots   shoes   trainers   sweater   blouse

REVISION FOCUS
Units 1–5 *page 20*

5 Illnesses

Key
headache   temperature
cough   stomach-ache   toothache   backache
stiff neck   flu

6 Sports

Key
tennis   hockey   golf   football   boxing   skating
swimming   basketball   cricket   motorcycling   rugby
rowing   table tennis   cycling   skiing   fencing

7 Functions

● Students have a list of functions in their books. On the cassette they hear short dialogues demonstrating these functions. They write the number of the conversation next to the function.

Key
3 Describing people
2 Giving personal information
9 Talking about the past
1 Talking about future plans
5 Making suggestions
7 Talking about obligation
4 Talking about permission
8 Talking about daily routine
6 Describing where things are

🎧 11

PRESENTER	Tapescript 11. Revision Focus Units 1–5. Listen.
	1.
MAN	What are you doing this year for your summer holidays, Margaret?
WOMAN	We're going camping in France.
MAN	That sounds nice. I hope it doesn't rain too often for you!
PRESENTER	2.
WOMAN	Good afternoon. Can I have your name please?
MAN	Yes. It's Granger. Tom Granger.
WOMAN	Is that G-R-A-I-N-G-E-R?
MAN	No, it's G-R-A-N-G-E-R.
WOMAN	I see. And your address, please.
MAN	86, Pemberton Road.
PRESENTER	3.
WOMAN	What's your new gym teacher like then Pat?
GIRL	Oh, she's OK. She's got really short hair, and she's very tall, taller than Dad, I should think. They say she's a fantastic basketball player.
PRESENTER	4.
BOY	There's a wonderful film at the Odeon tomorrow, Mum. All the boys in my class are going.
MOTHER	All of them?
BOY	Well . . . nearly all. Can I go?
MOTHER	Well, I don't know. It depends how much homework you've got.
BOY	I haven't got any. Our teacher said we should see this film so he didn't give us any homework.
MOTHER	Oh, well . . . In that case . . .

PRESENTER	5.
BOY	Hi, Mary. Why don't you come to my house on Saturday? I'm having a party.
GIRL	Thanks a lot. I'd love to come. What time is it? . . .
PRESENTER	6.
GIRL	Mum, have you seen my blue sweater?
WOMAN	Your what, dear?
GIRL	My blue sweater. I can't find it anywhere.
WOMAN	It's in the cupboard in your bedroom. I saw it on the top shelf when I was putting things away yesterday. You really must try to be tidier, you know.
GIRL	OK, Mum. I'll try.
WOMAN	Huh!
PRESENTER	7.
BOY	Are you coming to the football match, Jane?
GIRL	I wish I was, but I still haven't finished that French book we had to read. I've got to read it this evening or I'll be in trouble tomorrow.
BOY	Can't you do it when you get back?
GIRL	No, I really can't. I've still got about a hundred pages to read. As it is I'll probably be up all night . . .
PRESENTER	8.
WOMAN	Good afternoon. Do you mind if I ask you a few questions?
MAN	No, of course not.
WOMAN	Right then. First of all what time do you get up?
MAN	Usually at six o'clock, but on Sundays I stay in bed until about nine.
WOMAN	Do you do any sports?
MAN	Yes, I go running every morning and I play tennis on Saturdays.
WOMAN	And what time do you go to bed?
MAN	I'm usually in bed by eleven as I have to get up so early.
PRESENTER	9.
GIRL	Hi, John. Did you have a good holiday?
BOY	Yes, it was great.
GIRL	Did you go to Scotland afterwards?
BOY	Yes. We went to the Edinburgh festival and then on to Loch Ness. We didn't see the monster though . . .

8 Verb tenses

Key
Barbara Davies *lives* in London with her parents and her brother Edward. Barbara *is* eighteen years old and she *goes* to university in London. Edward *is* twenty-two years old and at the moment he *is working* in a bank but he *doesn't like* it very much. Last year he *bought* an old car and he and Barbara *went* on holiday together. The holiday *was* a disaster! They *stayed* on camp sites but the weather *was* awful: it *rained* every day! Then they *had* an accident when they *were going/were driving* along the motorway but fortunately it *wasn't* serious. They *were* very glad to get home!

9 Pronunciation

● The students are asked to divide the words into two groups depending on the pronunciation of *e* in the first syllable. *English* is the only exception in the list to the rule that the pronunciation is /ɛ/ when the first syllable is stressed, and /ɪ/ when it is unstressed.

🎧 12 ***Key***
1 /ɪ/ delicious   2 /ɛ/ centre

before 1	remember 1
seven 2	plenty 2
English 1	prepare 1
return 1	preparation 2
remind 1	every 2
terrible 2	decide 1
excellent 2	believe 1

Extra ideas for revision work: questionnaires

There are many reasons for doing questionnaires with your students:
- Students can decide the content and so become more autonomous.
- They are directly related to the students' interest.
- Question forms are particularly difficult to master and questionnaires give excellent practice.
- They are fun to do.

Included below are suggestions for seven questionnaires which you could use with your class. There are different ways of treating this material.
- Students could choose the questionnaire themselves, and work in groups putting it together. They then go and ask their questions to members of other groups.
- Alternatively, you could decide groups of students yourself. In this way, you can put weaker and stronger students together. This will be beneficial to both, as helping weaker students will fix the grammar better in the minds of stronger students and also weaker students will be helped without feeling exposed in front of the whole class.

While the various groups are preparing their questionnaires you should monitor their work but beware of over-correcting.
- Point out mistakes and encourage them to correct the mistakes themselves.
- Make notes of structures that the whole class does not seem to have absorbed. You can do a remedial session (or lesson) on these structures later.

After completing their questionnaires, you may like to get students to do some written work on the results. Students could do this after collating results with the other members of their original group.

Questionnaire 1: personal routine

This focuses on the use of the simple present tense and covers the vocabulary presented and practised in the first two units of Book 1.

Instructions

Find out about the other students' daily routines. Ask at least ten questions about these things:

time: get up – wash – have a shower – breakfast – lunch – dinner – go to
school – get home from school – do homework, etc.
activities: in the afternoon, evening, weekends, etc.

Here are some examples of the questions that you can use:
What time do you get up?
Do you get up at the same time every day?
What do you do in the evening after dinner?
Do you go to church on Sunday?

Questionnaire 2: life in the year 2000

Students will revise the use of *wh-* and *yes/no* questions with *will* used as the future.

Instructions

What do students feel about life in the future? Ask at least ten questions about these things:
houses – transport – health and medicine – education – political
situation – families – religion – technology – climate – ecology

Here are some examples of the questions that you can use:
Will people live in houses in the year 2000?
What will the climate be like?
Will people still go to church?
What type of government will there be?

Questionnaire 3: sports and hobbies

More use of the simple present with both *wh-* and *yes/no* questions.

Instructions

Which sports and hobbies are most popular in your class?
Ask at least ten questions about these things:
sports (winter/summer) – indoor hobbies (watching television – playing
with a computer) – outdoor hobbies (walking – cycling)

Here are some examples of the questions that you can use:
Do you like skiing?
Do you like watching TV?
Which programmes do you like?
How often do you go cycling?

Questionnaire 4: holidays

Students revise the simple past in a variety of question forms.

Instructions

Find out about the holidays that students in your class had last summer.
Ask at least ten questions about these things:
place – accommodation – cost – parents/friends – length of stay –
weather – transport – new friends – food

Here are some examples of questions that you can use:
Where did you go?
Did you enjoy yourself?
How long did you stay there?

Questionnaire 5: opinions

Students discuss their opinions on a range of topics using the verb *be* in the present tense and other verbs in the simple present.

Instructions

Find out the opinions of the other students in your class on *two* of these topics and ask at least five questions on each:
music – fashion – school – politics – religion

Here are some examples of the questions that you can use:
What type of music do you like?
What are the names of your favourite singers?
Do you buy records, cassettes or compact discs?

Questionnaire 6: ability

By asking a series of questions using *can* in the present tense, students find out about each other's abilities in a variety of fields.

Instructions

What can the other students in your class do? What can't they do?
Ask at least ten questions. Find out about these things:
sport – musical ability – domestic skills – languages

Here are some examples of the questions that you can use:
Can you play football?
What other sports can you play?
Can you sing?

Questionnaire 7: travel

This questionnaire focuses on students' travel habits especially their journey to school. They revise the simple present with a wide variety of questions.

Instructions

Find out about your fellow students' travel habits. Ask at least ten questions. Find out about these things:
distance – time – method – cost

Here are some examples of the questions that you can use:
How far is your house from school?
How do you travel to school?
What time do you leave home?
How much do you spend every week?

GRAMMAR FOCUS *page 21*

As with Revision Focus, a Grammar Focus section appears after every five units to give further practice of the grammatical elements students have been looking at.

For Units 1–5, Grammar Focus looks at the structural composition of a wide variety of functions. The subsequent Grammar Focus sections have the following pattern: In the first stage, students write a few sentences as examples of target structures or functions. Then, each structure or function is looked at in more detail with examples, an exercise and concept-checking questions. This should encourage students to adopt an analytical approach to their learning, and, when the exercises are complete, serve as a grammar reference section.

It should be noted that Grammar Focus sections are not suitable as testing material, and students should complete them in class or as homework with an opportunity to discuss any points arising afterwards.

GRAMMAR FOCUS
Units 1–5

Go over the functions in the right-hand column checking that students are clear on their meaning. You may need to ask students to give you examples of the various functions.

Explain that there is one model sentence for each function and that students must write the sentence numbers on the correct lines in the left-hand column. When they have done this, go over the example structure showing the grammatical form necessary for the function.

Students work in pairs to complete the middle column. (You may need to go through a couple of structures, or indeed, treat the whole exercise as a teacher-centred class activity if students appear unsure.) Make certain that students have the table filled out correctly, as they should use this page for reference.

Key

SENTENCE NUMBER	STRUCTURE	FUNCTION
9	*'have got to' + infinitive ('do')*	Talking about obligation
11	*'can' + infinitive ('swim')*	Talking about ability
7	*'will' + infinitive ('travel')*	Making predictions
3	*present continuous ('are staying')*	Talking about the present situation
1	*simple present ('is')*	Talking about personal information
5	*past continuous ('was walking') followed by simple past ('happened')*	Describing simultaneous actions in the past
2	*present continuous ('am playing')*	Talking about future arrangements
8	*'have got' ('has got') + noun ('a walkman', 'a calculator')*	Talking about possessions
4	*simple past ('went')*	Talking about the past
10	*'can' + subject ('I') + infinitive ('go')*	Asking permission
6	*present of 'be' ('am') + 'going to' + infinitive ('work')*	Talking about future intentions

Preparation
Ask students to complete WB 6.1–2 before starting Unit 6.

UNIT 6 *page 22*

> **New structures**
> Imperatives
> *will* future
>
> **New functions**
> Giving directions
>
> **Vocabulary**
> go straight down – go straight on – go across
> about – yards – metres
>
> **Revision**
> Prepositions of location

WB 6.1

- Before students begin the lesson, they should have completed
  WB 6.1–2 which revise prepositions of location. They complete the
  sentences with the correct preposition.

Key

1 The school is *opposite* the bank.
2 The cinema is *opposite* the hotel and *next to* the cafe.
3 The bank is *behind* the restaurant.
4 The station is *between* the car park and the post office.
5 The bank is *near* the post office.
6 The supermarket is *on the corner* of Lee Road and Park Avenue.

WB 6.2

- This exercise provides further revision of prepositions of place. Students
  write similar sentences to those in WB 6.1 but about places on a map
  they draw.

Where's the bank?

1 Pre-teach the word *landmark* by giving directions to a place students
  know using a landmark to help you.
- Explain that although England uses the metric system of measurement,
  people talk about *yards*. A yard is a little less than a metre. Tell them
  they will sometimes hear *metre* and sometimes *yard* in the listening
  exercises.
- Give students time to discuss the questions in the book either in pairs or
  groups or even with the whole class. This discussion is best done in
  English but if this is not yet possible with your class, do it in the mother
  tongue and make sure they understand the questions in English.
- This discussion helps to get students into the situation and identify with
  the characters in the dialogue, and encourages them to predict the sort
  of language which they will hear in the dialogue.
- Look at the map with the students. Get them to identify where places
  are so they become familiar with place names, etc.
2 Students read the three questions. Play the cassette once and check
  students' answers.

Key

1 Sinan visits a bank, a record shop, and the post office.
2 Yes, he gets what he wants – a cassette.
3 No, he doesn't manage to send anything to his sister because the post
  office is closed.

3 Draw attention to the second task and play the cassette a second time.

Key

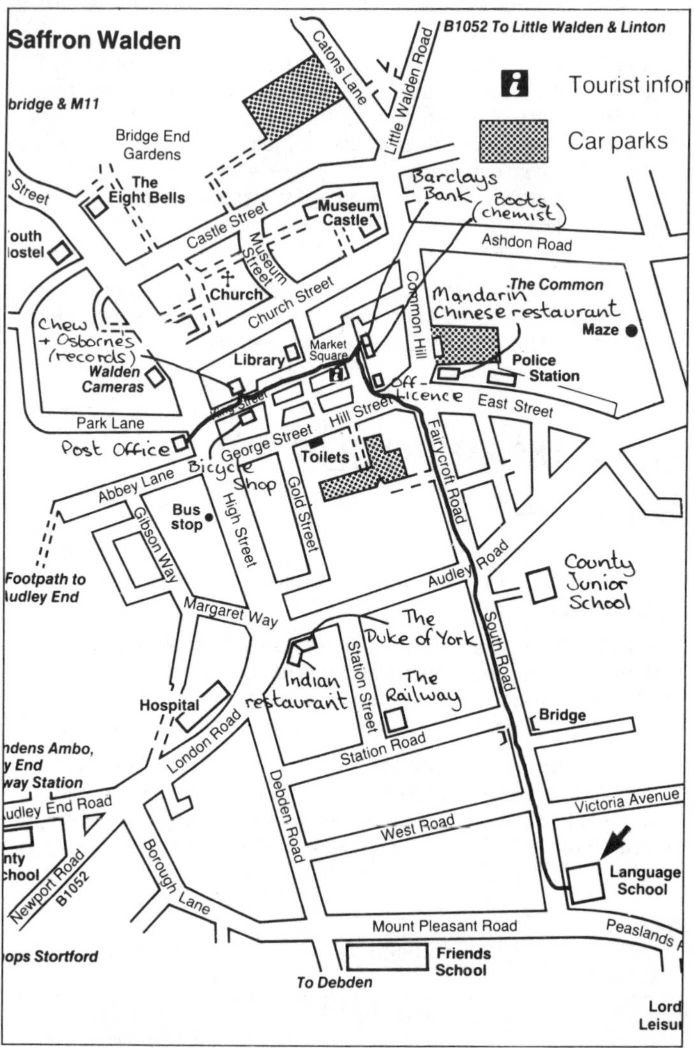

Sinan visits Barclays Bank, Chew & Osborne's and the Post Office.
Students should also have marked the County Junior School, the Mandarin
Chinese restaurant, the Off-licence, Boots (chemist) and the Bicycle shop.

Supplementary Exercise 5 *(SB page 118)*
Key
Refer to the map in the key to Exercise 3 above.
Sinan visits Barclays Bank, Chew & Osborne's and the Post Office following
the route as marked.

🎧 13 ▶ See Appendix for tapescript 13.

UNIT 6 *page 23*

1 *Language Focus*

1 Tell students to read the dialogue while they listen to the cassette. After listening they can mark the three places on the map.

● Play the dialogue with pauses and ask students to listen and repeat.

● Students should now practise the dialogue in pairs. After two or three times, encourage them to try the dialogue again with one of the two covering the dialogue and just referring to the map.

Key
Refer to the map in the key to Exercise 3 above.
Students should have marked The Railway, The Duke of York and the Indian restaurant.

PRESENTER	Tapescript 14. Unit 6. Listen.
JOHN	Excuse me. Is there an Indian restaurant near here?
MAN	Sorry, I'm a visitor here.
JOHN	Oh … thanks anyway. Er … excuse me. Is there an Indian restaurant near here?
WOMAN	Yes, there is. You go down South Road and take the second left, after the bridge. Take the first right. There's a pub on the corner called The Railway. Go down to the end of the road. Turn left at the end and the Indian restaurant's about 50 metres down that road on the left. It's just after a pub called The Duke of York.
JOHN	So that's second left, first right, left again and it's on the left after about 50 metres.
WOMAN	That's right.
JOHN	Thanks very much.
PRESENTER	Now Listen and repeat.

2 When you are satisfied that students are confident using the language of the first dialogue, move on to the second. There are two approaches to this. Either ask students to look at the map and try to fill in the gaps, and then listen to check their answers; or ask students to listen to the dialogue and then fill in the gaps after listening.

● When students have finished filling in the gaps, check their answers with the whole class. Now deal with the dialogue in the same way as the first one, encouraging students to roleplay it from memory as a final stage.

● Look at the tapescript for the answers.

PRESENTER	Tapescript 15. Unit 6. Listen.
ANNIE	Is there a good hotel in Saffron Walden?
MAN	Yes, *there's the* Saffron Hotel.
ANNIE	*Where's* that?
MAN	Well, you *go* down South Road and *turn* left after the bridge. Go straight *down* Station Road and *turn* right at the end. You're in *Debden* Road, then London Road. Go *straight* down London Road and after 50 metres it turns into High Street. You'll see the Post Office on your *left*.
ANNIE	OK, got that.
MAN	The Saffron Hotel is about 100 *metres* on your *right* after the *Post Office*.
ANNIE	I think I can remember that. *Thanks* very much.
PRESENTER	Now listen and repeat.

3 Students now work in pairs and take it in turns to give each other directions to get to the five places listed. Stress that they should use at least two landmarks to help their partner understand the instructions.

2 *Where do you live?*

In this part of the lesson, students have a chance to use the language they have learned.

● Tell students to read the instructions in the book. They have to imagine that they live in Saffron Walden. They choose an address and mark the location of their house on the map.

● Students work in groups or, where possible, they move round the class and ask for directions to each other's houses. They have to mark on their maps the routes to at least three other students' houses.

● Remind students to incorporate landmarks. Also remind them that their starting point is always the bus stop in High Street.

3 *Helping a visitor*

In this section, students apply the language they have learned to a possible real life situation: giving directions to visitors to their town.

1 One student in each pair takes the part of the visitor who asks for directions to three places. The other student gives directions. When they have finished, they change roles.

● You may have to adapt this exercise if your town hasn't got any of the places listed. Substitute other names or places.

2 Students listen to the two authentic unscripted conversations and tick the places on the list. The conversations are quite difficult to understand and students may have to listen several times. If you have a good class, ask them to make notes and write up the directions afterwards.

Key
The two places are: 1 police station 2 Eight bells pub

PRESENTER	Tapescript 16. Unit 6. Listen. 1.
WOMAN	Well, er … Yes, you turn left out of the car park, left again and it's just about 100 yards from that junction.
BARBARA	OK … so, out of the car park turn left, and then left again …
WOMAN	… and it's on the left, about 100 yards from that junction.
BARBARA	Thank you very much.
PRESENTER	2.
MAN	Yeah, right, erm … go out of the car park, turn right, carry on up to the top of the hill …
BARBARA	Yeah …
MAN	Come to a crossroads, turn left, carry on down the one-way system, right to the end, you come to the main High Street …
BARBARA	Yes …
MAN	Turn right on to the main High Street, and it's about two hundred yards up the road on your right.
BARBARA	OK. Thanks ever so much.

WB 6.3
Key
1 Take the first ____on____ the right, go straight ____on____ then take ____–____ the next left.
2 The swimming pool is ____on____ your right just after the bank.
3 Turn ____–____ right at the end of Staines Road, go straight ____–____ down London Road and Sainsbury's is at the end of the road ____on____ the right.
4 Turn ____–____ right outside the school and take the third ____on____ your left. Jo's house is ____on____ your right next to the pub.
5 Go ____–____ down this road and you'll see the park ____on____ your left opposite the car park.

WB 6.4
● Students read the note from Jake to Laura and write a similar note giving instructions to get to their house from the station or bus stop. There is obviously no fixed answer to this exercise.

Preparation
Ask students to complete WB 6.5 before starting the next section.

UNIT 6 *page 24*

New structures
too/enough with adjectives
Indirect statements
Modifiers – *a bit/very*

New functions
Expressing opinions
Agreeing and disagreeing

Vocabulary
too – enough – very – a bit – dramatic – boring – OK – lovely –
awful – nice – silly – good – banal – all right – peaceful – dark –
interesting – funny – depressing – beautiful – ugly – realistic –
wonderful – clear – terrible

Revision
Simple present *(What do you think of ... ?)*

WB 6.5
Before students begin the lesson, they should have completed this
vocabulary exercise.
- They categorise adjectives according to whether they are positive,
  indifferent or negative.

Key

POSITIVE	INDIFFERENT	NEGATIVE
lovely	OK	boring
nice	all right	awful
dramatic	dark	silly
good		banal
peaceful		dark
interesting		depressing
funny		ugly
beautiful		horrible
fantastic		terrible
pretty		
wonderful		
realistic		
clear		

Looking at photographs

- As a warm-up, look at the photos with the students. Get them to
  describe the photos and say whether they like them or not. Ask if there
  are any students who like photography, have been to a photographic
  exhibition, or who take a lot of photos. If they take photos, ask if they
  prefer taking one sort of photo rather than another.
- Tell students to look at the pictures on the page.
- Ask them what they think the dialogue will be about. Write these
  questions on the board:
  How many photographs do Bruce and Jan look at?
  Do they have the same opinion about them?
- Play the cassette and check the answers.
- Tell students to read the questions in their books. Play the cassette
  again. Check that your students have no comprehension problems with
  the dialogue. Tell them to answer the questions.
- Let them check their answers in pairs before you give them the correct
  answers.

Key
1. The dummy in the car.
   The window and the river.
   The mountains and mist.
2. He says it's depressing.
3. Yes.
4. It's very peaceful.
5. The mountains and mist.

Supplementary Exercise 6 *(SB page 118)*
- Students may give any answers consistent with tapescript 17.

Key
Bruce doesn't like the photo of *the dummy in the car* because it's
depressing. Jan agrees and says it's too *dark*. She thinks the one of the river
is *boring* and says you can't see the river *very well*. They both think the one
with the mountains and mist is *lovely*.

PRESENTER Tapescript 17. Unit 6. Listen.
JAN What do you think of this photo, Bruce?
BRUCE Which one?
JAN The one with the dummy in the back of the car.
BRUCE I don't like it. I think it's a bit depressing.
JAN Mmm ... I agree with you. I think it's too dark.
BRUCE What do you think of the one with the window?
JAN With the river behind it?
BRUCE Yes, that's right.
JAN Mmm ... I don't like it ... you can't see the river very well.
 I think it's a bit boring.
BRUCE Oh, I don't agree with you. I think it's very peaceful.
JAN Oh that's nice ... that one of the mountains and the mist.
BRUCE Yes, I agree, it's lovely!

UNIT 6 *page 25*

4 **Language Focus**

- If you have a good class, allow students to follow the procedure in the book, i.e. completing the dialogues before they listen to them. If this is too difficult, the class can complete the dialogues while listening once to the cassette.
- Students may work in pairs checking their answers before they listen to the cassette (or, in the case of weaker students, before they listen to it again).
- Play the cassette two or three times when students have completed the dialogues.
- Check the completed dialogues with the whole class.
- When you are satisfied that the whole class has a reliable written model, play the next section of the cassette and ask students to listen and repeat.

PRESENTER   Tapescript 18. Unit 6. Listen.
- A   *What* do you *think* of this *photo*?
- B   Which *one*?
- A   The *one* with the old man and the trees.
- B   I *think* it's beautiful.
- A   Yes, I agree with you. I *think* it's very good.

- C   *What* do you *think* of this *photo*?
- D   Which *one*?
- C   The *one* of the *man* singing.
- D   I don't *like* it. I *don't think* it's clear enough.
- C   Oh, I *don't agree* with you. I *think* it's nice.

PRESENTER   Now listen and repeat.

5 **Discuss the photographs**

- In this section students have the chance to express their own opinions about the photographs.
- Tell students to write a positive or negative adjective for each of the photographs. They must do this individually without discussing with each other, choosing a different adjective for each one.
- Students now practise the dialogue in the example, discussing the photographs. It is a good idea to practise the activity with a student before going into simultaneous pairwork.
- When students have finished the activity, ask two students to repeat one of their conversations. If students know that they may be called upon to do this, it will encourage them to work more carefully.

6 **What's your opinion?**

1. In this section students use the language they have learned in a slightly freer context.
- Put students into groups of three, four, or five.
- Explain that they must choose *one* of the pictures from the book to hang on the classroom wall.
- They must talk about the photographs and come to a majority decision.
- When they have finished and decided on a picture, compare the decisions of the groups.
2. Read the model paragraph from the book while students look at it.
- Tell students to write a brief description of their favourite photograph.
- This is quite a free writing exercise and you should monitor carefully and give assistance with vocabulary where necessary.
- Allow students to exchange paragraphs and read about their partners' opinions.

WB 6.6
- Students have first to put the words in each sentence in order. They then have to order the sentences to make a logical dialogue. There may be some degree of variation in their answers. The main thing is that the dialogue should read logically.

Key
- A   What do you think of this photograph?
- B   Which one?
- A   The one with the two men sitting on the bench.
- B   I think it's terrible. It's silly.
- A   I don't agree. I think it's very funny.

- In the second part students have to write a similar dialogue about one of the photographs in the Student's Book. This will help fix the language that they have studied in the lesson.

WB 6.7
Students' own answers.

UNIT 7 *page 26*

The power seekers

1 *Skills Focus: Reading*

1 As with other skills lessons, there is a certain amount of preparatory work to be done before students open their books and read the text.

● Firstly, brainstorm nuclear energy vocabulary – ask students to come and write any words which have to do with nuclear power on the board. They will know some as a result of reading the serial *Moondown*. They may ask you for translations of words from their language.

2 The second exercise consists of a series of questions for discussion.

● Students can work in groups or you can discuss them with the whole class.

● When you get to question four, write the results on the board, as this will make it more interesting and easier for students to check their hypotheses after they have read the text. Obviously, there are no right or wrong answers to these two exercises.

3 Students have to look for specific information in the text while they read it for the first time. Tell students to read the three sentences carefully before they read the text.

Key

1 Eight. (Paragraph 3: 'Elizabeth Abrahams ... (and) ... her seven companions'. However, only seven young people are actually named.)
2 Billericay School.
3 Safety and radioactive waste. (Paragraph 10.)

UNIT 7 *page 27*

4 Before your students read the text again, tell them to look at the chart and check that they understand what they have to do. This exercise is quite demanding and requires a close reading of the text.

● Students can work individually and compare their answers before referring to you for the correct answers.

Key

NAME	AGE	FAVOURABLE TO NUCLEAR POWER			REASON
		Yes	No	Unsure	
Elizabeth Abrahams	16			×	● hidden fear (Chernobyl)
Katie Nibbs	14			×	● over simplification of dangers ● safety
Kala Subbuswany	14			×	● sales talk ● Chernobyl – safety
Ian Hammond	14	×			—
Zafar Sarfraz	17	×			● no radiation detected
David Thomas	—	×			● people's fear is dictated by lack of knowledge
Colette Gilmore	16		×		● expensive ● waste disposal

5 There is quite a lot of difficult vocabulary in the text. In this exercise, students work together to produce a translation of the key words.

● It is important to emphasise to students that they must look at the words in context if they want to make an accurate guess at the meaning of the words.

● An alternative approach to vocabulary is to write the words on the board at the end of the previous lesson and tell students to look them up for homework.

Supplementary Exercise 7 *(SB page 118)*

● There are a number of things that the management has done to reassure people about nuclear energy. Students should find the sentences and clauses which explain these things.

Key

1 A large clump of trees desperately tried to hide the huge white buildings.
2 ... descriptions like 'glorified kettle' and 'the object of the controversy is boiling water' were perhaps meant to set our minds at rest.
3 I couldn't help feeling like a customer who had been subjected to a lengthy sales talk.
4 We took around a device to measure radiation – all the levels were harmless.
5 The managers we talked to thought that the most dangerous part of their jobs was driving to and from work.

2 *Skills Focus: Listening*

Students listen to an authentic recording of a representative of the CEGB talking about the advantages and disadvantages of nuclear energy.

● Play the cassette at least three times while students make a list of the advantages and disadvantages discussed.

Key

Advantages	Disadvantages
economic	people's fear of nuclear bombs
safe	possibility of radiation leaks
diversify our fuel supply	possibility of melt-down

Supplementary Exercise 8 *(SB page 118)*

● Students have to answer a series of questions which require a deeper understanding of the conversation.

● Play the cassette again as many times as your students ask you to, in order to give them time to answer these questions. Don't worry about inaccurate English in their answers as the important thing is for them to show that they have understood the text.

Key

1 He says that there is no hazard to the local environment, they don't dispose of waste near the power station.
2 The oil and coal industries.
3 Oil, coal, gas, solar, wind, wave and tidal power.
4 He says that they can't replace nuclear power.
5 Only coal and oil could substitute for nuclear power.
6 It would be very expensive to use them.
7 They build a concrete wall several feet/metres thick around the reactor.

◄ 19 ►

PRESENTER Tapescript 19. Unit 7. Listen.

SARAH Hello. Mr Leach, you represent the Central Electricity Generating Board, the company which controls nuclear power stations in Britain. Is that right?

JIM LEACH Hello, yes, that is correct.

SARAH Many people are very worried about the use of nuclear power, especially after the Chernobyl disaster, and they ask themselves, why nuclear power stations? What in your opinion are the main advantages of nuclear power?

JIM LEACH Well, firstly Sarah, I would say there is no need for people to be concerned. Nuclear power stations are economic, they are safe, and they help to diversify our fuel supplies.

SARAH Yes, could you expand on, on your reasons for saying that nuclear power is economic. What about the terrible problem about waste which seems to be so difficult to er to get rid of?

JIM LEACH Yes, that is a problem and it is something difficult to get rid of, but it is a very small proportion of the cost of running the power station so it does not affect the economics.

SARAH But what about the problems that that causes in the community at large, erm, we hear a lot about the disposal of nuclear waste and of course we know, we all know, that it has to be disposed of somewhere, but nobody really wants it to be disposed of near their own homes.

JIM LEACH   I quite agree, I quite agree. Our policy is to ensure that there is no hazard to the local environment, to the people who live close to the nuclear plant and that is how we do it now, that is how we will continue to do it in the future.

SARAH   I see. And to go on to your comment about safety. Erm, surely that's something we really can't claim, particularly after the Chernobyl disaster.

JIM LEACH   Well, I agree that was an awful disaster and I hope it will never be repeated but even so compared with other industrial or other activities it still has, nuclear power still has a safety record which is second to none, particularly when compared with exploration for oil or mining of coal.

SARAH   Mmm ... Right. And again you mention diversity, that nuclear power provided a very valuable additional source of energy, but surely we can do without it, there are all sorts of other sources of power that we haven't really exploited fully yet. For instance, wind power and sea power.

JIM LEACH   Yes, there are, yes, there are, but we still need it now as a vital contribution to our present power supplies. Worldwide a sixth of all our electricity comes from nuclear power. If we cut it out now, that would make a huge extra burden on other fuels.

SARAH   And in your opinion that couldn't be, that gap couldn't be taken up by other sources of power.

JIM LEACH   Well, it could not be taken up by the wind, the waves, tidal power, solar power. It could be taken up by fossil fuels such as coal, oil and gas. But if it did, it would make the price of those fuels very much higher. We would need six hundred million tons every year more to meet the same needs of electricity. And that would make those fuels much more expensive.

SARAH   I see, I see. And what about the aspect of conservation?

JIM LEACH   Yes, I agree it's a most important aim for us all to save as much fuel as we possibly can. If we use nuclear fuel, like uranium, which cannot be used for any other purpose, then we are helping to conserve fuels such as coal, oil and gas, which are finite. They will not last for ever. So nuclear power can help our conservation.

SARAH   Right. Well, thank you very much. You've given a very positive picture of nuclear energy, but there must surely be some clear disadvantages even in your own opinion. Can you tell us about those?

JIM LEACH   Yes. There are many people who are increasingly concerned about using nuclear power, they fear the possibility of creating nuclear bombs, they fear the radiation produced from nuclear power stations and I would wish to allay those anxieties and concerns by inviting anybody to come and see the nuclear power station and see what happens there how it works.

SARAH   And what about melt-down?

JIM LEACH   Yes, that is a possibility, a very remote possibility in a nuclear power station. But what we do in the power station is build several feet, several metres of concrete around the core of the reactor, so that even if that did happen, it would not cause a hazard to people outside the power station.

SARAH   Fine. Thank you very much Mr Leach. That was a very interesting account.

JIM LEACH   Thank you.

3 *Vocabulary Development*

Encourage the students to be autonomous when they are working through these study skills lessons. They are intended to be done by the students with little, if any, teacher participation.

● Your students will probably have their own dictionary. At this stage of their learning they should be encouraged to use a monolingual one, e.g. *Cobuild Essential English Dictionary*, published by Collins. If your students do not have access to a dictionary, bring some into class so

they can work in groups on the vocabulary study.

● When they are discussing the pattern in these changes, they will possibly notice that —*y*, —*ic* and —*ful* appear frequently to make nouns into adjectives. Ask them to find some more.

● Encourage the students from now on to write the noun and adjective alongside each other as they write them in their vocabulary books.

Key

NOUN	ADJECTIVE
beauty	*beautiful*
drama	*dramatic*
danger	dangerous
interest	interesting
friend	*friendly*
peace	*peaceful*
cloud	cloudy
athlete	athletic
fame	*famous*
health	*healthy*
freedom	free
fun	*fun**

*The adjective *funny*, meaning *humorous* (or *peculiar*), should not be associated with the noun *fun*, meaning *enjoyment*, the adjective *fun* means *enjoyable*.

WB 7

● Refer students to the questions before they read the article.

● The last question is intended as a discussion question and could be used as the title of a short composition. To do this, go through the exercise in class and ensure that students fully understand the article before setting question 9 for homework.

Key

1   26 years ago. (In fact it opened in 1962.)
2   Gloucestershire, Britain.
3   Anti-radiation tablets.
4   It will save time if there is an emergency as the people will be able to take the pills immediately.
5   It is sufficient to have the pills stored in police stations; also, the CEGB is concerned about causing alarm and frightening people.
6   Police stations.
7   Two years ago (1986) when workers were in danger from a leak of radioactive gas.
8   People who live near or work at the power station.
9   Students' own answers.

Preparation

Ask students to complete WB 8.1 before starting Unit 8.

UNIT 8 *page 28*

<table>
<tr><td>

New structures
Present perfect
Simple past

New functions
Talking about experiences

Vocabulary
Students will need vocabulary in the areas of sport, food, travel and/or music for the questionnaire in Exercise 3.

Revision
Simple past
Past participles of verbs

</td></tr>
</table>

WB 8.1

Before students begin the lesson, they should have completed WB 8.1, which is on the simple past and past participles.

- Students first look at the way the simple past and past participle of regular verbs are formed and then complete the chart.
- They then repeat this procedure for irregular verbs, but this time they just fill in the infinitive of the verb.
- Finally they fill in a table containing a mixture of regular and irregular verbs. They may have to refer to the verb table at the back of the Workbook before they are able to do this.
- If your students have already studied the present perfect tense, this exercise may be used for revision.

Key

	Infinitive	Simple past	Past participle
Regular	stay	*stayed*	*stayed*
	listen	*listened*	*listened*
	start	*started*	*started*
Irregular	*buy*	bought	bought
	be	was	been
	do	did	done
Mixed	visit	*visited*	*visited*
	teach	*taught*	*taught*
	learn	*learnt/learned*	*learnt/learned*
	think	*thought*	*thought*
	go	*went*	*gone*
	swim	*swam*	*swum*

Break away!

- Students look at the pictures and say what they think the text is going to be about.
- Tell them to read the text once or twice and ask you questions about any vocabulary difficulties they may have.
- Tell them to answer the questions, and then check the answers with the whole class.

Key

1 The questions are:
Have you ever been on holiday without your parents?
Have you ever done a job during the holidays?
Do you feel independent of your parents?
2 No, they didn't.
3 40%.
4 No, many young people pay for their own holidays.
5 Because you can improve your ability to speak the language.
6 Because it is cheaper and more convenient.
7 Before they are twenty years old.

Supplementary Exercise 9 *(SB page 119)*

- Tell students who are doing this exercise not to look at the text. In this way they will really be testing comprehension. Otherwise the exercise is rather mechanical.

Key

1 They are going on holiday without their parents.
  They have holiday jobs.
2 Language study holidays.
  Youth hostelling.
  Camping.
3 Charter flights.
  Inter-rail cards.
4 To work.
  To study.

UNIT 8 *page 29*

1 Language Focus

- Students look at the exchanges and listen to the cassette.
- Draw attention to the use of the present perfect and the simple past. Elicit from students the rule for use: that the present perfect is used when the time of the action is indefinite, whereas the simple past is used when the time is specified.
- Tell students to listen and repeat after the tape. Practise the two exchanges first where appropriate, then between two students and finally with the whole class practising simultaneously in pairs.

PRESENTER	Tapescript 20. Unit 8. Listen.
BOY	Have you ever been on holiday without your parents?
GIRL	Yes, I have.
BOY	Where did you go?
GIRL	I went to France.
GIRL	Have you ever been on holiday without your parents?
BOY	No, I haven't.
BOY	Have you ever had a holiday job?
GIRL	Yes, I have.
BOY	What did you do?
GIRL	I worked in a supermarket.
GIRL	Have you ever had a holiday job?
BOY	No, I haven't.
PRESENTER	Now listen and repeat.

2 Have you ever been to Rome?

This is a slightly freer activity in which students talk about their own travel experiences.

- Students make a list of ten towns or cities that they have visited in their country.
- Tell them to ask and answer questions in pairs trying to to find a city that they have in common, at which point the dialogue is to be extended as in the example.

3 Questionnaire

1 Students choose a theme, and in pairs or groups prepare a questionnaire for the other members of the class.
- While they are preparing their questionnaires, offer students help and advice and correct where necessary.
2 When the questionnaires are ready, invite students to form new groups and try them out on the people in the new group.
- An alternative to this activity is to elicit questions for one questionnaire for the whole class and write it on the board. When it is complete, ask various students to ask the questions and record the results on the board. Students may write up the results in paragraph form. For example: *In my class ten people have never been to France, but five have been to Germany…*
3 Students listen to the cassette and make notes about the four people's travel experiences. The recording is authentic and students will find it quite demanding.
- Allow them to work in pairs or groups and listen to the cassette as many times as they need to in order to complete the task.

Key

	Countries visited	Cities visited	Interesting experiences
Nick	Russia China	Moscow Peking	Trans-Siberian train
Jane	China	Beijing (Peking)	Great Wall Forbidden City
Paul	Greece	Athens	Moped accident Broken collar bone
Judy	Sweden	Upsala	Au-pair

21 See Appendix for tapescript 21.

WB 8.2

- The second exercise in the workbook is best done after the lesson to reinforce students' grasp of the structure and formation of questions. Some variation in answers is permitted.

Key

1 Have you ever done/had a holiday job?
2 Have you ever been on holiday alone/with your friends?
3 Have you ever been abroad?
4 Have you ever eaten Chinese food?
5 Have you ever been skiing?
6 Have you ever been horse-riding?
7 Have you ever played tennis?

WB 8.3

The third exercise in the workbook encourages students to talk about themselves using the new tense.

- Students write sentences describing things they have never done but which they would like to do.
- There are no fixed answers to this exercise.

WB 8.4

Key

1 Shakespeare *wrote* many plays.
2 Look at my sister. She *'s bought* a new jacket. It looks very nice.
3 I *'ve seen* that film. I *saw* it last week.
4 'Have you finished' your homework?' 'Yes, I *did* it yesterday.'
5 I *'ve never eaten* octopus. You don't often see it on menus in England.
6 My best friend *played* with a band a few years ago but he *hasn't had* time recently.
7 I *waited* for a long time and then I *went* to the cinema.
8 Maria *has been* in Paris for a long time. She lives on the Ile St Louis.

UNIT 8 *page 30*

New structures
Comparative adverbs
New functions
Comparing abilities
Vocabulary
fast – well – far – throw – jump – run – hurdles – pole vault – high jump – long jump – shot – javelin – discus – decathlete – decathlon

Who can cycle faster?

- Ask students if they practise any sports. Ask them how fast, or how far, they can swim, run, or cycle.
- Students read the puzzle and try to work out the names of the people. It may be useful for students to do this exercise in pairs.
- When students have the answers, check them with the whole class.

Key

Name	Wendy	Sid	Alice	George	Ann
swim	2 km	1 km	5 km	3 km	4 km
run 10 km	40 min.	50 min.	44 min.	36 min.	52 min.
cycle 30 km	1 hr	55 min.	1 hr 10 min.	1 hr	1 hr 5 min.

Supplementary Exercise 10 *(SB page 119)*
Key
(Accept any answers which are realistic.)
1 Wendy can't *swim* as far as *Alice, Ann or George.*
2 George takes *36 minutes* to run *10 kilometres.*
3 Alice takes the *longest* time to cycle 30 kilometres.
4 Ann can *swim* further than *George, Wendy and Sid.*
5 Alice can *swim* the *longest* distance.
6 Sid can *cycle* 30 kilometres in the *shortest* time.
7 George is very *good* at running.
8 Ann *runs* 10 kilometres in the *longest* time.

4 *Language Focus*

- Students listen to and read key sentences from the problem-solving activity. Check vocabulary at this point.
- Students listen to and repeat the sentences. Make sure that students are pronouncing the target structures accurately.
- Make sure that they are producing the weak shwa vowel /ə/ correctly in *can* and *than*.
- Students mark the statements in the second part of this listening *true* or *false*. A listen and repeat exercise of the true statements follows.

PRESENTER Tapescript 22. Unit 8. Listen.
Sid can cycle very well. He can cycle faster than all the others.
George can cycle quite well. He can cycle as fast as Wendy.
Ann can't cycle very well, but she can cycle faster than Alice.

Now listen and repeat.

Listen. True or false?	**Key**
1 Alice can run faster than Sid.	*True*
2 George can swim further than Sid.	*True*
3 Sid can't swim very well.	*True*
4 Ann can cycle faster than George.	*False*
5 Ann can run faster than Wendy.	*False*
6 Alice can cycle very well.	*False*
7 Wendy can swim further than Sid.	*True*
8 George can't run very well.	*False*
9 Alice can run faster than Ann.	*True*
10 Alice can cycle faster than George.	*False*

Now listen and repeat

The final phase of the Language Focus section is a game in which students produce three true and three false statements about the completed chart. Ask them to do this individually.
- Students then work in pairs with their books closed and read their statements in turn. The other student has to try and remember if the statements are true or false.
- If he or she gets the answer right, he or she gets a point. If he or she gets it wrong, the other student gets a point. The one with most points is the winner.

5 *How well can you swim?*

In this section, students use the adverbs in a slightly freer context and assess and compare their ability in certain sports.

- Tell students to fill in the charts for themselves.
- When they have finished, tell them to find out about another student's ability and complete column B. If you have a weak class, practise the exchange under the chart before students work together simultaneously in pairs.
- When they have completed the whole chart, students write sentences as in the example comparing themselves with their partner.

6 *Two decathletes*

1 Before the students begin this section, ask them if they know what a decathlon is. Get them to give you the names of the events in the decathlon. If no one in the class knows, then explain that there are ten events. Look through the list of events with them and make sure they understand what they are. Give a mother tongue translation if they have any difficulty.

- Play the cassette as many times as students need to be able to fill in the chart.

Key

	Daley Thompson	Jürgen Hingsen
100 m	10.44 sec.	*10.91 sec.*
110 m hurdles	*14.34 sec.*	14.29 sec.
1500 m	4 min. 35 sec.	*4 min. 22.6 sec.*
Pole vault	5.00 m	*4.50 m*
High jump	*2.03 m*	2.12 m
Long jump	*8.01 m*	7.80 m
Shot	15.72 m	*15.81 m*
Javelin	*65.24 m*	60.54 m
Discus	40.56 m	*50.82 m*
400 m	*46.97 sec.*	47.69 sec.

2 When they have finished and you have checked their answers, ask students to make sentences about the two athletes as in the example.

PRESENTER Tapescript 23. Unit 8. Listen.

Daley Thompson is faster than Jürgen Hingsen over 100 metres: Thompson's time is 10.44 seconds while Hingsen's is 10.91 seconds. Hingsen can throw the shot further than Thompson: he can throw it 15.81 metres while Thompson can throw it 15.72 metres. In the long jump, Thompson can jump further at 8.01 metres while Hingsen can jump 7.80 metres. In the high jump Thompson can jump 2.03 metres and Hingsen 2.12 metres. Thompson can run the 400 metres in 46.97 seconds while Hingsen runs it in 47.69 seconds. Over the 110 metres hurdles the German is faster at 14.29 seconds while the Englishman has run 14.34 seconds. The German is also superior in the discus with a throw of 50.82 metres against Thompson's 40.56 metres, but in the pole vault Thompson has a best of 5 metres while Hingsen can only pole-vault 4.50 metres. Thompson can throw the javelin 65.24 metres against Hingsen's 60.54 metres, but in the 1500 metres Hingsen is faster with a best time of 4 minutes 22.6 seconds against Thompson's 4 minutes 35 seconds.

Optional activity: adverbs game

You may wish to give your students extra practice in the use of regular adverbs by playing this game at the beginning or end of the lesson.

- One student goes out of the room. The other students think of an adverb of manner, e.g. *slowly*. The student comes back into the room and tells members of the class to perform actions (e.g. Dance! or Speak English!) in the manner of the adverb. The student has to guess the adverb that

the class has chosen from the way they perform the actions. You could compile a list of adverbs before you start the game.

WB 8.5
Key

1 George can run *faster* than Henry.
2 Judy can swim very *well*.
3 Laura can ride a bicycle *farther** than the others.
4 Melanie can speak French *better* than her mother.
5 Paul can't ski very *well*; he only started last year.
6 George can ride a bicycle *faster* than Sally but she can ride *farther*.
7 My sister can type *better* and *faster* than I can.
8 Although Dave doesn't study Italian he can speak it quite *well*.

* Both *farther* and *further* are comparatives of *far*; however, *further* has many other meanings as well.

WB 8.6

- Students write sentences about their family using the adverbs to describe and compare the ability of members of their family in certain activities.
- Encourage students to use the connectors *and* and *but* in their sentences as in the example. There is of course no fixed answer to this exercise.

Moondown: Episode 2

Skills Focus: Reading and Listening

Ask students a few questions about the previous episode before they open their books. E.g.: What was in the letter that Cathy received? Who sent the letter? What did Cathy intend to do with the letter? What would you do? What do you think will happen in this episode?

1 Students open their books and look at the picture. Let students answer the questions individually, in pairs or the whole class together. (It is a good idea to vary your approach to exercises to provide more stimulation for students.)

● Students listen to and read the text to check their answers.

Key
1 Cathy is in the editor's office at the *Westfield Gazette*.
2 The man is the editor of the newspaper.
3 She is talking to the editor about the letter.
4 They are talking about the possibility of publishing an article about Moondown.

UNIT 9 *page 33*

2 Students read the sentences in the exercise carefully and then reread the text and decide if they are *true* or *false*. Tell them to do this exercise individually, then compare their answers in pairs.
● Check the answers.

Key
1 True 2 True 3 False 4 False 5 True 6 False
7 False 8 True 9 True 10 False

● 24 ● See Student's Book for tapescript 24.

3 Students read the sentences before hearing the cassette.
● Play the cassette and allow students time to compare answers.

Key
7 Star Point's only three miles from Westfield!
2 It says that security measures at Moondown power station are inadequate.
5 I've got something really important to tell you!
6 She says they're dumping it in the sea about 2 miles from Star Point.
8 1.00 on a Saturday night! They really don't want people to know about it, do they?
4 Let's go and see George Parker at the town hall.
9 Go to Star Point tomorrow night, of course.
3 It also says that the people of Westfield are in terrible danger from radioactivity!
10 Mmm ... I suppose you're right.
1 No, Frank ... What letter?

Supplementary Exercise 11 *(SB page 119)*
● Tell students to answer the questions individually then check their answers in pairs. The questions are quite difficult and you should not worry too much about the accuracy of the grammar in the answers.

Key
1 They are shocked/surprised/disgusted/worried.
2 Yes, they do.
3 Because they built Moondown very quickly.
4 They decide to go and see a friend at the Town Hall and ask for a public enquiry.
5 The person who wrote the letter about Moondown.
6 At Star Point.
7 Because Star Point is very near Westfield.
8 Once a month.
9 1.00 the following Saturday night.
10 Because Mr Eastwood told them not to investigate.

4 The second listening exercise requires students to complete sentences after listening.

Key
1 ... one year to build.
2 ... wants to know about it.
3 ... a public meeting.
4 ... the woman who wrote the letter.
5 ... once a month.
6 ... interviews at Moondown.

Supplementary Exercise 12 *(SB page 119)*
This exercise is very demanding for students of this level; it would be wise to attempt this first one in class, building up the summary on the board.
● Write the headings on the board and elicit sentences from students. Write them up complete with any mistakes and allow the others to correct them.
● Encourage use of simple linkers: *so, but, then, and.*

● Then, either rub out the summary and ask students to write their own version or allow them to copy it.

● 25 ●

PRESENTER	Tapescript 25. Unit 9. Listen.
NARRATOR	On Friday, Pete is waiting for Cathy in the White Horse pub. He hears some people discussing the letter about Moondown.
FRANK	Have you seen this letter in the local paper, Alan?
ALAN	No, Frank ... What letter?
FRANK	This one here ... it says that security measures at Moondown power station are inadequate.
ALAN	Hmm ... that doesn't surprise me. They built it in about a year. But do you think it's true, Frank?
FRANK	Quite possibly, quite possibly ... it also says that the people of Westfield are in terrible danger from radioactivity!
ALAN	Well, I think it's disgusting, Frank. If I'm in danger from Moondown, then I want to know about it.
FRANK	Quite right, Alan. We need a public enquiry!
ALAN	Yes ... Let's go and see George Parker at the town hall.
FRANK	Good idea ... we can call a public meeting to discuss it.
CATHY	Hello, Pete.
PETE	Hello, Cathy. Did you hear those people?
CATHY	Yes ... but listen, Pete, I've got something really important to tell you!
PETE	What, Cathy? What's happened?
CATHY	Well, there was a message on my answerphone when I got home this evening!
PETE	Uhuh ... who from?
CATHY	From the person who wrote that letter!
PETE	No! What did he say?
CATHY	It was a woman. She phoned to tell me that they're dumping nuclear waste in the sea near here.
PETE	Really? Where?
CATHY	She says they're dumping it in the sea about 2 miles from Star Point.
PETE	Star Point's only three miles from Westfield! When do they do it?
CATHY	She says that they usually go there once a month. She's not sure ... but she knows the date and the time of the next dumping.
PETE	When is it?
CATHY	It's tomorrow night at 1.00 a.m.
PETE	1.00 a.m. on a Saturday night! They really don't want people to know about it, do they?
CATHY	No, they certainly don't!
PETE	What are we going to do, Cathy?
CATHY	Go to Star Point tomorrow night, of course.
PETE	But what about Mr Eastwood?
CATHY	We don't tell him anything. He said no to interviews at Moondown – he didn't say anything about Star Point.
PETE	Mmm ... I suppose you're right.
CATHY	Oh, come on Pete, don't be so wet.
PETE	Yes, sorry, Cathy. Right ... what time shall we meet, then?

WB 9.1
Key
1 False 2 False 3 False 4 False 5 False

WB 9.2
Students' own answers.

Skills Focus: Writing

Formal Letters (1)

1 Point out the layout of a formal letter, and ask them to tell you what is different from an informal letter.

  a They will see that they still write their own address in the top right-hand corner of the page, but this time they should also write the name and address of the people they are writing to, on the next line and on the left-hand side of the page.

  b, c, d, e, f, g The notes are the same as for informal letters. Refer students to page 18.

  h In formal letters they do not often use the shortened forms as in normal speech.

  i The ending of the letter is also different. If the letter begins *Dear Sir,/ Madam*, then the ending is *Yours faithfully,*. If the beginning is *Dear Mr Smith*, the ending is *Yours sincerely,*.

● Read through the letter with them and help them with any difficulty they have in understanding it.

● Tell students that they write their signature at the end of the letter but that they must make sure their name is also written absolutely clearly underneath.

2 Students now have to examine another letter of application for a job and rewrite it. The letter does not contain any grammatical mistakes but it is a very bad example of a formal letter.

- By reworking it, you will be able to see how well they have understood the principles of writing formal letters. It is probably a good idea for them to do this exercise with another student.
- When they have finished, check their work, making sure that their final version is well set out and does not contain any irrelevant information.

3 Tell them to read the advertisements and write a letter of application. Make sure they are aware of the kind of information that they have to put in.

WB 10
Students' own answers.

REVISION FOCUS
Units 6–10 *page 36*

1 Giving directions

- If you wish to provide further revision of directions, you may like to ask for directions to or from the school to other places in your town either before or after students do the exercise in the Student's Book.
- If you have a weak class, you may like to elicit all the language for directions again and write it on the board before they do Exercise 1. This will give them more confidence. The map in the exercise is a section of a map of Cambridge.

Key

Police station: Turn right and go down East Road. After about 100 metres you will see the fire station on your right. Turn right there and the police station is on your right next to the fire station.

Peter's house: Turn right and go down East Road. You will see the College of Arts and Technology on your left. Bradmore Street is the second on the left. Peter's house is about 50 metres (yards) down on the right.

Anne's house: Turn left into East Road and take the first right. Go down Norfolk Street and take the first right. That's Blossom Street. Ann's house is about thirty metres (yards) down on the left.

Car park: Turn left and take the first left. That's Burleigh Street. Go down Burleigh Street and turn right at the end. You'll see the car park at the end of that street.

Karen's office: Turn right and take the first right. Go down John Street and you'll see City Road at the end. Turn right into City Road. Karen's office is on the left after about forty metres (yards).

Terry's house: Turn right and take the first right. Take the first left, then turn right at the end. Warkworth Terrace is the first on the left and Terry's house is the first house on the right.

2 Expressing opinions

- Here again if you have a weak class, it may be a good idea to elicit the question form asking for an opinion and the ways of agreeing and disagreeing that the students have studied, as well as a range of adjectives appropriate to describing clothes. You could also usefully revise clothes vocabulary here.
- For variety, you could bring in your own photos cut from magazines or catalogues or ask students to bring some in.

3 What have you done?

- Demonstrate the way the game works by doing it with a student. Decide yourself whether you want to give the students all the verbs first or leave them free to choose their own.

4 Talking about experiences

- Use the exercise in the book as an introduction to your revision work.
- If your students are still making mistakes with the two tenses, and this is quite likely as it is a complex difference to grasp, you may like to continue with some oral revision on the same lines.
- Do not worry if at the end of this sequence of units your students are not using the two tenses perfectly, as they will have further chances to practise them later.

Key

1 Have you ever been on holiday alone?
2 Did she go on holiday (this year)?
3 Did you go abroad / on holiday last summer?
4 Have you ever done a holiday job?
5 Have they ever been abroad?
6 Did she go to the cinema last night/Saturday/week?
7 Has she ever been to France?

5 Comparing abilities

- Students can either do this exercise orally or in writing. Encourage good students to produce a paragraph about their family.
- You can help them by writing a model paragraph about yourself and your family on the board. The paragraph can be true or absolutely absurd, as you wish!

6 Vocabulary

- Students will need to be trained to write sentences which illustrate the meaning of words. For example, *'I arrived at about six'* does not show whether *about* means *before, exactly, after* or *approximately.* A good sentence would be: *'I don't know how many people were at the meeting, I think there were about 60.'*

7 Pronunciation

- The pronunciation exercise in this revision section concentrates on the different values of the letter *a*. Students will probably be producing the letter accurately but few will have realised that it has three different values (apart from exceptions like *was*).
- Students look at the three model words and pronounce them. Play the cassette and ask students to listen and repeat. Ensure that their pronunciation is accurate at this stage.
- Students classify the twelve words in the list then listen to the cassette and check their answers. You may wish to have students listen to and repeat the words as a final stage.

26 **Key**

1 /æ/ map   2 /eɪ/ late   3 /ɑː/ dance

play 2	can 1	than 1	past 3
stay 2	have 1	bath 3	date 2
car 3	black 1	day 2	grass 3

GRAMMAR FOCUS
Units 6–10 *page 37*

1 Directions

a The imperative should provide no problems for your students as it is very straightforward in English. The problem may be convincing your students that it is so easy! Using the future tense for instructions will probably be more difficult if they do not use it in their own language.

b *Turn* left at the supermarket. *Take* the second right and you *'ll see* the bank opposite you.

c We use the imperative, which is the infinitive without *to*.
There is no change in the verb depending on whom we are speaking to.
We often use the *will* future to give a landmark.

2 'I think . . .'

a,b,c Students sometimes have trouble understanding what is happening in this type of sentence – showing them that the word *that* is missing may help them understand better, but beware that students may start putting in *that* where English people leave it out. Most other European languages require *that* in indirect sentences.

3 *Present perfect with simple past*

a The difference between the simple past and the present perfect is one of the biggest problems that students have to face at this stage of their study. Do not worry if they have not grasped the difference immediately – it takes some students a long time to use the present perfect correctly. It will be re-presented in the next sequence of units.

b A *Have* you ever *been* to France?
B Yes, I *have*.
A When *did* you *go*?
B I *went* there last August.

c The main point of the presentation here was to show the use of the present perfect with *ever* to talk about indefinite time, while the simple past tends to be used with definite time or finished actions. Students also learn a number of past participles. (The past participle of the verb *go* in spoken use is usually *been*.)
The present perfect is formed with the present simple of the verb *have* and a past participle.

4 *Irregular adverbs*

a,b Students have seen regular adverbs in skills lessons already and do not normally have problems with them. For this reason, students are exposed to the irregular adverbs here and they concentrate on the problem of word order. It is also useful for students to realise that there are no rules for the formation of many adverbs – they just have to learn them as they occur.

c Generally, adverbs follow the verb.

UNIT 11 *page 38*

> **New structures**
> Qualifiers – *little, much, few, many, a lot of, plenty of*
> Countable and uncountable nouns
>
> **New functions**
> Talking about quantity
>
> **Vocabulary**
> survey – fashions – entertainment – video recorder –
> washing machine – freezer
>
> **Revision**
> *there is / there are*

This unit recycles the use of *there is* and *there are* taught previously in book one. Teachers who have not used Mode 1 should check that students are familiar with these structures.

Spending habits in Britain

This information is based on a survey carried out in 1987.
- Give students time to read the article. Tell them to discuss with another student any vocabulary difficulties they may have.
- Tell the students to underline *little, much, few, many, a lot of, plenty of,* when they appear in the text. Write the words on the blackboard and ask the students to read you a sentence for each. Ask them if they can now give you a different sentence for each.
- Tell them to do the comprehension exercise. They have to say whether the sentences are *true* or *false*.

Key
1 False   2 False   3 True   4 True   5 False   6 True

Supplementary Exercise 13 *(SB page 119)*
Students have to explain what certain words and expressions mean. This exercise is demanding and should not be attempted by weaker students. There is no set answer here. Accept suitable suggestions.

UNIT 11 *page 39*

1 *Language Focus*
- Students look at the sentences and listen to the cassette.
- Play the cassette and tell them to repeat the sentences.

PRESENTER   Tapescript 27. Unit 11. Listen.
A lot of families in Britain own a video recorder.
Very few people had one.
They don't seem to spend much money on going to the cinema.
Most families spend very little money on any kind of entertainment at all.
Not many people have a swimming pool in the garden.
There are plenty of families who have two cars.

Now listen and repeat.

- Tell students it is possible to make sentences which have the same meaning as those in the text by putting different words in the spaces. Ask them to try to do this, working in pairs.
- When they have finished, play the cassette for them to check their answers.

PRESENTER   Tapescript 28. Unit 11. Listen.
1 *Plenty* of families in Britain own a video recorder.
2 Not *many* people had one.
3 They seem to spend very *little* money on going to the cinema.
4 Most families don't spend very *much* money on entertainment.
5 *Few* people have a swimming pool in the garden.
6 There are *a lot of* families who have two cars.

- Ask them what they notice about these new sentences. They should be able to tell you that:
    plenty of and *a lot of* are interchangeable
    little and *not much* mean almost the same
    few and *not many* mean almost the same.

2 *Young people*

1 You can tackle this section in two ways. Either tell students to make their statements about young people in their country without any previous discussion, or talk about it with them first.
- There is more opportunity for real discussion between students when they have made their lists using the first suggestion but a weaker class would probably need the assurance that previous discussion would give them.
2 When students have finished the oral part of this activity, take time for the class to pool their ideas before they write their paragraphs.

3 *Weekly eating habits*

1 Go through the items on the list and check that students are aware which are countable and which are uncountable. Point out that in the answers they should not give numbers but use the expressions listed. Explain the meaning of *none*.
- Tell them to write their answers first and then ask another student and record his or her answers.
2 They will hear a radio interview with a dietician who talks about young people's eating habits with reference to items on the questionnaire. Ask them to make notes while they listen.
3 Tell them to use the notes to write a paragraph about British teenagers' eating habits.

 **29**

PRESENTER	Tapescript 29. Unit 11. Listen.
MAN	Good morning. Welcome to *Medical Matters*. With me today is a dietician, Doctor Bathurst, …
DR BATHURST	Hello.
MAN	… who has recently been studying the eating habits of teenagers. Doctor Bathurst, is there such a thing as a typical British teenage diet?
DR BATHURST	Well, yes, yes indeed. Although there is variation between er individuals and across the country. Let's erm break er food into er specific categories, erm we'll start with protein. Erm, in terms of protein, teenagers today eat er quite a lot of meat er both varieties, er red and white, er though we're not a meat-eating nation in the same way as say er the U.S.A., Australia or New Zealand, erm … Teenagers eat er a lot of cheese and erm a lot of eggs as well, although they do tend to fry the eggs, which of course is very fatty.
MAN	And how much carbohydrate do they eat?
DR BATHURST	Teenagers today? Well, they eat a lot of, a lot of bread er usually white, er they don't seem to like the wholemeal variety. They eat a lot of er potatoes, er, usually in the form of chips … and er well rice and pasta are becoming more popular, and of course er teenagers like er cakes and biscuits.
MAN	Ah yes. How many vitamins do they eat nowadays?
DR BATHURST	Well vitamins in the erm form of fruit, er they only eat er a little fruit, er though there tend to be er seasonal trends, for instance, er strawberries in summer and er tangerines, satsumas at Christmas …
MAN	Yeah.
DR BATHURST	… and so on. Erm, vegetables … well, not many and they do tend to be overcooked. Er salad is becoming more popular, and er especially with er weight-conscious people, erm particularly girls of course. On top of all this erm … well, teenagers eat a lot of junk food, unfortunately, erm hamburgers er chips … chips again of course.
MAN	Mmm.
DR BATHURST	Icecream and er sweets and chocolates between meals.
MAN	Oh dear …

WB 11.1

● Tell them to do the first part of the exercise either for homework or in class.

Key

little / much	*few / many*	*a lot of / plenty of*
information	icecreams	can be used with
icecream	friends	both categories
spaghetti	women	
traffic	children	
cheese	cars	
chocolate		
meat		
fruit		
sugar		

● When students have completed the table, tell them to try to work out which words are sometimes countable and sometimes uncountable. Make a list of these words.

Key

icecream(s) cheese(s) chocolate(s) meat(s) fruit(s)
They may be able to give more.

WB 11.2
Key
1 I like school but I think we get *too much* homework.
2 My sister went to the doctor yesterday. He said she eats *too many* chocolates and is too fat.
3 Very *few* people in England learn Italian.
4 There isn't *much* fruit in the basket. I'll buy some more today.
5 I eat very *little* meat. I prefer fish or vegetables.
6 She doesn't have *many* friends. She doesn't get *much* free time to go out.
7 There isn't *much* spaghetti in the house, certainly not enough for five people.
8 There are *too many* children in Ethiopia who are hungry.

WB 11.3
● This involves writing a paragraph about the ingredients for making a banana cake. Students have to decide which quantifiers to use. It is a real recipe so they can make the cake if they want to.

WB 11.4
Key
1 Two.
2 25–30 minutes.
3 One (the other one is on top).
4 Bananas and lemons.
5 a spread
   b decorate
   c mix
   d divide
   e sprinkle

WB 11.5
● Students look at the shop window and note the quantity of each item. You may need to translate the word *sale* in this context.
● Check students' sentences, especially that they are accurate descriptions of the picture.

New structures
Present perfect with *for* and *since*

New functions
Talking about experiences

Vocabulary
since – ago – journalism

Revision
Present perfect taught in Unit 8

John Nutting: motorcycle journalist

- Prepare students for the listening exercise by asking them to look at the photographs of John Nutting and make predictions about him. They could guess his age, his interests, what kinds of education he had, etc. This should then make the listening task easier.
- Tell them to listen to the dialogue but not to try to do the exercise yet. When they have listened, tell them to read through the information required in the curriculum vitae.
- Now play the cassette a second time and ask students to fill in as much information as they are able to.
- Play the cassette again. At this point they should have completed most of the information. Tell them to compare their answers with another student before going through it with you.

Key

CURRICULUM VITAE

NAME	John Nutting
DATE OF BIRTH	January 6th 1947
PLACE OF BIRTH	London
SCHOOL	comprehensive school
UNIVERSITY	Newcastle upon Tyne

WORK EXPERIENCE
1 Computer programmer
2 Design engineer
3 Journalist in 1972, then assistant editor

OTHER ACTIVITIES   Visited the States, worked for other magazines, edits own magazine, *London Biker*

PRESENT JOB   Assistant editor

NAME OF MAGAZINE   *What's New in Marketing*
STARTING DATE   1986

Supplementary Exercise 14 *(SB page 119)*
Key
1 Motorcycles and journalism.
2 London.
3 Mechanical engineering.
4 *Motor Cycle Weekly* and *London Biker*.
5 He enjoys it so much that he says, 'It doesn't really seem like work. It's a pleasure.'

🎧 30 ▶

PRESENTER Tapescript 30. Unit 11. Listen.
MELANIE Good afternoon Mr Nutting. Do you mind if I ask you a few questions?
JOHN No, of course not. Fire away!
MELANIE Well, you're a motorcycle journalist, aren't you?
JOHN That's right. I've been interested in motorcycles and journalism for many years and this is a good way of combining my two interests.

MELANIE I see. Well let's start at the beginning. You're in your forties, I believe.
JOHN That's right. I was born on January 6th 1947.
MELANIE In London?
JOHN Yes, I've lived in London all my life.
MELANIE Where did you go to school, John?
JOHN I went to a comprehensive school for seven years and then to the University of Newcastle upon Tyne.
MELANIE And did you decide that you wanted to become a journalist while you were at university?
JOHN Yes, but I didn't become a journalist immediately. I studied mechanical engineering at university and when I left, I worked first as a computer programmer and then as a design engineer.
MELANIE A computer programmer, a design engineer and then finally a journalist. Is that right?
JOHN Yes. I became a journalist for *Motor Cycle Weekly* in 1972 and later assistant editor.
MELANIE But you are not working for that magazine now, are you John?
JOHN No. Since then I've been to the States and I've worked for various other motorcycle magazines.
MELANIE And what are you doing at the moment, John?
JOHN I'm assistant editor of *What's New in Marketing* but in my spare time I'm editing my own magazine, *London Biker*.
MELANIE Mmm, I see. And how long have you had this job, John?
JOHN I've worked here since 1986.
MELANIE And do you enjoy your work?
JOHN Yes. It doesn't really seem like work. It's a pleasure.
MELANIE Lucky you, John. Well now...

4 Language Focus

● Students listen to and repeat sentences taken from the text.

PRESENTER	Tapescript 31. Unit 11. Listen.
JOHN	I've been interested in motorcycles and journalism for many years.
	I've lived in London all my life.
	I've been to the States and I've worked for various other magazines.
MELANIE	And how long have you had this job, John?
JOHN	I've worked here since 1986.
PRESENTER	Now listen and repeat.

● For the second part of the exercise, tell them to read the text about John Nutting and try to guess what the missing words might be. Then play the cassette while they complete the exercise. Note that the exercise paragraph is not a transcript of what is actually said on the cassette.
● Play the cassette a second time and tell them to check their work with another student before you give them the correct version.

Key

I've known John *for a long time*. I first met him *many years ago* when we were at school together. I *lived* in London too, then, but I don't live there now. We both got our first bikes at about the same time, about twenty years *ago*. I think John's been interested in bikes *since* he was at nursery school! I *haven't seen* him recently but I know *he has been in* his present job *for* a couple of years.

PRESENTER	Tapescript 32. Unit 11. Listen.
PAUL	Yes, I've known John for a long time. I first met him many years ago when we were at school together. He's lived in London all his life, of course, and I lived in London too at that time although I don't live there any more. I remember going round the showrooms together looking for our first bikes. That must have been about twenty years ago now. John's always been interested in bikes of course. We used to laugh at him and say he's been interested in them since he was at nursery school. I haven't seen him recently. It's more difficult when you don't live near each other any more but I know he's doing very well for himself and has been in his present job for a couple of years now.

5 The interview

● Tell students to read through the job description. If they have any difficulty with vocabulary, help them.
● Before you put the students into groups, go through the information sheet with them and ask them to give you ideas of the kind of information they could give.
● Put the students into groups of three. If they are of mixed ability, make sure the more-able students take the role of the interviewer. While they are working out the questions they are going to ask, go round helping or advising them. Check that students B and C are filling in their charts correctly.
● When they are ready, tell them to carry out the interview. Let the activity go on as long as is necessary.

6 What would you like to be?

1 Before asking students to carry out this activity, talk about what they would like to do in the future, their hopes, dreams, etc. Get them to be as imaginative as possible. When you feel the students are ready, tell them to make notes under the headings given.
2 Tell students to talk to the student sitting next to them and to imagine that they are meeting that person for the first time since leaving school. They should find out as much information as possible about him or her and make notes. When they have finished, they change roles.
3 As a conclusion to this section, they should use the notes they have made to write a paragraph about the student they talked to.

WB 11.6

● Tell students to read the passage and ask you for help in understanding vocabulary.
● Explain that they will obviously use their own language to find out the information. They must then use that information to write a paragraph in English similar to the one in the example.

WB 11.7

This is a substitution exercise and will require careful preparation with the class.
● Explain that not only do they substitute *ago*, *for*, or *since*, but they also have to change the verb. Prepare a few sentences with them to make sure they understand.
● If they have a lot of difficulty, it will probably be worth going through all the sentences orally and then setting the exercise for homework.

Key

1 Mary has had her car since (*year*).
2 She has lived in Paris for (*number*) years.
3 They have known each other for ten years.
4 He hasn't seen her since (*year*).
5 We've been on the bus since ten o'clock.
6 She's been married for five years.
7 He hasn't cut the grass for five weeks.
8 She hasn't worked in the New York office since (*month*).

UNIT 12 *page 42*

Angry lesson on freedom

1 *Skills Focus: Reading*

1 Ask students to open their books and read the questions in exercise 1. They may look at the photograph but not at the article. Discuss and answer the questions with the whole class.

- Richard Attenborough is the man on the right. He is famous as an actor, for example in his role in the 50s film of the Graham Greene book *Brighton Rock* and more recently as a film director with his films *Oh, What A Lovely War!*, about the First World War, and *Ghandi* (1982).
- Students can now look at the title of the article. As they know Attenborough's profession, they will probably guess that the article is about a film.
- Elicit hypotheses about the type of film it could be.

2 Read the questions about apartheid. Give a brief explanation if students have no idea what it is, but don't go into too much detail as you may spoil the listening exercise which follows the reading.

3 Discuss these points with the whole class. Write their suggestions on the board. Explain they are to use them as headings when they make notes while they are reading the article.

- The sort of thing that students should predict are: characters, the story, the name of the director, the names of the principal actors or actresses.
- Tell students to read the article now and make notes under their headings. Tell them not to worry about words they don't understand as these will be dealt with later.
- When they have finished, write the class's answers under your headings on the board.

UNIT 12 *page 43*

4 Students read the text again and find the listed information in the text and write the number of the paragraph in which they found it in the space. Students should work individually then compare answers before you check their work.

Key
5 South African attitudes to Sir Richard during his visit.
8 The names of some famous people's children who have attended the Waterford Kamhulaba School.
3 A description of the apartheid camps.
9 A comment on racism amongst British young people.
4 Sir Richard's comment on Steve Biko's death.
6 Sir Richard's connection with the Waterford Kamhulaba School.
1 Sir Richard's opinion of the South African regime.
2 An introduction to the characters of *Cry Freedom*.
7 A decription of the different races who attend the Waterford Kamhulaba School.

5 This vocabulary exercise requires a different approach to those you have encountered until now. Students collaborate to produce a translation of the key vocabulary items without using dictionaries. If you think there are any other words which may cause the students difficulty, add them to the lists.

- Tell students to read the instructions for the exercise and explain back to you what they have to do. (They have to write a translation of the four words in their group, pass the translation on to the next group, while they receive a different list from another group. Each group discusses the new list and agrees or disagrees with the translation given and adds their translation if they disagree. They then repeat the procedure until all groups have seen a translation of all 16 words.)
- At this point discuss the words and write a definitive list of translations on the board.

Supplementary Exercise 15 *(SB page 119)*
You may think that you have done sufficient work on the text by now and wish to move on to the listening section. If not, this is a difficult *true* or *false* exercise which you can do in class or set for homework.

Key
1 False   2 False   3 True   4 True   5 True   6 True   7 False
8 False   9 True   10 True

2 *Skills Focus: Listening*

- Recall what you said about apartheid at the beginning of the reading part of the lesson. Ask students to imagine what it would be like to be black and living in a country where there was apartheid.
- Tell students to open their books and read the introduction to the listening exercise.
- Tell them to look at the list of examples of apartheid and see if they correspond to those that they listed. Make sure that they understand all the vocabulary.
- Ask them to guess what sort of things Sir Richard Attenborough will say about each of the various categories.
- Play the cassette of the interview with Sir Richard Attenborough and tell students to put the various manifestations of apartheid in the order in which Sir Richard mentions them. Students can compare results before you play the cassette a second time.

Key
1 voting rights
2 freedom of movement
3 curfew.
4 the division of black families
5 educational opportunities
6 health facilities
7 apartheid on the beach
8 apartheid in public parks
9 career opportunities for black people
10 living conditions for black people

- Check students' answers and tell them to read the instructions for the second part of the exercise. Play the cassette again while students make notes.
- If you think that the listening text is rather difficult for your class, divide the class into groups and allocate different things for each group to listen for.

Supplementary Exercise 16 *(SB page 120)*
Students have to answer questions about the listening. Students will find this exercise relatively easy if they have done part two of the previous exercise.

Key
1 Blacks make up the vast majority of the population.
2 Three times a year.
3 He says that they can go into public parks on Tuesday and Thursday afternoons.
4 He says that they have no possibility of advancement in their work as the result of education.
5 They have to live like animals in camps.
6 That this situation is stated by the law.
7 That black people are inferior to white people because of the colour of their skin.

PRESENTER Tapescript 33. Unit 12. Listen.
JUDY While you were there presumably you witnessed apartheid at first hand and erm, must have seen a number of examples of it. What were the most striking examples you saw? How are black people treated differently from whites?
SIR RICHARD Well, I mean, I er, I think the extraordinary thing about apartheid is that it is unbelievable.
JUDY Yes …
SIR RICHARD Er … It's so extraordinary, it is so bizarre, it is so obscene, that it's almost beyond one's comprehension. For instance, I mean, people do not actually recognise that no black person has a vote. They are the vast majority of the population of the country, and they have no voting rights whatsoever. They have no freedom of movement. They are not allowed to travel after certain hours within a twenty-four hour period. Families are split up. Er a mother and children are in a homeland somewhere. The father has to work a thousand miles away, in order to earn a living. And he lives, lives in a, in a, in a ghetto camp in any event and he perhaps sees his wife and children three times a year. Or indeed it might be the other way round, the father might be with the family and the mother is able to earn in domestic service, a job somewhere. There are no equal educational opportunities. There are no er hospital opportunities of any sort of equality in terms of the facilities that exist. You will go into, I mean it's unbelievable, you'll walk on to a beach, which is totally divided by an artificial line down from the shore down to the sea and whites are on one side and blacks are on the other side. You'll walk into a public park and it will say on a notice that black people are only allowed in that park on Tuesdays and Thursday afternoons and at other times they're not allowed to go in there. Their capability of advancement in terms of work erm emanating from education obviously are negligible. But the most staggering thing is the way in which they are herded like animals, into compounds and areas and that they are only allowed out of those areas with particular permits to go into white areas and only particular times of day and night. Now all that is shocking enough enforced by a totalitarian, security-police-operated er constitution, but what is really disgusting and what is really unbelievable is that that is enacted in the law. The law says since 1948, that this person, and this person is black, shall remain forever inferior to that person on all the areas that we've just mentioned and in all those circumstances simply by virtue of the colour of their skin, which is, I would have thought, one of the most revolting concepts and manifestations of prejudice that one could ever imagine.

3 *Vocabulary Development*

- Explain that a *prefix* is a letter or group of letters added to the beginning of a word to change its meaning. (A *suffix* is added to the end of a word.)
- *un —*, *in —* and *im —* change an adjective into its opposite.
- Let the students work through this exercise in pairs, using a monolingual dictionary.

Key

un —	in —	im —
untidy	independent	imprecise
unhappy	inexpensive	impossible
unfriendly	inadequate	impolite
unrealistic	inhuman*	imperfect
unsafe	incompetent	immature
uninteresting		impatient
unhuman*		
unexciting		

*inhuman is more common than unhuman, but the latter may appear in the students' dictionaries. There is a slight difference in meaning, but for the students' purposes, they are interchangeable.

- Encourage students to keep their vocabulary books up to date. They can begin their prefixes section with the words from the exercise.

WB 12.1
Key
1 Pretoria Central Prison.
2 They will be hanged*.
3 Yes.
4 Because there is discrimination against black people.

*Point out that the regular verb to hang, hanged, hanged is only used to mean killing a person in this way. For all other meanings, students should know, to hang, hung, hung (e.g. I have hung the picture on the wall.)

WB 12.2
Key

hangman	executioner
amazement	great surprise
currently	now
threatens	menaces
estimated	calculated roughly
crimes	offences
reckoning	calculation
a further	another
granted	given
ashamed	embarrassed and guilty

WB 12.3
Key

Number of prisoners on death row in May 1988 excluding the writer of the letter	273
Number of black people	197
Number of coloured people	56
Number of white people	20
Number of people hanged January–May 1988	59
Number of black people	44
Number of coloured people	14
Number of white people	1
The death sentence in South Africa exists for	robbery with aggravating circumstances, rape, murder, political crimes
Recently there has been an increase in the number of people facing the death sentence for	political crimes

- The level and value of the discussion which follows will depend on the students' maturity.

UNIT 13 *page 44*

> **New structures**
> *shall* for offers
>
> **New functions**
> Making offers
>
> **Vocabulary**
> war – starvation – gifts – devastating – sale
>
> **Revision**
> Suggestions: *Why don't you …?*
> Future: *Will* + infinitive

War on Want

- Students look at the advertisement for *War on Want*. Tell them to read the information to understand the gist of what it is about, but tell them that it is not necessary for them to understand every word.
- Ask them a few questions about the advertisement in order to highlight the problems in Ethiopia, and to check their understanding.

Key
1 Ethiopia.
2 Starvation.
3 Getting food through.
4 Food and transport.
5 War on Want, Ethiopian Emergency, Room 17D, 37–39 Great Guildford Street, London SE1 0YU.

UNIT 13 *page 45*

- Students listen to the dialogue. Ask them to tell you what the connection is between the advertisement and the dialogue. (The advertisement sparks off their desire to do something themselves to get money for the famine victims.)
- Students then do the *true* or *false* exercise.

Key
1 False   2 True   3 False   4 False   5 True (probably)   6 True

Supplementary Exercise 17 *(SB page 120)*
Key
1 Jane and Mike
2 Tom
3 Mike
4 Jane
5 Mike

PRESENTER	Tapescript 34. Unit 13. Listen.
JANE	Have you seen the advertisement in the paper today?
TOM	No, I haven't. Let me see it.
MIKE	Oh, yes I saw that. It's terrible isn't it?
JANE	Yes, and terrible to think there's nothing we can do about it.
TOM	There must be something we can do.
MIKE	Well, they need money and we haven't got any.
TOM	I know, but perhaps we could do something to get some money. Why don't we organise something? A Bring and Buy sale perhaps?
MIKE	What on earth is a Bring and Buy sale?
JANE	It's what it says. You bring things and buy things. I think that's a brilliant idea, Tom. We could get people to bring things that they don't need anymore, as long as they are in good condition, and then sell them. The money we get could go to the people in Ethiopia.
TOM	That's right. Now how do we go about it?
JANE	First of all we need to decide where we can have a sale.
TOM	I'm sure we could have it in the local church hall. Shall I ask Mr Jones at the church?
MIKE	No, I'm going to church this evening.
JANE	Would you mind asking him then Mike? And we'll need to advertise the sale. Shall I make the posters?
TOM	Yes, that's a good idea.
JANE	And what are we going to do about distributing the posters? We want as many people as possible to see them.
TOM	We'll take them round to shops, the library, schools and anywhere else we can think of.
MIKE	Shall I keep the things we get at my house?
TOM	No, it's OK. I'll keep them as my house is nearer the church than yours.
MIKE	Then we'll get some more people to help us. I'll speak to the others in our class.
JANE	Yes, OK Mike.
TOM	And I'll see what we have to do about sending the money when we get it.
MIKE	Great. I'm glad we can do something to help …

1 *Language Focus*

- Students listen to the cassette and repeat the phrases from the dialogue. Watch their pronunciation. Get them to repeat in groups and then in pairs.

PRESENTER   Tapescript 35. Unit 13. Listen.
TOM   Shall I ask Mr Jones?
MIKE   No, it's all right. I'll ask him.
JANE   Shall I make the posters?
TOM   Yes, that's a good idea.
MIKE   Shall I keep the things at my house?
TOM   No, I'll keep them at my house.

PRESENTER   Now listen and repeat.

- Tell them to read the offers and make suitable answers. When they have finished, check their answers.
- Play the cassette and ask students to note the model answers.
- Tell them to practise the exchanges with another student.

🎧 36

PRESENTER   Tapescript 36. Unit 13. Listen.
  1 Shall I buy the bread?
     No, thanks. I've already bought the bread.
  2 Shall I ask John?
     No, I'll ask him.
  3 Shall I open the window?
     No, thanks. It's not very warm in here.
  4 Shall I bring some cassettes?
     Yes, please. I haven't got many.
  5 Shall I invite Mary?
     Yes, I'd like her to come.

2 Making offers

- Students work in pairs. One asks the questions and the other finds suitable answers. They change roles when they have finished.
- Point out to them that sometimes more than one answer is possible. Tell them to check with you if they are in doubt about any of the answers.
- When they have finished the exercise, tell them to make up similar questions and answers with another student.

Key

Shall I open the window?	No, it's quite cold in here.
Shall I phone Peter?	No, he's coming later.
Shall I write to Sarah?	No, I wrote to her last week.
Shall I buy some sugar?	No, there's some in the kitchen.
Shall I get your books?	No, I'll get them.
Shall I tidy the bedroom?	Yes, please. It's very untidy.
Shall I go to the station?	Yes, the train is due in twenty minutes.
Shall I order the drinks?	Yes, please. I'm really thirsty.
Shall I put on a cassette?	No, I'll put it on.
Shall I do the washing up?	No, I'll do it later.

3 The school trip

1 It would be fun if it were possible to make this activity lead up to a real school journey but obviously this depends very much on your school organisation.
- Explain to the students that you want them to discuss the topic as much as possible.
- Point out to them the kind of language structures you want them to include, but tell them that they are not to think of the exercise only as practising structures.
2 When they have finished, tell them you want a detailed description of what they have decided to do.

Extra practice idea: offers chain-game

Students work in groups of four. Suggest themes: (e.g. tidying a bedroom, preparing to go for a day out somewhere, etc.)

1 Each student has to offer to do something towards the preparations.
2 All members of the group must agree that the suggestions are valid.
3 Suggestions must not be repeated.
4 A student is out of the game if he or she repeats or cannot think of any more suggestions.
5 The winner is the last person left in the game.

WB 13.1

- In this exercise students have to make comments and suitable suggestions. Accept any reasonable offers.

Preparation

Ask students to complete WB 13.2 before starting the next section.

UNIT 13 *page 46*

> **New structures**
> Modal verbs – *must, should, have to, mustn't, shouldn't,*
> *don't have to, needn't*
>
> **New functions**
> Expressing obligation
>
> **Vocabulary**
> maths – history – behaviour – teenager –
> teenage – uninhibited – at the same time

WB 13.2

Before students begin the lesson, they should have completed WB 13.2
which pre-teaches modals. Extra time may need to be spent on this area if
students have difficulty doing the sentences.

Key

1 You *mustn't* touch electric wires with wet hands.
2 Children *don't have to* go to school in Britain after the age of 16.
3 We *should* visit our dentist regularly.
4 You *must* drive on the left in England.
5 You *needn't* go to the supermarket if you haven't got much time.
6 Students *shouldn't* go to bed late when there's school the next day.
7 I *have* to study every evening because I want to pass my exams.

The good language student

- Tell students to read the sentences and decide whether they think the
  statements are true about language learners.
- When they have finished, tell them to check their answers in pairs. If
  their answers do not coincide with those of their partner, they should try
  to defend their choices.
- Before going on to Language Focus, ask them to suggest other
  statements that could be made about the good language student. Write
  their suggestions on the board.

4 *Language Focus*

Some of these statements may have already been suggested by students.

- Tell them to put in the modal they consider most suitable in the spaces.
  In some cases more than one version is possible.
- When they have finished, play the cassette for them to check their
  answers.

PRESENTER   Tapescript 37. Unit 13. Listen.

    1 You *should* go to your English lessons regularly.
      You *must* go to your English lessons regularly.
    2 You *mustn't* translate everything into your language.
    3 You *should* ask your teacher to help you if you don't
      understand.
    4 You *mustn't* be afraid of making mistakes.
      You *needn't* be afraid of making mistakes.
    5 You *should* try to revise something before each lesson.
    6 You *don't have to* do examinations to learn a language well.
    7 You *needn't* understand every word when you read a foreign
      language.
    8 You *should* try to speak as much as possible.

Now listen and repeat.

5 *Maths and history students*

1 Students make sentences about the good maths student and the good history student using the modals given. They should complete the sentences individually.

2 Tell them to compare their answers in pairs. Encourage them to defend their choice of modal if it differs from that of their partner. They should also add any statements that their partner made to their list.

3 They should write a paragraph about one of the topics using the information they wrote down.

6 *Job applications*

1 Before students begin work on this activity, ask them to look at the categories and suggest any others they think could be there. Include these if possible.

● Students should now work individually writing comments as in the example.

2 When they compare their comments with other students, encourage them, as before, to defend their opinions when they are different from the others.

3 The next part of the activity is a listening exercise. Students will hear two adults talking about what they consider to be important when interviewing school leavers for their first job.

● They will use the headings in the first exercise. They should make notes while they listen.

 **38**

PRESENTER	Tapescript 38. Unit 13. Listen.
MAN	You don't have to have confidence, but it certainly helps, in my opinion.
WOMAN	Yes, I quite agree.
MAN	In mean, you shouldn't be aggressive, but it helps certainly to come in with some, er, belief in your own abilities.
WOMAN	Absolutely. You don't want to, erm, erm, think that a person is nervous.
MAN	No. No. Polite certainly, but er…not nervous.
WOMAN	Absolutely…Not nervous. And what about experience? I think experience is very, very important – certainly for the sort of people that I want to place.
MAN	Yes, erm, I mean I think they should certainly have erm work experience and they must have good references.
WOMAN	Yes, I think two references. One from erm, a teacher, possibly, and one from someone who's known them for a long time.
MAN	I'm also more interested in the, in the personality, the more rounded personality of the applicant. I think they should certainly have an interest in, in, culture and art, er music and literature.
WOMAN	Yes…yes, I agree with that. And the theatre, I think is important, too. And their appearance…
MAN	I'm not so sure about that, but erm, that's a personal opinion. Appearance is of course extremely important…
WOMAN	Appearance…yes I like a man to be well dressed, wear a suit, er, a tie…
MAN	They should wear a tie, of course.
WOMAN	Yes, and nice clean shoes, and short hair…clean…
MAN	Well, I don't worry too much about the length of the hair as long as it is well, it, it, must be well groomed, and it must be well bleaur, looked after…care.
WOMAN	Yes…What about erm the nationality? Do you mind if er… they're foreign?
MAN	Increasingly: No. I think erm, Brit…the, the, the days of the 'Ah, he's British, he must be the best!' er, I'm afraid are long gone. Ha-ha-ha! Which is rather good, I suppose, in a way.

WOMAN	All right…I also, I do think a language is important especially erm, nowadays…
MAN	Indeed, more and more so.
WOMAN	…er, you find the French, manage to be able to speak er all languages…
MAN	Quite.
WOMAN	…whereas we just speak English.
MAN	Yes, yes…they needn't necessarily all have er, travel experience, but obviously it is a, it is a great help.
WOMAN	It is, because it gives them an idea of what people in other countries er are like.
MAN	Yes, do you have any strong erm, er, erm, opinions about people with criminal records?…which do crop up.
WOMAN	Oh…yes, I certainly do…I, I wouldn't ever employ anybody…
MAN	You wouldn't…They mustn't have…a criminal…
WOMAN	They must not have a criminal record.
MAN	That's er, that's very hard I think er…

4 As a final phase, students write a paragraph about teenage behaviour from their own point of view and from the point of view of adults, using the notes they made.

WB 13.3

● In this exercise students have to complete the sentences. Point out to them that there can sometimes be various answers. Accept any reasonable suggestions.

Key

1 There's a holiday tomorrow so I *needn't* get up early, but I *must* go to school the day after tomorrow, so I'll *have to* get up at seven o'clock.

2 I *should* wash my hair this evening but I think I'll go to the cinema instead.

3 When you are in London you *mustn't* smoke on the Underground.

4 You *must* be over seventeen to drive a car in Britain.

5 You *shouldn't* go to bed very late when you have a test the next morning.

6 Mary went to the dentist yesterday. She *had to* make three more appointments.

7 My teacher said I *needn't* do my homework today as I've got an important tennis match but I *have to* do it tomorrow.

WB 13.4
Key

1 I must go to the dentist.

2 You needn't buy any bread. I've already got some.

3 You shouldn't play football near the windows.

4 You mustn't play with the electricity wires.

5 I should do my homework.

6 You must drive on the right in France.

7 You shouldn't eat so much chocolate.

UNIT 14 *page 48*

Moondown: Episode 3

Skills Focus: Reading and Listening

1 Students read and discuss the questions before they look at the text. It may be a good idea to write the questions on the board and do them away from the book to ensure that students do not look at the text.

Key
1 At the end of the last episode Cathy had received the phone call telling her about the dumping of nuclear waste at Star Point and telling her the time and date of the next dumping.
2 Cathy and Pete decided to go to Star Point, although Pete was a little worried about going.
3 Encourage students to make predictions in English about this episode and write them on the board.

● Students look at the text as they listen to the cassette and check their hypotheses. If they have any serious problems with vocabulary, you may deal with them now.

UNIT 14 *page 49*

2,3 These two exercises and Supplementary Exercises 18 and 19 should
be done together. The latter two are more difficult and may be omitted,
depending on the ability of your class.

- Students work through the exercises individually and then check them in
  pairs, before you go through the answers in class.
- While they are doing the exercises, monitor their progress and give
  assistance where necessary.

Key to Exercise 2
1 False   2 True   3 True   4 False   5 True   6 True   7 False

Supplementary Exercise 18 *(SB page 120)*
Key
1 To go to Star Point.
2 Because he had to wait for his mother to go to bed.
3 His father is dead and his mother relies a lot on Pete.
4 She would worry about him.
5 The students will have varying ideas here. Encourage them to make
  hypotheses.

Key to Exercise 3
4 The lorries arrived.
6 A man saw Cathy and Pete.
2 Cathy and Pete went to the harbour.
7 Cathy and Pete ran away.
1 Cathy and Pete arrived at Star Point.
5 Pete took some photos.
3 Cathy and Pete hid behind a wall.

Supplementary Exercise 19 *(SB page 120)*
Key
1 True   2 False   3 True   4 True   5 True   6 True   7 False

 See Student's Book for tapescript 39.

4 Allow students time to read the summaries and discuss the differences
between them.

- Play the cassette and let students identify the correct paragraph; play
  the cassette a second time if necessary, but do not help the students
  reach the answer.
- You may wish to supplement the discussion with comprehension
  questions of your own.

Key
The correct paragraph is the second.

Supplementary Exercise 20 *(SB page 120)*
This may be used as an alternative way of approaching the listening, or as
the comprehension questions mentioned above.
- Let students read the questions before they listen to the cassette, after
  which they discuss the answers in pairs.

Key
1 Because the bags that he was carrying were very heavy.
2 Because he fell over.
3 Yes, he did.
4 Because he was a friend of Pete's father.
5 No, he didn't.
6 A film from his camera.
7 Because she didn't wait for him.
8 Because she thought it was silly for both of them to be caught.
9 Because she found out that Pete still had the film with a photo of the
  lorries.

40

PRESENTER	Tapescript 40. Unit 14. Listen.
PETE	I *am* running, Cathy, but these bags are a bit heavy!
CATHY	Give one to me, then!
MAN	Come here, you two! Stop!
PETE	Oh no!
MAN	Got you! Well, I never, this *is* a surprise! Peter Chisman!
PETE	Who are you? How do you know my name?
MAN	I used to work with your father, we were good friends, that's why.
PETE	Oh yes, I remember you ... you're Jack Sims.
MAN	That's right ... now, what are you doing down here at 1 o'clock in the morning taking photographs?
PETE	I came here with my friend ... we wanted to go for a walk and ...
MAN	A likely story! With a camera! I'm not that stupid, Peter! Now, you'll have to give me the film.
PETE	All right. Here you are. But what are you doing here? What are those lorries doing here?
MAN	That's none of your business, Peter. You just forget you saw them and everything will be all right. OK?
PETE	All right. Good night, Mr Sims.
MAN	Good night, Peter. And remember what I told you.
CATHY	Hey, Pete, over here!
PETE	Oh, there you are. Thanks very much for stopping to help me!
CATHY	There was no point in two of us getting caught, was there? Now, who was that? Why did he let you go?
PETE	His name's Jack Sims. He worked at the factory with my father.
CATHY	What did you give him? I saw you give him something.
PETE	I had to give him a film.
CATHY	Oh no! That means we haven't got a photo of those lorries.
PETE	Er, Cathy, I said I gave him *a* film not *the* film! We *have* got a photo of those lorries!
CATHY	Oh, well done, Pete! You're not so stupid after all.
PETE	Oh, thanks very much, Cathy, thanks very much.

WB 14.1
This is a reading comprehension based on a brief description of the British
political party system. The text is extremely difficult for students of this level
and should only be given to them if they are able and confident.

- Approach WB 14.1 by asking students as a class what they know about
  British politics. They should know Margaret Thatcher, Winston Churchill,
  etc.: use the discussion to elicit and provide as much vocabulary as
  possible, e.g. *prime minister, government, sovereign, parliament.*
- Let students read the questions and discuss the answers in class.
- They should be able to make predictions for all of the questions,
  (question 3 is not actually answered in the text, but the situation is
  referred to).
- Impress on the students that when they look at the text, they should
  only find the information necessary to answer the questions.

Key
1 Conservative and Labour.
2 Before 1945.
3 Some constituencies have fewer voters than others and Britain does not
  have a proportional representation system of voting.
4 The sovereign.
5 To contribute to the formulation of policy; to oppose proposals where
  necessary; to prepare for the next election.

- Afterwards, go over the students' answers to WB 14.1 in class and
  discuss any points arising. Guide the discussion to cover the three
  questions in WB 14.2.

WB 14.2
- Refer the students to the questions and discuss the differences in your
  country.

UNIT 15 *page 50*

Skills Focus: Writing

Narrating

1　A lot of the things we can say about story writing also apply in the students' own language. The problem in the foreign language is that students tend not to draw analogies with their own language and don't make full use of their vocabulary. That's why it's necessary to make the points set down in the Student's Book.

2　Encourage students to use a dictionary (preferably monolingual) when writing, not so much to find the meanings of words as to find alternative words instead of repeating the same ones.

● Give them help on how to use the dictionary.

Key

twelve o'clock at night – *midnight*
fallen asleep – *dropped off*
in my direction – *towards me*
speaking very quietly – *whispering*
trying very hard – *straining enormously*
'Be quiet.' – 'Sshhh!' or 'don't make a noise.'
closer – *nearer*

3,4　Students need to be encouraged to use linking words when they are writing a continuous piece of prose.

● Ask them to name as many linking words as they can before they start. Put these on the board and encourage students to use them.
● Point out the value of varying sentence lengths by using linking words.
● The linking words in the story are: *when, as, so, but, unless, and, before.*

5　These comprehension questions will help students understand the first part of the story.

● Let students work in pairs.

Key

1　Harry is the man in bed.
2　Timber.
3　It is at the side of the house, probably on the ground floor, with a window on to the drive.
4　Harry's light is on.
5　So he can walk quietly.
6　Students' own answers.

6　Give students the chance to predict in groups how they think the story will end.

● The sentences are in order and are given to help students come to a version reasonably close to the original.
● Do not help too much or regard their answers as *right or wrong*, the value of the exercise is in working out a story, which need not be the same as the original.
● They should write their version of the story, again in groups, using the sentences as guidelines.

Key

Who do you think says this?　*Harry.*
What do you think 'it' is?　*The danger; an animal.*
Who is 'I'? Why do you think he wants a knife?　*Timber. To kill/cut the animal.*
Who says this?　*Harry (could also be Timber).*
What do you think his profession is?　*Doctor.*
What do these things do?　*Make people/animals unconscious.*
Whose face?　*Harry's (could also be Timber's; whoever was afraid).*
What is likely to happen after fifteen minutes?　*The danger will have gone;*
the animal will be unconscious.
Why do they need to do this?　*To find the animal, but carefully, in case it is not unconscious.*

7　This exercise builds on the dictionary practice in Exercise 2 above.

● Tell students to look up the adjectives if they do not know them, and try to imagine the ending of the story using these adjectives. A group or class discussion would be useful here.

8　The writing should be done individually, after the group discussion.

● Encourage students to swap papers when they have finished to look over each other's work. Any comments or suggestions written by a student on another's work should be in light pencil so that they can be erased.

UNIT 15 *page 51*

- This story, *Poison*, by Roald Dahl, is about a man who is convinced that a poisonous snake has crawled under the bedclothes. It is imperative that the man doesn't move. A doctor is called and he attempts to kill the snake by giving it a dose of ether. At the end of the story they find out that in fact there was no snake there at all.
- *Poison* is from a selection of short stories by Roald Dahl, called *More Tales of the Unexpected* published by Penguin. Try to get hold of a copy so that students can be encouraged to read it for themselves after they have done the exercise. Alternatively you could read it to them.

WB 15

- Remind students of the value of this unit (and other *Skills Focus: Writing* units) as a reference for their written work.
- In correcting students' compositions, look for the elements of narrative writing studied in this unit.

REVISION FOCUS
Units 11–15 _page 52_

1 *Talking about quantity*

- Before students begin this exercise, tell them to look at the example. Show them how the second sentence has the same meaning as the first.
- Tell them to point out what changes were made to produce this sentence. Go through some more examples with them and then let them do the exercise.
- Other answers may be acceptable.

Key

1 *Not many* people in Britain go to church regularly.
2 There are *a few* people in the room.
3 There are *a lot* of eggs in the fridge.
4 There *is very little* milk in the bottle.
5 I *haven't got much* free time today.
6 We *have very few* history lessons a week.
7 *Plenty of* people are studying English. (accept *many*)
8 She *ate very little* food yesterday.

2 *Talking about personal experiences*

- This exercise contrasts the simple past and present perfect tenses.
- It is advisable to do the exercise before giving students a lot of explanation in order to find out whether they have grasped the differences, especially when they are used to using a different tense in their own language.
- If you find the students are having a lot of difficulties, refer them to the relevant grammar sections (WB pages 18–19 and 29) again as a homework study and then give them more examples of a similar kind in class.

Key

1 I *have seen* that film twice and I don't want to see it again.
2 I *studied* French for two years when I was at school.
3 I *'ve been* in Paris for two weeks. I'm going home tomorrow.
4 I *have lived* in Italy for ten years. I like it here.
5 I *have been* here since half past six but he hasn't arrived.
6 I *played* tennis last week but I don't want to play this week.

3 *Making offers*

- In this exercise students are asked to make offers for which the answers given are reasonable. They get an idea from the replies what offer to make.
- There is no key to the exercise as there are various possibilities for each sentence.

4 *Obligation*

- Students will have seen in the modal lessons (pages 46–47) that there is usually more than one right answer, so set the exercise for them to do and accept any solution that is reasonable.
- Treat the following as a suggested but not definitive paragraph.

Key

YOUNG CHILDREN

Young children *should* go to bed early as they need a lot of sleep. They *must* go to school regularly but at least they *don't have* to go to work! They *shouldn't* watch television all the time although there are some very good programmes which they *should* watch. They *needn't* get up early on Saturdays and Sundays. They *should* help their parents in the house and certainly *should* keep their rooms tidy!

5 *Vocabulary*

Students' own answers.
Refer to the teacher's notes for Exercise 6, page 36.

6 *Pronunciation*

- The pronunciation exercise in this lesson deals with the letter *u*.
- Ask students to look at the four examples and pronounce them.
- Play the cassette and get them to listen and repeat. Check the accuracy of their pronunciation.
- Students now classify the words in the list. Play the cassette and tell them to check their answers.

41 *Key*

1 /ʌ/ lunch   2 /juː/ music   3 /uː/ blue   4 /ɜː/ church

much 1	surname 4
fruit 3	butter 1
supermarket 3	hundred 1
Thursday 4	excuse 2
bus 1	Tuesday 2
June 3	nurse 4
computer 2	true 3
burn 4	

GRAMMAR FOCUS
Units 11–15 *page 53*

1 Qualifiers

a The difficulty here comes from students trying to use *many* or *much* to replace *a lot of* as they would in their own language. If this problem arises, tell students to use *many* and *much* in negative sentences, which is the most common use in English. They will later come across times when they can be used in positive sentences.

b There aren't *many* people in England who go to university.
People don't spend *much* money on entertainment in England.
There are *a lot* of people in England who have a television set.
People spend *a lot* of time watching television.
Very *few* English people have a swimming pool in the garden.
We've got very *little* free time this week.

c *much* and *many* are used with uncountable and countable nouns respectively, but *a lot* and *plenty* can be used with both.

2 Present perfect with *for* and *since*

a The structure was first introduced in Unit 8 and students should be beginning to feel confident about when to use the present perfect.

b I *am* in the classroom.
I came in five minutes *ago*.
I *have been* in the classroom *for* five minutes.
I *have been* in the classroom *since* ten o'clock.

c This obviously depends on your language. In many languages the present perfect is used when in English we would use the simple past (sentence 2) and the simple present is used when we use the present perfect (sentences 3 and 4).

3 shall *for offers*

a In English we use *shall + infinitive* when making offers (in contrast to other languages). Once the students understand this they should have no difficulty using the form as it is very straightforward.

b *Shall* I buy some bread?   *Shall* I invite Mary?

c Many languages use the present tense for this function.

4 Modal verbs for obligation

a The students are asked here to think about when and why one modal verb is used instead of another. The choice depends on how strong the obligation is. If they have understood this, they should have no difficulty matching the sentences in *b* to the most suitable sentence in *a*. If they do have difficulty, refer them back to exercise WB 13.2.

b It's Saturday. You needn't get up.
You're very ill. You mustn't get up.
It's a lovely day. You should get up.
You're late. You must get up.

c No, modals always remain the same.
It depends on your language. Ask the students to give you the equivalents in your language.

UNIT 16 *page 54*

> **New structures**
> Long numbers
>
> **New functions**
> Talking about statistics
>
> **Vocabulary**
> spacecraft – tail – dust – spread – lifetime – satellite – diameter –
> nucleus – surface – orbit – scientist
>
> **Revision**
> Dates
> How to say the year in English

Guide to the galaxy

- Before reading, tell students to look at the two photos, one of Halley's
  Comet taken in the early twentieth century and the other during the
  1986 sighting. Teach words like *tail, dust, spacecraft, satellite, diameter,
  nucleus, surface, orbit*, which are needed for this unit. A lot of technical
  words are very similar in other languages so students should be able to
  make reasonable guesses.
- Ask general questions about the pictures and give students a chance to
  tell you what they know from their science lessons, if possible in English,
  and if not, in their langauge. Let this go on as long as the students have
  something to say as it is good preparation for the rest of the unit.

Halley's Comet

- Tell students to read the passage about Halley's Comet. If the ground
  has been well prepared, they should have little difficulty with the
  specialised language.
- Do not ask them to read the passage aloud. Let students answer the
  true or *false* exercise.

Key
1 True   2 False   3 True   4 False   5 False

Supplementary Exercise 21 *(SB page 120)*
This is a reading comprehension, based on the text.

Key
1 About every 76 years.
2 Vega 1, Vega 2, Giotto, (and also Pioneer Venus Orbiter).
3 It's made of gases and dust, about 20,000,000 km across.
4 Because it's losing material from the surface during every orbit.
5 In about 2062.

UNIT 16 _page 55_

1 Language Focus

● Play the sentences on the cassette as students follow in their books. Then play the version with pauses, which students repeat.

PRESENTER   Tapescript 42. Unit 16. Listen.
Vega 1 and Vega 2 came within 10,000 km (6,200 miles) of the nucleus.
The Giotto space probe passed within 600 km (372 miles) of Halley.
The cloud of gases and dust which make up the tail spread over a region about 20,000,000 km across.

Now listen and repeat.

● Get them to repeat the numbers in groups and individually, and make sure they are putting the _and_ in where necessary.
● When you feel they are confident, tell them to practise reading the numbers with another student. Go round and monitor them while they are doing this.

PRESENTER   Tapescript 43. Unit 16. Listen.
Five hundred and sixty-four.
Five thousand, nine hundred and sixty-seven.
Eight thousand.
Twenty-five thousand.
A hundred and twenty-three.
Three hundred and forty thousand, five hundred and twenty.
Nine million.
Seven million, eight hundred and twenty thousand, six hundred and forty-five.

● Tell them to read the information about the planet Uranus before they listen to the cassette.
● Then play the cassette and tell them to put in the missing numbers. Play the cassette a second time and allow them to check their answers with another student. Finally check the answers with the whole class.

PRESENTER   Tapescript 44. Unit 16. Listen.
William Herschel discovered Uranus in 1781 but little was known about it until January 24, 1986, when the Voyager 2 spacecraft passed within _82,000_ kilometres of its surface. They found out that the rotation period of the planet was 17.2 hours and the atmosphere contained _88%_ hydrogen and _12%_ helium. The atmosphere rotates in the same direction as the planet with winds of about _200_ km/hr (_125_ mph). Before the arrival of Voyager there were five known satellites of Uranus ranging from about _500_ to _1,600_ kilometres in diameter. Voyager found ten more satellites with diameters of _40_ to _80_ kilometres.

2 Area and population

In this part of the lesson students practise reading more numbers, this time referring to the area and population chart for the UK. Monitor this activity carefully and correct errors immediately.

● Students do this exercise in pairs. One student will transfer the information about area to his or her chart and the other student the information about population.
● In turns they should read the information from the chart in their books. The other student puts the information he or she hears on his or her chart.
● When they have finished, tell them to check their answers in pairs and then check in their books.

● It is probably a good idea to ask one or two students to read the numbers out to the class as a final check.

3 Geography quiz

Explain in class what you want students to do in this section (make up their own quiz.) It is important to get students to work out the areas they want to base their quiz on beforehand so that students who have to answer the questions have time to revise!

● Depending on the situation in your school you can either get students to prepare their questions at home before the next lesson or give them time in class to consult their geography books and prepare the quiz.
● If they work at home, then at the beginning of the next lesson put them into teams and tell them to make their final choice of questions together.
● If they are going to consult books in class, put them in teams and tell them to work out the questions they want to ask.
● They should have at least fifteen questions in case the other team is asking questions on the same topic so they have alternative ones ready. You may prefer to avoid this problem by making sure each team has a different country to ask questions about.
● They now take turns to ask questions. The team with most points at the end wins.

WB 16.1

● The numbers are given above the exercise and students have to write them out in full.

Key

The diameter of the sun is _a hundred and nine_ times the diameter of Earth and it is _three hundred and thirty-three thousand_ times as massive. The temperature at the surface of the sun is about _six thousand_ K*, and it is believed to increase to perhaps _twenty million_ K at the centre. The sun loses _four million_ tons of hydrogen a second but it is generally believed that it will continue to radiate for another _two or three hundred million_ years. The solar wind blows at a speed of about _two thousand_ kilometres per second.

* 1 K, or kelvin, is the basic unit of thermodynamic temperature.

WB 16.2
Key
1 100,000 million.
2 Stars.
3 Epsilon Eridani and Gamma Cephei.
4 The Space Telescope and Hipparchus.
5 Search for Extraterrestrial Intelligence.

WB 16.3
Key

1	nearby	6	unseen
2	are common	7	further
3	hampered	8	vastly
4	tiny, minute	9	life-supporting
5	dimly		

WB 16.4
Key
1 Planets are so small.
   They only reflect light dimly.
2 High-resolution spectroscopy.
3 It measured accurately any variations in a star's light.
4 They were being affected by large bodies around them.
5 By the end of the century.

WB 16.5
Students' own answers.

UNIT 16 *page 56*

New structures
used to
didn't use to
Did you use to...?

New functions
Describing previous habits and situations

Vocabulary
complain – strange – drive – knit – sew – household

Revision
Present simple to describe habitual actions
Adverbs (sometimes, never, often, usually)

I *used to live in Italy*

- Tell students to look at the picture but cover the text in their books.
- Ask some general questions about what the girl is doing, where she is, if they have a lot of homework, where they do their homework, how long they take, etc.
- Play the cassette once and then tell them to read the questions under the dialogue. Play the cassette a second time and tell students to answer the questions. Weaker students may prefer to look at the text as they listen the second time.
- It is a good policy to let students be more and more responsible for their own learning. Encourage them to decide for themselves whether they want to do the exercise without the text or if they want to see the text while they do it.

 **45** See Student's Book for tapescript 45.

Key
1 In Italy.
2 Three.
3 The number of subjects she had to study.
4 Because they didn't do many sports at school.
5 Yes.

Supplementary Exercise 22 *(SB page 120)*
Key
Jane's mum went to school in *Italy*. She had a lot of *homework* every day and she also had to do it in a *foreign language*. She had more *subjects* to study than Jane, too – about *sixteen*. She did quite a lot of things in the afternoon. She went to the *sports centre* and she also had *piano* lessons in the afternoon.

4 Language Focus

● Play the cassette and tell students to listen and repeat.

PRESENTER   Tapescript 46. Unit 16. Listen.
JANE   Did you use to have a lot of homework when you were at school?
You used to live in Italy, didn't you?
MUM   We used to go to the sports centre two or three times a week. We didn't use to do many sports at school.

PRESENTER   Now listen and repeat.

● A good class should attempt the exercise which follows without hearing the cassette first. Give a weaker class the back-up of the cassette from the beginning.
● Play the cassette for the students to check their paragraph.

PRESENTER   Tapescript 47. Unit 16. Listen.
PAOLA   We *used* to go to school at nine o'clock but we stayed there until four o'clock in the afternoon. Of course we *didn't use* to go on Saturdays so that was a good thing. One thing I found difficult about living in England was the fact that we *used* to eat so early in the evenings! I was always hungry by about ten o'clock, and *used* to have a sandwich or something before I went to bed. I *didn't use* to drink as much tea as English people but I didn't think it was too bad.

5 Thirty years ago

In this section students have the chance to give their views on men's and women's roles thirty years ago and today.
1 Tell them to complete the chart for themselves first. Point out to them that in some cases, things will be different now and in some cases they will be the same.
2 When they have done this, tell them to ask another student questions to find out what he or she thinks. This will hopefully lead to some exchange of views as not all students will agree on the way things are now.
● Encourage any discussion that may come out of it.
3 As a follow-up activity there is a writing exercise. Point out to students that we generally use *used to* with the linker *but* when there has been a change of habit, and *and* with the simple past tense, when there has been no change of habit. Students must put the conclusions they have come to, into a continuous piece of writing.

6 When I was ten

1 Before the students do the writing exercise, spend some time on a class discussion of the kind of things they used to do when they were ten.
● This will encourage those who are more reluctant to begin to start thinking about themselves.
2 Students listen to two British teenagers discussing the same topics.
● Tell them not to expect to understand everything but they should understand enough to make some notes under the different headings. Play the tape a second time.
3 Put students into groups after they have finished the writing and listening exercises and get them to discuss what they used to do and compare this with what the two English people said.

PRESENTER   Tapescript 48. Unit 16. Listen.
GIRL   So where did you use to live before you came to Sevenoaks?
BOY   Oh I used to live in Edinburgh. Used to live in a small flat and share it with my family er my mum, my dad, my sisters. I, I used to share a room with my brother.
GIRL   Oh, you shared a room?
BOY   Yeah.
GIRL   Oh.
BOY   Why – didn't you use to share a room?
GIRL   No, no I, I didn't. I had my own room. I used to live in my grandparents' house you see and it was, it was enormous and er...
BOY   Wow.
GIRL   ...I had my own room.
BOY   It was a bit posh, huh?
GIRL   Well yes, yes it was, but erm you know my, my school was a little bit like that, my primary school. Did erm did you use to go to a nice school?
BOY   Oh...used to go to a very strict school. It was er that you know primary school I went to, it was, it was very strict. We used to have to stand up when the teachers came in. It was sort of monks that brought us up, you know, sort of walking round with...canes you know, like that, sort of give you whack over the, over the legs or whatever you know, if you, if you...
GIRL   Oh I think I would have hated that. Did you use to like it?
BOY   No, I hated it. I did hate it. Did you use to like school?
GIRL   Oh...I used to love my primary school. Erm, I mean you know we didn't have any exams or homework and it was all very sort of, free and easy, well we were very young you know...
BOY   Sure.
GIRL   ...it's a little bit different to er to going to um a secondary school.
BOY   Sure...sure...
GIRL   Erm, what did you use to do in your spare time?
BOY   We used to play in the street, you know, football, that was the best part of the day, you know after school. It was great. And we used to, well, I say we, I mean I used to read a lot, but my friends used to think I was a wimp because they didn't bother reading.
GIRL   Oh I didn't use to read, no. I never used to like it.
BOY   Do you play sports though?
GIRL   Oh well, I used to play rounders and erm hopskotch. Do you know hopskotch?
BOY   'Course I do yeah. Used to used to play that all the time.
GIRL   Did you?
BOY   Mmm.
GIRL   Mmm. Well, I, you see, I don't know because we didn't have any boys at that school, so er so I don't know what boys do when they're at primary school.

WB 16.6
● Students first read the notes about how the American Indians used to live and how they live now and then use those notes to write a paragraph about the American Indians.

WB 16.7
Key
1 She used to read a lot but now she doesn't read at all/much. She prefers to watch television.
2 He used to smoke but now he doesn't smoke at all.
3 She used to live in Venice but now she lives in London.
4 There used to be a park next to the hospital but now there's a supermarket.
5 She didn't use to drink coffee but now she really enjoys it.
6 She used to have long hair but now it's short.
7 He didn't use to have much money but now he's rich.
8 He didn't use to enjoy studying but now he really enjoys it.

Message in a bottle

1 *Skills Focus: Reading*

1 You may do the first phase of the lesson with the books closed. Write the headline of the article *Message in a bottle* on the board. Invite students to speculate on the content of the article. (They may hypothesise that it has something to do with pop music, as the title is borrowed from a pop song by The Police, or messages in bottles found on beaches.)

● You can guide students' hypotheses by asking them what bottles usually contain.

2 Now ask students to open their books and look at the questions for discussion.

● Students should first read and answer the questions individually before discussing them in pairs or groups.

● When they have finished their discussion, compare results with the whole class and write some of the findings on the board.

3 In this exercise students are asked to speculate on the content of the article by reading a series of statements on the subject of children's drinking habits and deciding if they think they will be included in the article.

● Students now read the article individually and check their answers.

● The statements not included in the article are:
The age at which children begin drinking.
The opinions of some parents on alcohol abuse.
The names of the drinks that young people prefer.

4 The vocabulary load in this text is not particularly heavy. Most of the topic-specific vocabulary can be dealt with before students actually read the text: *hard and soft drugs – illegal – booze (alcoholic drink) – alcohol – drink (i.e. alcoholic drink) – pub drinkers – cider – lager – beer – wine – spirits*.

● There are also some interesting adjectives, which may cause comprehension problems. By looking at these carefully in context, students will have a better chance of understanding them. Their meaning will be reinforced or clarified when they complete the gap-fill exercise. Allow students to work individually or in pairs.

Key

1 legless	2 hard, soft	3 staggering
4 cheaper	5 parental	6 brainless

(Note that questions 5 and 6 are on page 59.)

5 Students match the numbers to the phrase which best describes their significance.

Key

15,000	The number of children interviewed in the survey.
74	The percentage increase in the number of arrests of under-18-year-olds for drunkenness in the last 30 years.
90	The percentage of boys of 17 who regularly go to the pub.
14	The safe maximum of units of alcohol a week for women.
1000	The number of under-18-year-olds killed by alcohol in 1985.
15,700 million	The amount of money in pounds that the British spend on alcohol every year.
71	The number of deaths caused by illegal drugs in 1985.
300 million	The amount of money in pounds that under-18-year-olds spend on drink every year.

Supplementary Exercise 23 *(SB page 121)*
This exercise is very demanding and you should only allow very able or advanced students to tackle it.

● Tell them to underline what they feel to be the most important sentences in the text.

● They then rewrite these sentences in paragraph form to make a summary of the text.

2 *Skills Focus: Listening*

1 Students listen to an authentic unscripted conversation between one of the authors, Paul, and Fionnoula Coulson who works for the Alcohol Advisory Centre in Bath. As the conversation is unscripted students will find it quite difficult and it may be necessary to play the cassette several times for them to be able to complete the tasks.

● Tell students to look at the exercise and read the instructions. They have to decide which of the questions they would ask if they were doing the interview. This helps them to recognise the questions when they listen. They mark their questions with a tick.

● Play the cassette as many times as necessary for students to hear which questions Paul asked Fionnoula. Allow students to compare their answers in pairs before supplying the correct answers.

Key

1 How much alcohol is it safe to drink?
2 When does drinking become a problem for people?
3 Why do people drink to excess?
4 How old are the people who come to your centre?
5 How many people on average come to you in a year?
6 What do you do to help them?

● When you have checked their answers, play the cassette again and tell students to write down Fionnoula's answers in note form. Again allow students time to compare answers before going over them.

● If your students find the exercise difficult, divide the class into groups and allocate a question to each group. Better still, allow students to listen to the text in a language laboratory where they can control the machine.

Key

1 14 units for women, 21 for men, per week.
2 If they drink before a test or difficult moment, before driving, if they are spending too much money on alcohol, if their friends are encouraging them to drink too much.
3 To give them confidence, to make them feel better, to forget their problems.
4 15–80 years of age.
5 Several hundred.
6 Every person is an individual, work out an individual programme – some people have to stop drinking altogether, they help others to come down to a safe limit.

Supplementary Exercise 24 *(SB page 121)*
Better students should be able to tackle this. They decide if the statements
are *true* or *false*.

Key
1 True   2 True   3 True   4 True   5 False   6 True   7 False
8 False

 49

PRESENTER Tapescript 49. Unit 17. Listen.
PAUL Erm ... Fionnoula, you work for the Alcohol Advisory Centre, and
you help people who have a problem related to drinking alcohol.
Erm ... one of the questions which people often ask is this: Erm,
just how much alcohol is it safe to drink?
FIONNOULA Well, over the years the amount of safe alcohol has been
coming down and at the moment what is recommended is that
women should drink up to, should keep below 14 units a week
and men below 21 units.
PAUL Erm, you say units. Erm ... what is a unit? How much alcohol is
one unit?
FIONNOULA Well, if you think in terms of the measures you get in a pub, one
glass of wine, or one measure of spirit or half a pint of beer, or
one small glass of sherry. They're all equivalent to one unit.
PAUL So, um, er, a bottle of wine is about erm six units, is it?
FIONNOULA About six, seven or eight units depending on the size. I would
mention one thing here about beer. Some of the very strong
beers like export and double X and those can be up to three
times the strength of an ordinary beer ... so that's a point to
bear in mind.
PAUL Yes, and they're very popular now. Erm ... when does drinking
become a problem for people?
FIONNOULA That's a very difficult question to answer because everybody will
have a different level where they find drink a problem, but if you
find that you're drinking, having to dri- have a drink before you
face any test or any difficult moment, that might be worth
looking at. If you're drinking and driving, that's quite a
serious problem. If you're spending more money on alcohol
than you can afford, that's a problem, or if you feel that your
friends are encouraging you to drink more than you really feel
happy about, that could be a problem.
PAUL Mmm ... I see. But, why, why do people drink to excess, do you
think?
FIONNOULA Well, people often drink more than they want to because of their
friends, friends encourage them to drink more than they want
to. They sometimes drink more to give themselves confidence
and they feel better when they've had a drink. Or they've got
problems and if they drink enough they forget about their
problems. But they only end up having another problem.
PAUL Yes ... of course, yes. Now, how old are the people who come
to your centre?
FIONNOULA They cover quite a wide age range – the youngest was 15 and
the oldest was 79. So from 15 years of age to 80 years of age.
PAUL Yes, and how many come in on average in a year?
FIONNOULA Well, every year we have, well, over the past four years the
numbers have gone up and last year we had about 220 new
people coming ... er ... and we are working with those as well
as the people who've already been to see us and who are still
coming to see us.
PAUL Yes. So, overall how many clients do you have, approximately?
FIONNOULA Oh, er, several hundred clients come in over the year ...
PAUL Uhuh ...
FIONNOULA And interestingly enough this, half are men and half are female,
about the same number ...
PAUL Mmm. So it's about the same number. And what do you do to
help them?
FIONNOULA Well, everybody's problem is different. We look at each
individual's problem and work out a special programme for each
person. For some people it might mean having to stop drinking

all together, if they have very severe problems. Other people we
will be trying to work with them to get back to drinking at a safe
limit.
PAUL Yes, down to the 21 or 14 units.
FIONNOULA Yes.
PAUL OK, well thank you very much. That was very interesting.

2 In this section students are given the chance to express their own
opinions about under-age drinking and compare drinking habits in their
own country with those in Britain.
● You may like to discuss the matter in small groups or with the whole
class, but if you wish to give the discussion more direction, it is wise to
use the activity in the book. Students write a short simple questionnaire
about their drinking habits.
● There are some hints as to the questions they can ask in the book but it
is better if the students themselves decide what information they want
to ask about.
● When they have finished their questionnaire, which they can write in
pairs or groups, they can ask the other students in the class. You can
then have a class feedback session and write the information on the
board.

3 Vocabulary Development

As we have said in previous units, students should be encouraged to do
these lessons by themselves. They should also be encouraged to use a
dictionary. For this lesson it will obviously be an advantage for them to have
access to a dictionary which gives synonyms and antonyms.
● Give help with the exercise if the students seem really stuck but
encourage them to try to find a solution with other students first.
● The words below are only suggestions.

Key

	SNYONYM	ANTONYM
surface	outside	inside
spread	extend	decrease
large	big	small
finish	end	start
difficult	hard	easy
cheap	economical	expensive
fed up	miserable	excited
remove	take away	add
forbidden	prohibited	allowed
get on	board	get off
take off	leave	land
friendly	amicable	hostile
tidy	neat	messy
strange	peculiar	normal

WB 17.1
Students' own answers.

WB 17.2
Key
1 Dropping litter.
2 Damaging garden plants.
3 Spraying graffitti.
4 Vandalising bus shelters.
5 Torturing a pet.
6 Setting fire to a building.

WB 17.3
Key
1 They are not anti-social but often sociable, cyclists, and football fans.
2 Setting fire to a building.
3 Dropping litter.
4 They said they were not strict enough.
5 Give them more to do, inflict punishments and have more police on the
streets.

UNIT 18 *page 60*

> **New structures**
> *too much/many*
> *not enough*
>
> **New functions**
> Complaining
>
> **Vocabulary**
> not enough – too much – too many – sports facilities – toilets –
> dining-hall – sports equipment – maintenance – administration –
> football pitches – tennis courts – science laboratory – subjects
>
> **Revision**
> Countable and uncountable nouns

Students have already practised countable and uncountable nouns in Unit
11 but it is a good idea to revise them before beginning this unit.
- Write the titles *uncountable* and *countable* on the board and ask
  students to give you nouns to write in the lists.
- You may like to divide the class in two and do this as a team game or
  you may like to invite students to come and write the nouns on the
  board themselves.

Fed up!

It is possible to use the dialogue presentations as extra listening material.
- Write some easy questions on the board (How many people are
  speaking? What do they do? Are they pleased with their situation? Why
  not?)
- If your class is not particularly advanced and all the language presented
  is new to them, then you are advised not to use the dialogue for
  listening practice. In this case, you should allow your students to read
  the dialogue while they are listening to it.
- Play the cassette two or three times and ask students to write
  sentences as in the example using the numbers taken from the text.
  They should do this without referring to the text.

Key
1 Peter has to do at least four hours' homework every night.
2 Pam is doing six GCSEs.
3 There are 42 students in Peter's class.
4 There are 32 students in Pam's class.
5 There are 1200 students in Peter's school.
6 There are 90 teachers in Peter's school.
7 There are only three tennis courts in Peter's school.

Supplementary Exercise 25 *(SB page 121)*
Key
1 False   2 True   3 False   4 False   5 False   6 True   7 True
8 True

50 See Student's Book for tapescript 50.

Language Focus

- While students read the model sentences, play the first part of the
  cassette two or three times. Discuss any comprehension problems
  relating to vocabulary or the meaning of the target structure.
- Play the next part of the cassette and allow students to listen and
  repeat.
- Draw students' attention to the pronunciation of *enough* /ɪnʌf/. Ask
  them if they know any other words ending in *-ough* and if they are

pronounced in the same way. (They should know *although* and may
know *rough* and *cough*).

PRESENTER Tapescript 51. Unit 18. Listen.
  PETER I've got too much homework and I have to study too many
  subjects.
  I haven't got enough free time.
  There are too many students in my class.
  There aren't enough teachers.
  I like tennis and there aren't enough tennis courts.
  They haven't got enough money to build any more.

PRESENTER Now listen and repeat.

- Tell students to read the sentences for completion and work out the
  missing words. Students should work on their own at this stage.
- Play the next part of the cassette and allow them to check their
  answers. Elicit the answers and write them on the board.
- Finally students listen and repeat.

PRESENTER Tapescript 52. Unit 18. Listen.
  PETER There aren't *enough* toilets.
  There are *too many* football pitches.
  There aren't *enough* places in the library.
  They spend *too much* money on administration.
  They don't spend *enough* money on sports facilities.

PRESENTER Now listen and repeat.

UNIT 18 _page 61_

2 Complaining

- Allow students a few minutes to read the information in the chart. Discuss any difficulties they may have with vocabulary.
- Tell students to look at the examples of sentences written about the chart. Tell them to write at least six more sentences about Peter's school.
- When students have finished writing their sentences, divide the class into pairs and allow them to read their sentences to each other to see if they have written the same things.
- Follow this up with a class discussion and comparison of the sentences.

3 Difficult situations

1 Divide the class into groups and ask students to discuss conditions in their school. They must write a list of complaints.
- Allow a representative of each group to come up and write the group's complaints on the board.
- Discuss the complaints with the whole class.
2 Draw students' attention to the photograph. Ask them where they think it is. Ask them what they know about Ethiopia and conditions there. Refer them back to Unit 13 where they will already have done some work on the problems affecting people in Ethiopia.
- Give students a few minutes to read the questions and discuss any vocabulary problems. Explain words such as _famine, spreading, corn, cattle grazing, seed, drought._
- Play the cassette at least three times and tell students to choose the correct answers.
- Allow them to compare their answers before supplying the correct ones.

Key
1 b 2 b 3 a 4 b 5 a 6 c 7 a 8 a

PRESENTER Tapescript 53. Unit 18. Listen.

GREG And now it's just coming up to 1 o'clock and time for the news and this is Greg Norman reading it. Famine in Ethiopia is spreading from the highlands in the north to the food-growing areas in the south and east according to Mr Fred Cuny, chairman of the disaster assessment consultancy Intertect. The highlands of Harage are usually prime cereal lands producing sorghum and corn. The lowlands provide good grazing land and last year did not suffer badly in the drought. But in recent weeks large numbers of both highland and lowland tenants are entering food distribution centres in the region. There are crops in the fields according to the relief agency but the lack of rain means they do not produce seed. An estimated 1.2 million people in Harage are now without food – part of the total of 5.8 million Ethiopians who are in need of aid this year. The twenty African countries worst hit by the drought will need a total of $1.03 billion worth of aid this year.

3 Using the answers to Exercise 2, students should work alone on their paragraphs. Ask them to discuss their work in pairs when they have finished.

WB 18.1
Key
1 The government spends _too much_ on defence and _not enough_ on social services.
2 People eat _too much_ meat and _not enough_ vegetables.
3 There is _too much_ pollution in the north-east of England.
4 There are _not enough_ jobs in the north of England and _too many_ people who are out of work.
5 In our hospitals there are _too many_ patients and _not enough_ doctors and nurses.
6 There are _too many_ cars on our roads and the government doesn't spend _enough_ money on public transport.
7 There is _not enough_ rain in Ethiopia and _not enough_ food either.
8 There are _too many_ people in London and _not enough_ houses.
9 There were _too many_ people at the concert and _not enough_ seats.
10 Children eat _too many_ sweets and _not enough_ fruit and vegetables.

WB 18.2
- You may like to discuss this with students before they attempt to write the sentences.

UNIT 18 *page 62*

> **New structures**
> Present and past passive
>
> **New functions**
> Talking about processes
>
> **Vocabulary**
> LP – cassette – compact disc – produce – introduce – record –
> develop – invent – plastic – aluminium – recording – shellac – cut –
> coat (*verb*) – focus – remove – transfer – apply – press – print – sell
>
> **Revision**
> Formation of past participles

Before you start the lesson on the passives it is a good idea to revise the
formation of the past participles.

- You may do this in a traditional way by giving students the infinitive of a
  verb and asking them to supply the past and the past participle.
- You can make this into a game with the class divided into two teams
  and award points for each correct answer.
- Alternatively, you may like to revise the participles in a more
  communicative way by asking questions in which students have to use
  the present perfect tense.

The history of hi-fi

Before allowing students to open their books, do the following warm-up
activity.

- Find out with a show of hands what sort of audio equipment the
  students and their families have. (This provides useful revision of *have
  got*.)
- Discuss with them the quality of the equipment, the advantages and
  disadvantages of cassettes and records. Find out if they lend each other
  records or cassettes to record.
- There is a certain amount of difficult vocabulary in the text, although
  your students shouldn't have too much trouble with it as technical
  vocabulary is fairly international.
- You may adopt a *group* approach to this vocabulary. Tell students to
  make a list of the difficult words individually then compare lists within
  the group before they refer to you for confirmation of the meanings.
- When you have cleared up any vocabulary problems ask students to
  read the text and complete the chart. They may compare answers
  before you supply the correct answer.

Key

	DATE	ADVANTAGES	DISADVANTAGES
78s	1888	×	poor sound quality
LPs	1948	good sound quality	dust and scratches still a problem
Cassettes	1963	small, portable, possibility of recording	sound quality not as good as LPs
Compact Discs	1982	excellent sound quality, long life	high cost, no home recording possible
DAT	Now!	excellent sound quality, home recording possible	very high cost

Supplementary Exercise 26 *(SB page 121)*
Key

1 Louis Armstrong made his first recording on *78s*.
2 The Beatles recorded their first songs on *LPs*.
3 Cassette recorders were first shown at the *Berlin Show* in 1963.
4 Compact discs have a long life because there is no direct *mechanical contact*.
5 DAT is going to revolutionise *home recording*.

UNIT 18 *page 63*

4 Language Focus

- Tell students to look at the model sentences. Play the cassette twice.
- Play the next part of the cassette and ask students to listen and repeat. Make sure that students pronounce the various —*ed* endings correctly. They practised this when studying the present perfect tense.

PRESENTER Tapescript 54. Unit 18. Listen.
78s were made of shellac and were first produced in 1888.
LPs were first produced by Columbia Records in the U.S.A. in 1948.
Compact Cassettes were introduced by Philips at the Berlin Show in 1963.
Compact Discs are made of plastic and aluminium.
With DAT, studio-quality recordings can be made on small, portable recorders.

Now listen and repeat.

- Ask students to look at the second part of the Language Focus section. They have to try to match the first and second half of the sentences. Let students compare answers before playing the cassette. Better students can do this exercise away from the books.
- Write the beginnings and the endings of the sentences on the board without the verbs – ask students to give you the verbs in the passive.
- When you have checked their answers, play the cassette and ask students to listen and repeat.
- The correct sentences are shown in the tapescript.

PRESENTER Tapescript 55. Unit 18. Listen.
The Dolby system was invented by Dr Ray Dolby.
LPs were invented by Dr Peter Goldmark.
CDs were developed by Philips and Sony.
CDs are produced in Japan and Germany.
DAT is made in Japan.

Now listen and repeat.

5 Compact disc production

- Write the verbs for the section on the board. Ask students to give you the past participle of each verb. Check that students understand the meaning of the verbs.
- Tell students to look at the diagram showing the sequence of CD production. Discuss any difficult vocabulary.
- Students complete the paragraph using the verbs you have looked at. Let them compare answers before checking.
- You may like to ask extra comprehension questions at this point to be answered in the passive. E.g. *What is the first stage in the production of CDs?* (A master tape *is recorded*.)

Key

CD production is a highly technological process but it is basically quite simple. As with LP and cassette production a suitable master tape is *recorded* first. This is *transferred* to a new kind of master disc, made of glass. This glass disc is *coated* with light sensitive 'photo-resist'. A laser beam is *focused* on the disc and a track of 'pits' is *cut* from the disc centre outwards. (60 of these tracks would fit into one single track on a traditional LP). The disc is then *developed* and the photo-sensitive layer is *removed* chemically. The surface which remains is then *given* a thin metal coating. A 'stamper' is *produced* from this master and then *pressed* into transparent plastic to make the CD itself. A reflective aluminium surface is *applied* and then a protective plastic film. The label is *printed* directly on to the finished disc.

6 Blank cassettes and the record industry

1. Discuss with your students the possible effects of the sale of blank cassettes on the record industry.
- Tell them they are going to hear a talk by Michael Gilbert about these effects. They do not fill in the chart the first time they listen.
- The second time they listen, they should fill in the numbers in the spaces. This exercise also revises long numbers studied earlier, in Unit 16.
- Supply the correct answers when students have completed the chart.

Key

Sales of LPs and cassettes in the UK

Year	LPs	Cassettes	Total
1977	*81,673,000*	*18,500,000*	100,173,000
1980	67,398,000	*25,200,000*	*92,598,000*
1983	*56,000,000*	*36,500,000*	*92,500,000*

PRESENTER Tapescript 56. Unit 18. Listen.
MICHAEL Both records and cassettes are produced by the record industry but the industry is not very happy about the number of blank cassettes which are sold. With the introduction of double deck cassette recorders it has never been easier to copy friends' records or cassettes and as you can see from the chart this has had a profound effect on LP sales. In 1977, 81,673,000 LPs were sold against 18,500,000 cassettes making a total of 100,173,000. In 1980 cassette sales increased to 25,200,000 while LP sales fell to 67,398,000 making a total of 92,598,000. In 1983 LP sales were down to 56,000,000 and cassette sales were up to 36,500,000 making a total of 92,500,000. It's not just the record industry which is losing money but also musicians, artists, writers and publishers. It's been proposed to make people pay a royalty on blank cassettes as a way of offering partial compensation to those losing money from royalties on pre-recorded material.

2. When you have finished the first part, ask students to write sentences based on the chart as in the example.

WB 18.3

This exercise requires students to insert the correct verb in the passive form. They have also to decide if the verb should be present or past.

Key

1. The first CDs *were produced* in 1982.
2. Spaghetti *is made* in many countries, particularly in Italy.
3. America *was discovered* by Christopher Columbus.
4. English *is spoken* in many countries in the world.
5. *The Divine Comedy was written* by Dante.
6. Cricket *is played* in many countries, including Britain, India, Pakistan and Australia.
7. In Britain, English and mathematics *are studied* by all schoolchildren.
8. Radium *was discovered* by Marie and Pierre Curie.
9. Sony cassette recorders *are made* in Japan.

WB 18.4

The second workbook exercise is very demanding and should only be set if you have a very good class.

- Students choose one of the processes from the list or any other in which they are interested.
- They must find out about the process and write a paragraph similar to the one on CD production in the Student's Book.

UNIT 19 *page 64*

Moondown: Episode 4

Skills Focus: Reading and Listening

Before students open their books to look at the first part of the lesson discuss with them what happened at the end of the last episode. Ask a few questions. E.g. Where were Cathy and Pete at the end of the last episode? Who did Pete talk to at the harbour? What did Pete give the man? Why was he pleased?

● Let them make predictions about the action in the first part of this episode. If necessary, tell them that the action is still at Star Point. Write their ideas on the board so they can check them after listening.
● Play the cassette of the listening section (which comes before the reading section in this episode). Check students' guesses against the listening.
1 Students open their books and read the first exercise. They may be able to do the exercise without listening to the cassette again.
● Do not immediately give them the correct answers if they get any wrong. Rather, play the cassette another time.

Key
√ Cathy and Pete go to Cathy's house.
  A police car chases them.
  They go to Moondown power station.
  The police arrest Cathy and Pete.
  Cathy and Pete have an accident on the way home.
√ A car follows them.
√ Cathy manages to lose the other car.
  They sleep in the car at Star Point.
  Cathy and Pete go back to the harbour.
  They follow Jack Sims to his house.

Supplementary Exercise 27 *(SB page 121)*
Key
1 Half past two.
2 Cathy.
3 Pete.
4 No. At one point he shouted. 'God! Be careful!'
5 A Rover.
6 White.
7 Because of the car chase.

PRESENTER	Tapescript 57. Unit 19. Listen.
NARRATOR	Pete and Cathy are going home after their adventure at Star Point.
PETE	I'm so tired. Let's go home!
CATHY	Me too. It's half past two! Now, which way do I go here?
PETE	Turn left and then go left again . . . Here . . . Oh no!
CATHY	What's the matter, Pete?
PETE	There's someone following us! Get your foot down!
CATHY	Right! I'll go down the back lanes near Radford. I'll lose him down there.
PETE	God! Be careful, Cathy!
CATHY	Did you want to lose him, or not? Is he still with us?
PETE	He's dropping back . . . He can't stay with us!
CATHY	OK . . . left here . . . and right here. I'll stop in this drive.
PETE	Here he comes . . . Quick, switch the lights off!
CATHY	Ha! He's gone . . . Oh, thank goodness for that!
PETE	Well done, Cathy. What sort of car was it?
CATHY	It was a Rover, I think. It was white.
PETE	Mmm . . . Let's go home . . . although I'm not so tired any more!

2 Tell your students to read the instructions for the exercise. It is not necessary to use the books at this point and you may prepare for this activity with books closed and using the board.
● Divide the class into five groups. Assign one of the five roles to each group.
● Tell each to discuss, first the sort of person they think their character is, and second, discuss how it would feel to be this character in the story and what they would do in this character's position. If you have a good class, this discussion can be in English but do not worry if they can't. Any discussion about the story will still be useful – it will raise questions about what is going to happen and therefore raise their motivation.
● Students open their books now and read the episode while they listen to the cassette. Tell them to check their ideas about their character against what happens.

〔58〕 See Student's Book for tapescript 58.

UNIT 19 *page 65*

3 This is a vocabulary exercise.
- Divide the class into groups of four or five.
- Tell everyone to reread the story and find the words in the list.
- The groups now discuss the meanings of the words and write a translation of them on a piece of paper. They must make two copies of this list.
- They now exchange lists with another group and tick the words that they have translated in the same way. They must also look at the other words and see if the other group's translation is better than theirs. They make a new list incorporating the new translations.
- This procedure is repeated until you are satisfied that all groups have got a good idea of the meaning of the words.
- Finally, check the answers.

4 This exercise replaces the usual comprehension exercise in that the students write it themselves, which focuses students' attention on the most important facts in the story.
- Tell students to stay in their groups and imagine they were the writer and write five comprehension questions about the story.
- When they have finished, they pass on their questions to the next group who answer their questions.
- This procedure is repeated until everyone has seen everyone else's questions.
- Make a master list of the questions on the board and check that everyone knows the answers to all of them.

Supplementary Exercise 28 *(SB page 121)*
Students are given the beginnings of sentences which go to make a summary of the reading part of the episode. They finish the sentences to make their summary. Accept all logically correct answers.

Key
On Monday morning Mr Eastwood spoke *to the Board of Directors of the Westfield Gazette.*
Later, Cathy and Pete *went to see Mr Eastwood.*
Mr Eastwood *was very angry with them about Saturday night.*
They were *suspended for a month.*
Cathy was *very surprised and angry.*
Cathy and Pete went *to Cathy's house.*
When they got there, *they found the door open.*
There was a terrible mess and *someone had written a message on the wall.*
The message said *'Keep away from Moondown. Or else …'*
Cathy and Pete decided *to carry on with their investigations.*

WB 19.1
Key
1 New Covent Garden and Brixton.
2 Brixton Market.
3 Petticoat Lane.
4 Portobello Road.
5 New Caledonian Market.
6 Greenwich Antique Market and New Caledonian Market.

WB 19.2
Key
1 Very early in the morning.
2 Friday from dawn to 13.00.
3 Saturday.
4 Early Saturday morning.

WB 19.3
Students' own answers.

UNIT 20 *page 66*

Skills Focus: Writing

Summaries

Summary writing is something students are expected to do in school but
often without any clear idea of how to go about it.
- Tell them to read the notes under *DO* and *DO NOT* and to suggest any
  other points they might think useful.
1 Students read the article from the Observer and underline in pencil what
  they think is the important information. They then compare what they
  have underlined with that of other students and modify their version if
  necessary.
2 In this vocabulary exercise, students are given explanations or
  synonyms and have to find the correct word in the text.
- Tell them first to work on their own and then compare answers in pairs.

Key
a thing which has the shape of a ball   *sphere*
surprisingly   *astonishingly*
a sort of book which gives information, often about holidays   *brochure*
get on (an aeroplane)   *board*
a place where you sit   *seat*
enjoy   *relish*
journey   *voyage/trip*
travel and accommodation arranged by an agent   *package holiday*

UNIT 20 *page 67*

- Now tell them to read the summary of the article and see if the writer has included the information they would have included. If they have underlined other points, ask them to look at them again.
- Students should now say what other points they really think should have been included. Some of them might be valid. If so, try to decide whether they were more important than the points which were included.
- If they suggest points which you consider irrelevant, explain why they are not necessary to the summary.
3 Tell them to read the second article about a holiday in Sicily. They should do this without a dictionary and try to understand the gist of the article.
- There is a vocabulary exercise to help them focus on the main points.

Key
1 Sicily
2 large (largest), beautiful
3 friendly
4 perfect
5 fish (seafood), swordfish
6 tidy, well-maintained, uncrowded

4 Students read the article again and underline the essential information. As before, tell them to do this first on their own and then go through it in groups.
- As a group they discuss the various suggestions and decide on the information they are going to include in their summary.
- The summary writing can then either be done as a group or individual activity.
- There is obviously no set answer to this exercise but the summaries should include some general information about the island, its size, climate, how to get there, accommodation and food, beaches and excursions. Irrelevant information would be reference to the Mafia, details about other places in the Meditteranean, too much information about the individual items.

WB 20
Students' own answers.

REVISION FOCUS
Units 16–20 *page 68*

1 *Talking about statistics*

- Before asking students to do the revision exercise get them to look at the chart. Ask them to estimate how many there are likely to be in each category. It might be interesting for them to see afterwards how near (or wildly out) they were.
- You could ask them as a follow-up to find out what the statistics are for their own country and make a comparison. This would give them a further opportunity for using long numbers.

Key

	Schools	Teachers	Children/Students
Primary (5–10)	25,326	207,100	4,549,700
Secondary (11–18)	5,328	274,500	4,384,200
University	46	53,000	204,276

PRESENTER Tapescript 59. Revision Focus. Units 16–20. Listen.
In a recent survey carried out it was found that there are now 25,326 schools in Britain offering education for children aged between five and ten – 25,326 schools and a total of 4,549,700 children. With an average of 22 children in a class that means there are 207,100 teachers at this level. When we move into the secondary level there are fewer schools, only 5,328 state schools (figures are not included for private schools), but there are more teachers working in them – 274,500. These 274,500 teachers are responsible for teaching 4,384,200 students, a ratio of 16 students per teacher. At university level there are 46 institutions catering for a total of 204,276 students. The number of teachers at university level is 53,000.

2 Life in the past

- First look at the photos with the students. Ask them to tell you some of the things they notice which are different from today. Get them to use *used to* and *didn't use to* when talking about the photos if they don't do it spontaneously.
- Try to get them to say something about each of the categories mentioned. When they seem to have plenty to talk about tell them to do the exercise.

3 Complaining

- Students work in pairs or groups. They must imagine they are the headmaster or headmistress of their school. They must imagine the sort of things that students and staff may do which could irritate them.
- When they have finished their list, compare lists with the whole class. Students should use *too* and *not enough* structures.

4 *Present passive: statements and facts*

- There are a number of answers; accept anything reasonable.

Key
1. Giorgio Armani clothes *are made/designed* in Italy.
2. Japanese *is spoken/used* in Japan.
3. Maths is *taught/learnt/learned* in all schools.
4. Whisky *is made/distilled* in Scotland.
5. Boats *are used* instead of buses in Venice.
6. Rice *is eaten* by all Chinese people.

5 *Past passive: inventions and discoveries*

- Explain the difference between *invention* and *discovery*.
- You may approach this exercise in two ways. Either set the preparation for homework and ask students to read out their sentences in the next lesson, or do the first part of the activity in class followed by students individually writing the sentences out.
- You could also write the names of the inventors and scientists on the board, and ask students to match them to the inventions and discoveries if your students have no idea about the answers.
- In the same way you could either get the students to ask you for the dates; *When was radar invented?* and then give them, or put the dates on the board in random order and get students to match dates with people.

Key
1. radar – Sir Robert Alexander Watson-Watt, 1935 *(invention)*
2. X-rays – Roentgen, 1895 *(discovery)*
3. colour-blindness – Dalton, about 1787 *(discovery)*
4. gravity – Newton, 1684 *(discovery)*
5. electric battery – Volta, 1794 *(invention)*
6. photography – Daguerre, 1839 *(invention)*
7. chloroform – Liebig, 1831 *(discovery/invention)*
8. genetics – Mendel, 1866 *(discovery)*

6 Vocabulary

Students' own answers.
Refer to the teacher's notes for Exercise 6, page 36.

7 Pronunciation

In this exercise students see the link between stress and /ə/, the shwa (unstressed) vowel. Unstressed parts of the sentence tend to contain shwa since the lack of stress creates the need for it.

- Tell students to look at the model sentence while you play the first part of the cassette. Point out the stressed syllables and the shwa vowels. Ask students to listen and repeat.

Key

Compact discs are made of plastic and aluminium.

- Tell students to look at the six sentences, say them to each other and mark the main stresses.
- Play the cassette and check their answers.
- The cassette instructs students to listen and repeat. Work hard at trying to get them to repeat the target sentences with accurate pronunciation and stress.

60 Key

1. I've got too much homework and I have to study too many subjects.

2. 78s were made of shellac and were first produced in 1888.

3. It's Monday morning at the *Westfield Gazette*.

4. The telephone was invented by Alexander Bell.

5. People eat too much meat and not enough vegetables.

6. Compact cassettes were introduced by Philips at the Berlin Show in 1963.

GRAMMAR FOCUS
Units 16–20 *page 69*

1 *Long numbers*

a The way of writing numbers is often very different from one country to another. Make sure they are aware of the techniques involved when writing numbers in English. (Using commas, not full stops, putting *and* between the hundreds and the other numbers.)

b Five hundred and seventy-two.
A hundred and fifty thousand.
Two million, three hundred and ninety-three thousand, six hundred and twenty.

c You say *and*.
No, you only add *s* when you are saying *hundreds of people*, etc.

2 used to

a,b Students are likely to make mistakes with the question form and negative when they will probably want to add *d* as in the positive form. Point out the different spelling.

c No. (Except in the sense of a familiar habitual action, e.g. *As a doctor, I'm used to seeing great suffering.* Also, *to use* is a verb which may appear in any tense.)
No, the present perfect would be used here.

3 too much/many, not enough

a Draw students' attention to the model sentences. They should be quite familiar with them by now, but check that they have no comprehension problems.

b A lot of Ethiopians haven't got *enough* food.
A lot of children spend *too much* time watching television.
The disco was very hot and there were *too many* people.

c We may use *too much* with uncountable nouns and *too many* with countable nouns.
We can use the determiner *enough* with either countable or uncountable nouns.

4 *Present and past passive*

a Tell students to read the model sentences. Point out the fact that the use of the passive is very common in English.

b America *was discovered* by Christopher Columbus.
LPs *were invented* by Dr Peter Goldmark.
Barbera wine *is produced* in Italy.
Sony cassette recorders *are made* in Japan.

c The verb *be* is used to form the passive.
The auxiliary verb agrees with the subject.
The past participle follows the auxiliary.
Yes, the past participle never changes.

Preparation
Ask students to complete WB 21.1–2 before starting Unit 21.

UNIT 21 *page 70*

New structures
(much) too + adjective
Would you mind...?
Do you think you could...?
Could you...?

New functions
Complaining
Making polite requests

Vocabulary
Clothes vocabulary and sizes presented in Workbook.
advertised – pre-shrunk – label – complaints – colour fast

Revision
Too many/too much with countable and uncountable nouns
Would you mind...?

WB 21.1
Before the lesson, students should have completed WB 21.1–2 which
revise clothes vocabulary and English, American and Continental sizes.

Key

jacket	jeans	shorts	coat
shirt	sandals	T–shirt	trousers
skirt	dress	bikini	gloves
boots	sweater	socks	pullover
trainers	scarf	tights	shoes

WB 21.2
The purpose of this exercise is to practise clothes vocabulary and to show
the conversion tables.
● Students can say, *I take size 6 shoes, I am size 6 for shoes.*

You've got to do something

● As a warm-up activity give students the opportunity to talk about any
experiences they may have had of taking something back to a shop and
complaining. This should bring out some of the language that they will
then hear in the dialogue.
● Treat this material either as a listening comprehension (this is a more
demanding exercise and suitable for good classes) or as a listen-and-
read exercise which will give weaker students more confidence.
● Play the cassette twice and ask students to do the exercise.

Key
1 False 2 False 3 True 4 False 5 True 6 True

Supplementary Exercise 29 *(SB page 121)*
This can be given as an alternative exercise for more-able students and as
an extra exercise for homework for less-able students.

Key
1 Janet.
2 No, she didn't. (They were too small.)
3 Two weeks ago.
4 They are too small (they shrank) and they lost colour (they weren't
colour fast).
5 She followed the instructions on the label.
6 (There is no set answer to this question. Encourage students to
speculate and back up their opinions.)

 See Student's Book for tapescript 61.

UNIT 21 *page 71*

1 *Language Focus*

As there are two structures in this presentation, the Language Focus is in
two parts. The first part focuses on *too + adjective* and *much too*. Students
have previously met (Unit 18) the expression *too much*. In some languages
too much and *too* are expressed in the same way. Be aware of this
potential difficulty and if the students do confuse the two, spend more time
explaining that in English they need to use *too* and *much too* before an
adjective and *too much* before an uncountable noun.
● Play the first part of the cassette two or three times while students read
the target sentences. Check their pronunciation and intonation as they
listen and repeat.

PRESENTER	Tapescript 62. Unit 21. Listen.
JANET	They're much too small for me.
	They're too small for my little brother.
	It's too bad.
PRESENTER	Now listen and repeat.

● Tell them to complete the sentences which follow. Then play the
cassette for them to check their answers.

PRESENTER	Tapescript 63. Unit 21. Listen.
	I take size 5 in shoes. These are size 8. They're *much too big*.
	I take size 12 in jeans. These are size 10. They're *too small*.
	That watch is *too expensive*. I haven't got £80.

● Now deal with the second structure in the Language Focus. In English
we generally believe that the more words in the request, the more polite
the request is.
● Again tell them to listen and repeat. Insist on good intonation here.

PRESENTER	Tapescript 64. Unit 21. Listen.
JANET	Do you think you could ask the manager?
ASSISTANT	Could you wait a moment?
	Would you mind coming this way?
PRESENTER	Now listen and repeat.

● Students complete the sentences which follow and check their answers
by listening to the cassette.

PRESENTER	Tapescript 65. Unit 21. Listen.
	Do you think you *could open the window?*
	Could you *do the washing up?*
	Would you mind *going to the shops?*

2 Separate the dialogues

- Allow students time to read the sentences and discuss any vocabulary difficulties they may have, either with you or with another student.
- Tell students to sort out the two dialogues and to write them out in their exercise books. They should do this work individually.
- When students have finished writing their dialogues, divide the class into pairs and tell them to act out the dialogues with their partner. In this way they can check their work. If they have any problems, they should be encouraged to sort them out with their partner and come to you if they can't agree.
- Ask one or two pairs to perform their dialogues before the whole class.

Key
Dialogue 1
A Good afternoon. Can I help you?
B Good afternoon. Would you mind changing this record please?
A Why do you want to change it?
B I had it as a present but I've got too many Madonna records. I don't want another one.
A We don't usually change them you know. Would you mind waiting a moment?
B No, of course not.
A Yes, it's OK this time. Which one do you want?
B I'll have the latest U2 please.

Dialogue 2.
A Good morning. Do you need anything?
B Good morning. Yes. Could you change these shoes please?
A When did you buy them?
B I bought them yesterday but I think they're too small.
A What size did you want?
B I need size 6. And I don't really like the colour. They're too dark.
A So, what colour do you want?
B Have you got a size 6 in grey?
A No, I'm sorry. I haven't got them in grey. I've only got blue.
B OK. I'll try the blue ones please.

3 Roleplay

1 This is a full-scale role play and gives the opportunity of revising language learnt in previous units while practising the new structures in this unit.
- Put students into groups of three. If class numbers do not allow this, one or two groups of four could be formed and you could have two customers. The most demanding part is that of the customer who is the one who will keep the conversation going. Where possible give this role to a more-able student.
- Before they begin the role play give students time to work in groups with others who have the same role to discuss the kind of things they want to say. This is a phase which can be beneficial to everybody, particularly less-able students. While they are doing this, go round giving help when necessary. This also means you will need to interfere less while the role play is in progress.
- When they are ready, rearrange the groups for the actual role play. Give them as much time as you feel they need to carry out the activity. Find out at the end how many people managed to persuade the manager to change the sweater.

2 Check that students understand the questions. Treat this as a class discussion.

Key
Conversation 1
1 A computer.
2 The disk drive makes a clicking noise and doesn't work, and the printer sticks.
3 Don't know. She is going to see the manager.

Conversation 2
1 A clock.
2 It is broken. (It has been dropped).
3 No.

Conversation 3
1 A sweater.
2 It is too small and the wrong colour.
3 Yes, she gets a replacement.

 See Appendix for tapescript 66.

WB 21.3
Key
1 too	6 too much
2 too much … too	7 too
3 too many	8 too
4 too	9 too many
5 too many	10 too much

WB 21.4
Students write five questions asking people to do things for them. There are various possibilities here. Make sure the students use each expression at least once.

WB 21.5
Key
A Good morning. Can I help you?
B Yes. I bought this birthday cake here last night.
A Yes, I remember. What's wrong with it?
B It tastes really funny. Do you think you could give me my money back, please?
A Well, we don't usually do that, I'm afraid.
B In that case, would you mind getting the manager, please?
A Certainly. Mr Shaw, do you think you could come here, please?
C Yes, Mrs Green, what's the trouble?
A This man bought a cake here yesterday and it tastes funny.
C Oh, dear! Let me taste it. Mmm, yes, it does taste a bit strange.
B Do you think you could give me my money back, please?
C I'm sorry, sir, but we can't do that. Would you like another cake?
B All right, I suppose so. But I hope it's fresh this time!

UNIT 21 *page 72*

> **New structures**
> Relative clauses
>
> **New functions**
> Talking about people, places, things
>
> **Vocabulary**
> childhood – scholarship – album – relationship – rise – fame

Madonna

- As a warm up activity ask the students to tell you if they like pop music and if so, who their favourite singers are. They may or may not mention Madonna at this point! Ask them if they can give you any biographical information on any of the singers they mention. Save this information for later in the lesson.
- Tell students to read the text and discuss any vocabulary difficulties with the person sitting next to them. If there are any words which give trouble, help them.
- When they have finished reading the text, tell them to close their books. A weaker group could leave their books open.
- Write the comprehension questions on the board and tell students to answer them from memory if possible. If they cannot do this, tell them to refer to the text.

Key
1 In Michigan.
2 Contemporary dance.
3 A black musician.
4 *Everybody, Into the groove.*
5 *Desperately seeking Susan.*

Supplementary Exercise 30 *(SB page 122)*
Key
1 Madonna was born.
2 This was the name of one of her albums.
3 This was the year her mother died.
4 She made her first single.
5 This is the name of her most successful song.
6 This is the name of one of her films.

UNIT 21 *page 73*

4 Language Focus

- Ask students to read the sentences as they listen to the cassette. Point out the relative pronouns and explain how they are used to put additional information into a sentence.

PRESENTER Tapescript 67. Unit 21. Listen.
Madonna was born in Michigan, where she lived during her childhood.
Madonna, whose mother died when she was six, was unhappy when her father remarried.
Steve Bray was a black musician who wrote several songs for her.
It was the record *Everbody* which started her on the rapid rise to fame.
Madonna has also appeared in several films, of which the most successful is *Desperately Seeking Susan*.

Now listen and repeat.

- In the second part of Language Focus, they have to complete more sentences about Madonna. Tell them to check their answers with another student when they have finished, before listening to the correct version on cassette.
- Refer to WB 21.6 for an explanation of the difference between defining and non-defining relative clauses.

PRESENTER Tapescript 68. Unit 21. Listen.
Beautiful, talented and ambitious are three words *which* people use to describe Madonna.
Madonna, *whose* family is very large, is the eldest of the daughters.
In 1980 she went to Paris, *where* she stayed for only a few weeks.
Shanghai Surprise, *in which* she appeared with Sean Penn, was not well received by the critics.
She describes herself as a woman *who* knows what she wants and is determined to get it.

5 Boris Becker

- Tell students to read the notes about Boris Becker and ask about any difficulties they may have.
- Now ask them to give examples of words to introduce relative clauses. Give them time to work on their own version of the paragraph on Becker.
- The most important phase here is the checking phase with another student and the working together to produce an improved piece of writing. Encourage them to be critical.
- When they have finished, give the whole class the opportunity to create a version with you. At this stage in their language learning they should be starting to try to produce more complex sentences especially in writing. Encourage them also to add more information if they have it.

6 People, films, places

- Read through the sentence beginnings with the students. Make sure they understand them and also that they understand what they have to do. Give them time to fill in their sentences.
- Now tell them to exchange opinions with their partner and to make notes in their exercise books on what their partner tells them.
- They have to use these notes to write three paragraphs about their partners' opinions on people films and places.

Game: definitions
Students have to guess the object, person, or place, from the definition.
Example:
This is a place where there is a lot of sand and where it rains very little. *Desert.*
Others:
This is a person who . . .
This is a book which . . .
This is a thing with which . . .
etc.

WB 21.6
This exercise explains the difference between defining and non-defining relative clauses. Students then are asked to decide whether to insert commas or not.

Key
1 The woman who has long black hair is our English teacher. (*Defining.*)
2 Margaret Smith, who is our English teacher, has long black hair. (*Non-defining.*)
3 I spent a week in London, where I went to the theatre every night. (*Non-defining.*)
4 The woman whose daughter is in my class is sitting over there. (*Defining.*)
5 Italy, which lies to the south of Germany, Austria and Switzerland, is famous for all kinds of pasta. (*Non-defining.*)
6 I enjoyed the last part of the story, in which the police finally catch the murderer. (*Non-defining.*)
7 The place where I went for my summer holidays is on the coast near Trieste. (*Defining.*)
8 Robert Carr, whose brother lives next door to us, is going to live in Spain. (*Non-defining.*)
9 The exhibition which I visited was very interesting. (*Defining.*)
10 The new Woody Allen film, which I saw last week, is on at our local cinema. (*Non-defining.*)

WB 21.7
Key
1 This is the book *which* I bought last year.
2 Have you been to Venice, *where* the roads are made of water?
3 Madonna is a singer *who* appeared in *Desperately Seeking Susan*.
4 There is a very big swimming pool near my house *to which* (or *where*) I go every week.
5 I met an odd man last week *whose* hair was green.
6 Boris Becker is a tennis player *who* won the Wimbledon championship when he was eighteen years old.
7 I was reading about the Atacama Desert, *which* is the driest place in the world.
8 There's that new restaurant *where* I went yesterday.
9 Have you met John Smith, *whose* sister can speak fourteen languages?

WB 21.8
Key
1 Mary is the woman *whose mother lives in America*.
2 The north-west is a part of England *where there are a lot of lakes*.
3 Chinese is a language *which is difficult to learn*.
4 Shakespeare was a man *who wrote a lot of plays*.
5 The play *in which Desdemona appears is Othello*.

WB 21.9
This is a paragraph-writing exercise based on the Madonna text earlier. In correcting their work look for students' use of relative clauses.

UNIT 22 *page 74*

The dirty old man of Europe

1 Skills Focus: Reading

1 Before starting work on the text, introduce the topic by writing the two questions on the board: If you don't know what your country is doing, it's wise to find out before the lesson.

2 Tell students to read the article *quickly*, that is, without stopping at every word they don't know.

Key
1 Paragraph 3.
2 Paragraph 1.
3 Paragraph 5.
4 Paragraph 1.
5 Paragraph 2.

● When students have read the article they should be in a position to understand the headline *The dirty old man of Europe*. Ask students to explain in their own language if an explanation in English is still too difficult.

3 It is important, as always, for students to read the words in context. Encourage them to discuss the meanings of the words with other students.

● The sentences which follow should help them further understand the meanings of the words by showing them in a different context.

● If they still have problems with this vocabulary, they may use their dictionaries.

UNIT 22 *page 75*

4 Students have to match the numbers and the sentences. Get them to check their answers with another student before giving them the correct answer.

Key
1	$12 billion.	The sum of money that Europe spends because of pollution every year.
2	June 1988.	The date of a newspaper report about senile dementia.
3	1985.	The date of a survey by the Friends of the Earth.
4	70%	The amount of British pollution which falls on Europe.
5	30%	The amount by which the European club hopes to reduce pollution by 1993.
6	£2 billion.	The cost of reduction in sulphur production over 10 years.

Supplementary Exercise 31 *(SB page 122)*
Key
1 Britain.
2 No, it has done very little.
3 Acid rain takes aluminium from the soil and carries it into the lakes and rivers.
4 It may cause senile dementia.
5 It causes a chemical imbalance.
6 About two thirds.
7 CEGB.
8 In the rest of Europe.
9 No.
10 Yes, it's essential.

2 Skills Focus: Listening

As with other listening exercises in the reading and listening lessons of Mode 2, the listening text is thematically linked to the reading text which precedes it. This makes quite a difficult listening somewhat easier as the students are already familiar with the theme, structures and lexis.

Environmentalist David Job talks to one of the authors about acid rain. The conversation is unscripted and authentic, so the exercises are quite supportive.

● Tell students to look at the first task and try to imagine in what order the interviewer asks the questions. Deal with any difficult vocabulary at this stage.

● Play the cassette. Students listen and write the numbers of the questions in the spaces.

● Allow them to check their answers in pairs before supplying the correct answers.

Key
1 What is acid rain exactly?
2 What's the single most important cause of acid rain?
3 What are the main effects of acid rain in Great Britain?
4 What's the government doing about it?
5 What else needs to be done urgently about this problem?

● Tell students to look at the sentences for completion. Check that they understand the vocabulary in this exercise.

● Play the cassette again two or three more times while students fill in the missing words. Again, allow them to check their answers before supplying the correct answers.

● Ask them to decide which statements go with which questions. Play the cassette again if necessary.

Key

Question	Statement
3	There are two main causes of concern: one is to do with the effects on *rivers* and *lakes*, and the other is perhaps more to do with the effects on *vegetation*.
1	Rain is naturally *acid*.
4	Well, in Britain the government is doing very *little* at present.
2	We have coal- and oil-fired *power stations*, which generate a fair amount of oxides of *sulphur*.
5	… the most important thing is to recognise the *international* nature of the problem.
2	… we have vehicle fumes, which are particularly rich in oxides of *nitrogen*.
4	I think we're a long way *behind* other EEC countries and *North America*.
3	There are many causes, perhaps, of damage to *trees*, some of which may be due to *disease*, some of which may be due to *acid rain*.

Supplementary Exercise 32 *(SB page 122)*
● Students answer a series of questions which require a closer understanding of the text.

Key
1 Carbon, nitrogen and sulphur.
2 Acid rain in the water kills fish.
3 No, it isn't. Some is caused by disease.
4 Clean up the emissions of power stations.
5 It's very expensive.
6 Produced legislation to clean up exhaust fumes from cars.
7 Because the movement of air from one country to another doesn't recognise international boundaries.

 See Appendix for tapescript 69.

Extra activity: questionnaire
This exercise does not appear in the Student's Book, and the questionnaire form may be photocopied by teachers for use in their own classes. (No other part of this book or the Student's Book may be photocopied without permission).
● Check that students are familiar with the language in the questionnaire.
● Ask them to fill in their own opinions in the *YOU* column and then fill in the *YOUR PARTNER* column by interviewing their partners.
● As a follow-up, it may be interesting to discuss the findings of the class as a whole.

(Put ticks √)		POLLUTION QUESTIONNAIRE
YOU	YOUR PARTNER	
—	—	Which of these types of pollution is worst?
—	—	exhaust gas from cars
—	—	motorcycles
		buses and lorries
—	—	gas from factories
—	—	power stations
—	—	cental heating in houses
—	—	radioactivity from nuclear power stations
—	—	nuclear arms tests
—	—	noise from cars
—	—	motorcycles
—	—	lorries and buses
—	—	televisions and radios
—	—	detergent in the sea
—	—	rubbish and litter on land
—	—	Who is most responsible for pollution?
—	—	the government
—	—	local government
—	—	factory owners
—	—	individual citizens
		What kind of action is most effective in the fight against pollution?
—	—	organising demonstrations
—	—	writing letters to the government
—	—	increasing taxes
—	—	trying to change our own habits and attitudes.

3 Vocabulary Development

At first sight, students will think it is easy to form an adverb from an adjective: you just add *–ly* to the end of the adjective. In many cases this is what you do, but students should be aware that this is not always the case and also that sometimes there are two adverb forms of the adjectives, with different meanings.
● Let them work through the list below on their own using a dictionary to help them if they need it. Then get them to work out any patterns of how to form adverbs.

Key

ADJECTIVE	ADVERB
obstinate	*obstinately*
useful	*usefully*
fantastic	*fantastically*
fast	*fast*
good (better best)	*well (better best)*
bad (worse worst)	*badly (worse worst)*
careful	*carefully*
late	*late* or *lately**
separate	*separately*
terrible	*terribly*
probable	*probably*
easy	*easily*
real	*really*
formal	*formally*
hard	*hard* or *hardly**

lately and *hardly*, should not be associated with the adjectives or adverbs *late* and *hard*, as the meanings are quite different. *lately* means *recently*; *hardly* means *scarcely*.

Rules for forming adverbs:
   Adjectives ending in *–y* become *–ily*
                     –le become *–ly*
                     –e add   *–ly*
                     –l add   *–ly*
Two adverbs from one adjective:
   late or *lately*
   hard or *hardly*
Adverbs same as adjectives:
   better   *best*   *worse*   *worst*   *fast*   *late*   *hard*

WB 22.1
Key
1 Britain.
2 Germany and Scandinavian countries.
3 They both use coal with a high sulphur content.
4 Damage to the earth's ozone layer.

WB 22.2
This exercise may be done as a class activity: ask each student to write down eight words on the topic of pollution. Then, in groups get them to share their words, adding any new ones to their list. Encourage students to explain meanings to each other. Note that in the second part of this exercise, many vocabulary items will come up which are not directly associated with pollution.

WB 22.3
This exercise requires a more detailed understanding of the text than 22.1. Most of the problems should have been dealt with in the vocabulary exercise, nevertheless, it may be worth discussing the article as a whole in class before students attempt the answers.

Key
1 Spending £2 billion on fitting anti-pollution equipment to the largest coal-fired power stations.
2 No. Britain will cut emissions by less than other European countries.
3 Set tough new standards for new power stations.
4 Because Spain is planning to introduce large numbers of power stations.
5 Because of an increase in public awareness.
6 They are stopping the production of CFCs.

Preparation
Ask students to complete WB 23.1 before starting Unit 23.

UNIT 23 *page 76*

> **New structures**
> Modal verbs – *must, may, might, can't*
>
> **New functions**
> Expressing certainty/uncertainty.
>
> **Vocabulary**
> document – genuine – life – death – moon – oxygen – planet –
> exist – UFO – alternative – ghost – monster – cat – fox – badger –
> rabbit – snake – deer – seal – squirrel
>
> **Revision**
> *can*

Remind students that they have studied two of the modals before. They
have used *can* to ask for permission and to talk about ability. Elicit
sentences from students and ask questions about how *can* works in a
sentence. (Inversion for questions – use of the infinitive without *to* after.)
The other modal they have studied is *must*. Ask them to give you examples
of sentences using *must*.

WB 23.1
Before students begin the lesson, they should have completed WB 23.1
which revises (or teaches) a lexical set of animals.

Key

1 horse	2 snake	3 lion	4 rabbit	5 fox
6 squirrel	7 badger	8 cat	9 deer	10 seal

Close encounters

- Write the initials *UFO* on the board and ask students if they know what
  they mean (Unidentified Flying Object). Point out that *UFO* is
  pronounced as three separate letters.
- Ask them if they believe in the existence of UFOs. Ask them to explain
  their belief or disbelief.
- Students open their books and look at the text. Tell them to read it
  quickly; they don't have to understand every word, but just get the
  general meaning.
- When they have finished tell them to answer the comprehension
  questions in pairs or individually. Allow them to compare their answers
  before supplying the correct answers.

Key
1. In 1947.
2. To investigate the existence of UFOs.
3. In January 1947.
4. A man in New Mexico.
5. Four.
6. No, there weren't.
7. 75 miles north-west of Roswell Army Air Base.
8. No, they don't.

Supplementary Exercise 33 *(SB page 122)*
- Students write a sentence giving specific information about the text.
  There are no fixed answers to this exercise. The key is intended as a
  guide.

Key
1. Majestic 12 was set up to investigate the existence of UFOs.
2. The UFOs were sighted on 24th June 1947.
3. The dead aliens were found near Roswell Army Air Base.
4. The bodies of the dead aliens were found on 7th July 1947.
5. The committee decided that the spacecraft was a short range
   reconnaissance craft on 19th September 1947.
6. General Twining was part of the Majestic 12 committee.

- You may like to discuss the questions at the end of the article before
  moving on to Language Focus.

UNIT 23 *page 77*

1 *Language Focus*

- Ask students to look at the sentences and the percentages. Explain that
  the percentages represent degrees of certainty.
- Play the cassette while students look at the sentences.
- Play the next part of the cassette and ask students to listen and repeat.
  Explain that there is very little difference between *may* and *might* and
  that many English people would not be able to tell you which is more
  certain.

PRESENTER   Tapescript 70. Unit 23. Listen.
The document must be genuine – one hundred percent.
The document may be genuine – forty percent.
The document might be genuine – thirty percent.
The document can't be genuine – zero percent.

Now listen and repeat

- Tell students to look at the four sentences for completion. This is rather
  a subjective exercise, so be prepared for your students to come up with
  different answers from those recorded on the cassette.
- When they have completed the sentences, play the cassette, then allow
  students to listen and repeat.

PRESENTER   Tapescript 71. Unit 23. Listen.
There *can't* be life on the moon because there is no oxygen.
There *might* be life on other planets.
UFOs *may* exist.
I waited for three hours and the bus didn't come.
There *must* be a bus strike.

Now listen and repeat.

2 *Animal tracks*

- Check the names of the animals again. Point to the animals and elicit
  the names.

Key

A squirrel		E snake
B rabbit		F cat
C deer		G fox
D badger		H seal

- When you are sure that students can identify the animals, ask them to match the animals with their tracks. A certain amount of guesswork will be necessary here, although some tracks are quite obvious.

Key

1 F   2 D   3 E   4 C   5 A   6 H   7 B   8 G

- Students now compare their answers as in the example. Practise the exchange, T–S, S–T, S–S, in the usual way, ensuring that students use the modals in their exchanges, before allowing students to work in pairs.
- When students have finished, elicit their answers and correct them if necessary.

3 *Do these things exist?*

1 Students complete the chart according to their own beliefs, then work in groups comparing their opinions. Encourage them to justify their beliefs.
- When students have finished, you may like to extend the activity with a class discussion of the various topics. You may also like to draw up a chart on the board and plot percentages of the class who believe in certain things.
2 Students listen to two people discussing the same things. Play the cassette two or three times while they make notes.

 **72**

PRESENTER	Tapescript 72. Unit 23. Listen.
CHRIS	Paul, do you think UFOs really exist?
PAUL	I do, Chris, I, I think they must do.
CHRIS	Really?
PAUL	I mean, I think there have been so many cases of unidentified objects . . . I think they must do.
CHRIS	Oh! . . . I can't quite believe it, I must say.
PAUL	Well, I think it's more feasible than ghosts and stuff.
CHRIS	Oh, no. I, I believe in ghosts.
PAUL	Well, I think they might, possibly be ghosts, but it just seems so unlikely to me.
CHRIS	Oh, well, I know people who have seen them, so, you know . . . I think that . . .
PAUL	You have?
CHRIS	Yes. Yes, they must exist . . . I, I definitely believe in them.
PAUL	Maybe . . . they may do.
CHRIS	Oh and, you know, I mean, what about life after death then? How do you feel about that?
PAUL	Now, that might exist . . . I'm not sure . . .
CHRIS	Just . . . you're not sure . . .
PAUL	I think it might do, but, I don't know . . .
CHRIS	I think it definitely must.
PAUL	. . . reincarnation . . . yeah . . . it's a, it's a maybe.
CHRIS	I don't think people just die . . . and, and you know, sort of stay and rot in the ground. They must, they must go on to another life . . .
PAUL	You could be right. I think there could be life after death.
CHRIS	I don't feel that way about the Bermuda triangle, though . . . I'm very suspicious about that . . . no.
PAUL	Now that . . . that I don't believe in. No. I do not believe, I just can't . . .
CHRIS	No, there's not enough evidence really . . . You can't just believe that planes disappear . . .
PAUL	Planes disappearing . . . No, no, not at all. Um . . .
CHRIS	I don't believe in the Loch Ness monster either.
PAUL	I I I think that might exist.
CHRIS	No . . .
PAUL	I don't know, I'm a bit, I'm a bit of a romantic but . . .

CHRIS	It can't do.
PAUL	. . . I I like the idea of snakey monsters in lakes.
CHRIS	Yeah, well every photograph that's been seen, you know, they've proved that, that um they're either not real photographs or, or it's something else that looks like a monster . . .
PAUL	Well . . . I believe it. I think it, I think it must exist . . . I mean, if they'd, if they've been er talking about it for so long, it must . . . How can it not?
CHRIS	Well, life on another planet. How about that one? Definitely yes.
PAUL	Ah! No, no, no . . .
CHRIS	Oh, it must exist.
PAUL	No.
CHRIS	Of course, we can't be the only people in the whole universe . . .
PAUL	I think that humans are a superior race and . . . How can anybody else exist?
CHRIS	Oh, that's a ridiculous thing to say . . .
PAUL	No, they can't . . .
CHRIS	. . . I'm sorry . . .
PAUL	. . . they can't.
CHRIS	. . . I'm sorry . . . I can't go along with what you say, they must exist.
PAUL	We'll beg to differ, we'll beg to differ.

3 When students write their paragraphs, they should include modal verbs. The writing need not be more than a few sentences.

WB 23.2

Students insert *can't*, *may*, *might* or *must* in a series of sentences. Since native speakers are usually unable to tell the difference between *may* and *might*, in some of the sentences either will be acceptable.

Key

1 The lights are out and the door's locked. He *can't* be at home.
2 She has taken her swimming costume and her towel. She *must* be at the swimming pool.
3 It's half past nine on Monday morning. My father *must* be at the factory. He always starts work at nine o'clock on Mondays.
4 No, I haven't seen Anna. She *may/might* be at her friend's house or she *may/might* be at home.
5 They *can't* be English because they've both got American accents.
6 I *may/might* go to London this weekend, but I'm not sure.
7 Thousands of people say that they see them every year, so UFOs *may/might* exist, but I'll believe in them when I see one myself.
8 Mandy isn't at school today. She had a temperature and a headache yesterday. I think she *must* have flu.
9 Solar energy *may/might* be a valid alternative to nuclear energy, but the government doesn't spend enough money on research.
10 He *can't* be sixteen years old! He looks much younger!

WB 23.3

- Students make two sentences about each photograph, one with *can't* and the other with *may/might* or *must*.

Key

1 watch   2 camera   3 ruler   4 cassette   5 pencil
6 coin   7 book   8 film   9 diary

UNIT 23 *page 78*

New structures
First conditional

New functions
Talking about future possibilities (1)

Vocabulary
seaside – sunny – show – hear – put back – climb – holiday –
hotel – sightseeing – spend

Revision
will future

Check that your students remember the *will* future structure before you
begin the lesson. Write sentences on the board with the *will* omitted and
elicit the missing verbs both in the affirmative and negative forms.

Where shall we go?

- Ask students what they like doing at weekends, if they ever get bored, if
  they ever go away at the weekend with their friends.
- Play the cassette while students read the cartoon. Play the cassette a
  second time. Students may ask you for help with any vocabulary that
  they don't understand.
- Students may now tackle the *true* or *false* exercise. This is quite easy.

Key
1 True   2 True   3 False   4 True   5 False   6 True   7 False

🎧 73   See Student's Book for tapescript 73.

UNIT 23 *page 79*

4 Language Focus

- Tell students to look at the three sentences taken from the dialogue. Play the cassette while students read them.
- Ask students which verb tense is used in the *if* clause and which tense is used in the other clause. Explain that *will* and *shall* are never used after *if*.
- Students listen and repeat after the cassette.

PRESENTER   Tapescript 74. Unit 23. Listen.
GIRL   If it rains, we'll go to London.
   If it's sunny, we'll go to the seaside.
BOY   If we go by train, it'll cost a lot of money.

PRESENTER   Now listen and repeat.

- Students complete the sentences before they listen to the next part of the cassette.
- Play the next part of the cassette while students check their answers.
- Tell students to listen and repeat after the cassette.

PRESENTER   Tapescript 75. Unit 23. Listen.
   If it snows, I*'ll go* skiing this weekend.
WOMAN   If you *come* to my house, I*'ll show* you my new computer.
MAN   If you *go* to England this summer, you*'ll have to* speak English.

PRESENTER   Now listen and repeat.

5 Travel quiz

1 Tell students to try to fill in the gaps in the sentences individually. Monitor their progress and give assistance if there are students who are making poor progress.
- Students can now work in pairs or in groups. In turn they read out their version of each sentence while the others agree or disagree. If there is any controversy over the answers, you will have to act as mediator.
2 An alternative way of checking answers can be to play the cassette on which there is a recording of some English people doing the same exercise.

Key
1 If you go to Quebec, you will hear people speak *French or English*.
2 If you go to Rio de Janeiro in December, the weather will be *hot*.
3 If you go to the USA, you will have to put your watch back *seven* hours.
4 If you want to climb Mount Fuji, you will have to go to *Japan*.
5 If you want to see the Taj Mahal, you will have to visit *India*.
6 If you want to see the tallest building in the world, you'll have to go to *Chicago*.
7 If you want to visit the Forbidden City you will have to go to *Peking*.
8 If you want to go for a trip on the River Thames, you will have to visit *London*.
9 If you stay in Bangor, you will hear people speak *Welsh or English*.
10 If you go to *San Francisco*, you will see the Golden Gate Bridge.
11 If you go to Australia at Christmas, the weather will be *hot*.
12 If you want to see St Mark's Square, you will have to visit *Venice*.
13 If you go to *Barcelona*, you will be able to visit the Parco Gaudi.
14 If you go to Jersey, you will hear people speak *French or English*.
15 If you want to climb Mount Snowdon, you will have to go to *Wales*.

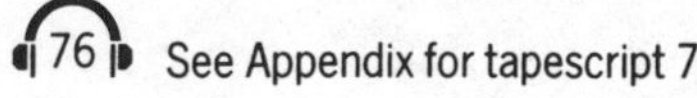

- See Appendix for tapescript 76.

3 Students have to invent similar sentences to the ones in Exercise 1. They exchange their six sentences with another student and say if they are correct.
- When they have finished, ask some students to write their sentences on the board and elicit comments from the rest of the class.

6 Consequences

In this exercise students have to use two consecutive word prompts to produce a conditional sentence in a limited time (ten seconds). The following student takes the second part of the sentence and makes it into the *if* clause.
- Tell students to read the instructions and tell you what they think they have to do.
- Monitor students while they work in groups.
- The game may be extended using another situation. Give students the beginning of another *if* sentence. For example: *If the weather is fine this weekend, I'll…* The first student in each group finishes the sentence then the next student takes the second part of that sentence and makes it into the *if* clause and so on. Here again any student who can't make a sentence in ten seconds is eliminated.

WB 23.4
Key
1 If he gets home late, his mother will be angry.
2 If she drives too fast, she will have an accident.
3 If they go to Moscow, they will visit the Kremlin.
4 If you train very hard, you will win the race in March.
5 If she gets a good job, she will earn a lot of money.
6 If they eat too much, they will get fat.
7 If I pass my exams, I will go to university.
8 If you spend all your money, you won't be able to go out this weekend.
9 If I earn enough money, I will buy a new motorbike.
10 If he smokes too much, he will get lung cancer.

WB 23.5
Students imagine that they are giving information to travellers in London. They consult the timetable and write sentences as in the example.

Key
1 If you want to be in Weston-super-Mare at 3.00 pm, you will have to catch the 12.30 train from London.
2 If you want to be in Bristol by half past two, you will have to catch the 13.00 train from London.
3 If you want to be in Hereford at six o'clock, you will have to catch the 3 o'clock train from London.
4 If you want to get to Bridgend by quarter to eight, you will have to catch the 5.25 train from London.
5 If you want to get to Bath by four o'clock, you will have to catch the 2.30 train from London.
6 If you want to be in Cardiff by seven o'clock in the evening, you will have to catch the 4.43 train from London.
7 If you want to get to Swindon by six o'clock, you will have to catch the 4.55 train from London.

Moondown: Episode 5

Skills Focus: Reading and Listening

Before students open their books to look at the first part of the lesson, discuss with them what happened at the end of the last episode. Ask a few questions. E.g. Where were Cathy and Pete at the end of the last episode? Who broke into Cathy's flat? What message did they leave?

1 You can either write the pre-reading questions on the board and remove the temptation for students to read the text, or you can tell students to open their books and discuss the questions. This activity can be done in pairs or groups. When your students have finished discussing, compare answers with the whole class.

● Students now read and listen to the story and check their hypotheses. Give them plenty of time to read but do not answer any questions they may have about vocabulary, etc. Let them try to work out meanings from the context.

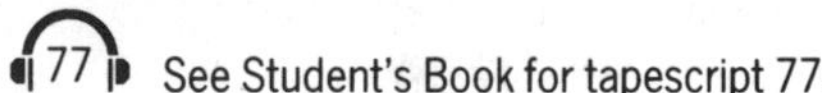 See Student's Book for tapescript 77.

UNIT 24 *page 81*

2 Although there is not a lot of difficult vocabulary in this episode, there are a number of new words. Students have to find words in the text which have the same meaning as the words or phrases given.

● Tell students to work individually before discussing their answers in pairs. When they have finished, check their answers.

Key

to not tell the truth	(v)	to	*lie*
to leave	(v)	to	*go away*
obstinate	(adj)		*stubborn*
with no job	(adj)		*unemployed*
the time spent working	(n)		*the hours*
not to take risks	(v)	to	*be careful*

3 This comprehension exercise concentrates on the first part of the reading.

● Students can work individually, in pairs or in groups.

Key

1 The photographs.
2 Because Pete secretly took a photo of her.
3 No, she doesn't.
4 She's going to send them to a friend of hers who works for the *Daily Clarion* in London.
5 Because she and Pete were followed by a white Rover on Saturday night.
6 No, he doesn't. He's going to visit Jack Sims.

4 This comprehension exercise concerns the second half of the reading; Pete's visit to Jack Sims.

● You may vary your approach to the lesson by asking students to do the first part of the reading and do the work on Exercise 3. Then tell them to read the statements in Exercise 4 and predict if they are *true* or *false* before reading the second half to check their answers. Or you may follow the usual procedure and allow students to do the exercise after they have read the text.

● At this point in the course, students should be able to explain why some answers are false.

Key

1 False	2 True	3 True	4 True	5 False	6 False
7 False	8 True				

Supplementary Exercise 34 *(SB page 122)*

Better students may like to attempt this exercise which is best done in class as it is rather free.

● Ask students to imagine Jack Sims' conversation with the director of Moondown. Elicit the type of question the director will have asked Jack, and his possible answers.

● Tell students to write the conversation or if you like you can get them to role-play it.

5 In the listening section you can again adopt one of two strategies. Either ask students to read the questions and try to predict the answers before they listen or let them listen to the cassette and answer the questions afterwards.

Key

1 No, she wasn't.
2 It belonged to the director of Moondown.
3 At Moondown.
4 Her informant at Moondown.
5 At the Old Ship pub.
6 No, she isn't.
7 Yes, he did.
8 A man.
9 Because Cathy's informant at Moondown was a woman.

Supplementary Exercise 35 *(SB page 122)*

This can be done in class if your students find summary writing difficult or at home if your class is very good.

● Students look at the list of important details from both parts of the story and write a sentence about each one. If you are doing the exercise in class, write the sentences on the board.

● When you have a sentence for each item, ask students to rewrite them putting them together in a paragraph making a summary of the episode.

At the end of the lesson, you may like to discuss what they think is going to happen in the next episode, what has happened to Cathy, who the strange man is and what Pete is going to do next.

PRESENTER	Tapescript 78. Unit 24. Listen.
NARRATOR	It's one o'clock. Pete is waiting for Cathy at his house.
PETE	Mmm … one o'clock. She's late again. I … That must be her. Hello, 67543.
CATHY	Hello, Pete?
PETE	Hi, Cathy, Where are you?
CATHY	I'm at Star Point. We were right about the Rover. It belongs to the director all right. But that's not all. When I got back to my house, the woman from Moondown phoned again.
PETE	Yes? What did she say?
CATHY	She couldn't talk much. She said it was too dangerous. She asked me to meet her here during her lunch hour. Can you get here straight away?
PETE	Yes, of course. I'll be there at half past, OK?
CATHY	OK. I'm at the phone box outside the Old Ship pub.
PETE	Right! I know that. I'll see you in about twenty minutes then. Bye.
PETE	Here we are … The Old Ship … and there's Cathy's car, but where's Cathy? Maybe she's inside … Excuse me, have you seen a young woman with blonde hair, wearing a brown jacket?
BARMAN	Yes, she was in here about half an hour ago. A man came into the bar and spoke to her and they both left. They were in a bit of a hurry …
PETE	Thanks … A man! But her informant in the power station was a woman! Who was that man, I wonder? I hope Cathy's all right!

WB 24.1
Key
1 ITV and Channel 4.
2 BBC 1 and ITV.
3 No, not yet.

WB 24.2
Key

1	BBC	*British Broadcasting Corporation*
2	ITV	*Independent Television*
3	IBA	*Independent Broadcasting Authority*
4	S4C	*Sianel 4 Cymru*

WB 24.3
Key
1 Controls ITV and owns Channel 4.
2 It is the same for each area.
3 No.
4 S4C broadcasts some programmes in Welsh.

WB 24.4
Students' own answers.

Skills Focus: Writing

Reports

This unit gives guidance to students on writing reports of events or incidents. A report is a formal piece of writing and very often is linked to note-taking.

1   Ask students to look at the two texts printed. One is a set of notes and the other a report written from those notes.
2   Look at the style of the report with the students. Get them to underline the passives and simple pasts and to circle the linking words.

Key

Passives: *were robbed   was pushed   was (then) snatched*
             are described   was recovered   (was) handed in
Simple past: *they heard   they turned round   saw   snatched*
             attempted   ran   wore   contained
Linking words: *as   before   when   and   but   then*

3   Show how the notes are converted into a report using linkers. Read through and discuss the other report writing guidelines.

UNIT 25   *page 83*

4   Students now read notes of another incident and complete the report of
it, bearing in mind the points about report writing.

Key

There *was* an accident *on Friday* at 3.15 pm on the A48 *near Chepstow*.
A car and a coach *were involved*. The car *was going* up the hill *while* the
coach *was coming down the hill*. There *was* a lot of snow and ice on the
road. The coach *skidded* on the ice *before* it *collided* with the car. The car
driver *is in* hospital *with* a broken leg *but* the coach driver *is not hurt*.
A pedestrian *was hit* by the car *and* is now in hospital. There *were* two
witnesses, one a woman who *was walking* along the street and the other,
a man who *heard* the crash and *went* to the window.

5   They finally write their own report.
- Ask them to look at the notes and make sure they understand them.
- When they have written their reports, ask one or two students to read
  their versions to the rest of the class and ask others what they could do
  to improve on them.

WB 25

As planning is so important in writing, emphasise the note-taking stage of
this exercise, either in class, or by awarding half the marks to the planning.

REVISION FOCUS
Units 21–25 *page 84*

1 Complaining

Students are asked to write simple sentences but if you have a good class, you can make the task more demanding by getting them to write two sentences for each picture. So the example could become: *I can't wear this hat. It's too big.*
- Tell them to be fairly imaginative about the sentences they make.
- Students read their sentences to another student when they have finished.

Key
1 There are too many people in this room.
2 This table is too heavy.
3 I've got too much homework.
4 This bed is too short.
5 These jeans are much too small/tight.

2 Polite requests

Key

1 Do you think you could close the window, please?	No, I'm sorry. It's too hot in here.
2 Would you mind changing this shirt, please? It's too small.	Certainly. Have you got a receipt for it?
3 Would you mind getting the manager, please?	No, I'm sorry. He's not here at the moment.
4 Could you turn the stereo down, please?	Yes, OK. I didn't realise it was so loud.

3 Relative clauses: talking about holidays

- Make sure students use relative clauses in their answers to this exercise.

4 Expressing certainty and uncertainty

- Explain to students that you want them to make two comments about each person as in the example.
- Tell them to try to use a selection of modal verbs, although their negative answers are always going to be *can't*.

5 Talking about future possibilities (1)

Explain to the students that you want them to make three sentences for each *if* clause and that the three sentences should follow on from each other. So in the first one, for example, they might say: *. . . I'll study medicine. Then I'll become a doctor. After that I'll work in a hospital.* When they go on to do the other set of statements, they must choose a different subject (e.g. languages).

6 Vocabulary

Students' own answers.
Refer to the teacher's notes for Exercise 6, page 36.

7 Pronunciation

- Play the first part of the cassette, making sure students can reproduce the five words correctly. These illustrate different sounds for the letter *e*.
- Play the second part as students listen and classify the words by the sound of the letter *e*. Draw students' attention to which *e* is to be examined in words with two: d<u>e</u>finitely, d<u>e</u>cent, d<u>e</u>compose, s<u>e</u>rve, d<u>e</u>cide, <u>e</u>xample.

 **Key**

1 /ɛ/ met   2 /ɜː/ verb   3 /ɪ/ departure   4 /ə/ absent
5 /iː/ female

fern 2	decide 3
definitely 1	sister 4
decent 5	invent 1
decompose 5	reply 3
help 1	example 3
serve 2	brother 4
she 5	afternoon 4

GRAMMAR FOCUS
Units 21–25 page 85

1 (much) too + *adjective*

a Students may have had difficulty manipulating the two constructions with *too* and *much*, but they should have mastered them by the time they come to the Grammar Focus section. After they have read the model sentences they have to complete other examples using *too*, *much* and *many*.

b Those shoes are very nice but they're *too* big.
That restaurant is very good but it's much *too* expensive.
There are *too many* cars on the roads these days.

2 'Would you mind . . . ?'

a It is important that students realise that there are various ways of saying the same thing in a language, and that both the form you use and how you say things, affect the degree of politeness of what you are saying.

b *Would you mind* opening the window?
Could you open the window?
Do you think *you could* open the window?

c The least polite is *Could you . . . ?* and the most polite is *Do you think you could . . . ?* However, all three are polite and the degree of politeness can be varied by changing the intonation.

3 Relative clauses

a Show students that you can use *that* instead of *which* when you are merely referring back to something already mentioned (i.e. in a defining relative clause), but when you are giving more information about something from the previous clause, you cannot use *that* (i.e. in a non-defining relative clause). Compare: *I work at the factory which/that is next to the station.* and: *I work at Bloggs Boot Factory, which* (not *that*) *is next to the station.* For a complete explanation of relative clauses and pronouns, refer students to the Workbook Grammar Summary Units 21–25.

b The book *which/that* is on the table is Mary's.
Mary is the girl *that/who* lives in New York.
She's the girl *whose* father is a postman.
The place *where* I went for my holidays is very beautiful.

c *whose* is an object pronoun, so while in the second example, the girl lives in New York, in the third, the girl is not a postman.

4 Modal verbs

a Elicit answers to the sentences for completion. Here, again, make it clear to your students that *may* and *might* are almost interchangeable.

b I saw Sue in town this morning, so she *can't* be in America.
I'm not sure about ghosts. They *may/might* exist.
Roger isn't at school today. He *may/might* be at home.
That girl speaks fluent German, so she *must* be from Germany.

c We use *may* or *might* to express uncertainty.
We use *can't* to express negative certainty.
We use *must* to express positive certainty.
We use the infinitive without *to* after the modal.

5 First conditional

a Remind students of the structure: *If* + present + *will* + infinitive. There may be some variation in students' answers. The key is for your guidance.

b If she *arrives* late, I*'ll go* to the cinema without her.
If it*'s* sunny on Saturday, I*'ll go* to the seaside.

c The main difficulty that students have with the conditional is in the *if* clause, where they tend to use the *will* future. It is important that they realise that this is wrong except in very specific circumstances (which it is best not to mention at this level). Although they have always used the *will* future in the lessons on the first conditional, you may like to point out that variations are possible in the second half of the clause. For example, when *if* means *whenever*, you can use the present in the second half. If you have a good class, you may like to point out that you can use *going to* or the present continuous in the second half as well.
E.g.: *If my friend arrives on time, we're going to the cinema this evening.*
The use of the imperative is also possible.
E.g.: *If you want to buy some bread now, go to the shops immediately! It's nearly six o'clock!*

UNIT 26 *page 86*

New structures
Past perfect

New functions
Talking about an earlier past

Vocabulary
diversion – delayed – helicopters – unconscious – upset

Revision
Past participles

What happened to you?

- Ask students to guess why Carol is ringing Bob. Ask them why she is ringing from a phone box and what the relationship between Bob and Carol probably is.
- If you think your students can treat this as a listening presentation rather than as a listen-and-read, then tell them to close their books while they listen to the dialogue. If you think your students need the back-up of the printed word, then tell them to keep their books open. They can do the exercise alone or with another student but in any case, they should check it with each other before you give them the correct answers.

Key
1 Bob went to the bus stop but he missed the bus.
4 They waited for the next bus.
2 He phoned Barbara.
6 They chased a thief.
3 He met Barbara at the Three Bells.
7 They went to the police station.
5 They walked past Brown's department store.
8 They missed the last bus.

Supplementary Exercise 36 *(SB page 122)*
Key
1 Carol hasn't got *a phone*.
2 Bob didn't know how to get to *Carol's house*.
3 Bob and Barbara met at *the Three Bells*.
4 The woman was running out of *Brown's department store*.
5 Bob and Barbara spent two hours at *the police station*.
6 It was ten o'clock when *they left the police station*.

 See Student's Book for tapescript 80.

1 Language Focus

Tell students to look at the sentences in the Language Focus and try to work out when the past perfect tense is used. (To express an action which happened in the past before another action.)
- Tell students to look at the sentences taken from the dialogue while you play the cassette. Then tell them to listen and repeat.
- Pay particular attention to the intonation and pronunciation of *had*.

PRESENTER   Tapescript 81. Unit 26. Listen.
BOB   When I got to the bus stop, the bus had already gone.
I looked in my pocket for the instructions you'd written for me but I'd lost them.
Because the bus still hadn't arrived, we decided to walk to the station.
They wanted to know exactly what had happened.

PRESENTER   Now listen and repeat.

- In the second part of Language Focus they have to complete similar sentences.
- Ask students to explain what would be the difference in the first sentence if they wrote: *When I arrived, she went to bed*. (That she went to bed as soon as he arrived. In the exercise example we understand that she was already in bed when he arrived.)

PRESENTER   Tapescript 82. Unit 26. Listen.
1 When I *arrived*, she *had gone* to bed.
2 I *wanted* to phone but I *had lost* your number.
3 His mother *asked* him what he *had done*.

UNIT 26 *page 87*

2 ... *the lesson had started*

1 Students work individually to find sentences to describe the illustrations. One half of each sentence is given. There may be some variation in their answers. Allow any reasonable solution.

● When they have finished tell them to read their solutions to another student to compare answers.

Key
1 When I arrived at the station, *the train had already left.*
2 *The party had started* before I arrived.
3 She wanted to know where I *had been.*
4 He arrived after the match *had finished.*

2 In this section they listen to a group of people talking about people they were at school with. Students write down what the people did as soon as they left school and details about their careers.

● Students are only required to get the information for the people on their list. Their partner will get the other information and then tell them.

Key

	AFTER SCHOOL	CAREER
Jack Beecham	Left school early, worked in a supermarket, got fed up, went to Australia, worked on a farm.	Hoping to farm in Australia.
Tim Brown	University (economics).	Worked in a bank, wanting to become a bank manager.
Margaret Green	A levels, went to US, various jobs while travelling.	Qualified as a nurse in 1985.
Ann Smith	University (medicine), became a doctor.	Applied for a job in Ethiopia as a doctor.
Tom Margam	Left school early, worked in father's factory.	Hoping to open his own factory.
Ian Blythe	University, excellent athlete, left university to train.	Won competitions, hoping to be chosen for British Olympic team.

The second part is a written exercise. The students choose only one of the characters and write a paragraph as in the example.

 See Appendix for tapescript 83.

3 *Story writing*

1 Put students into groups to do this exercise. Try to make sure that good students and weaker students are working together. They have to look at the suggestions in their books and invent a story. Give them plenty of time to do this activity and go round giving help where it is needed.

● Encourage them not to ask you for too many extra words although they should be free to add any words they know. Encourage them also to be critical of their work and aim to get as perfect a final version as possible.

2,3 When they have finished, get them to read their story to another group. Finally, tell them to write out the other group's story.

WB 26.1
Key
1 She *'s lived* in London for a long time. She likes it there.
2 When he *arrived* at school he realised he *'d left* his bag on the bus.
3 My brother says he *'s finished* the book I gave him last week.
4 She *rang* after she *'d spoken* to my father.
5 They *'d wanted*/They *wanted* to go to the States for many years before they finally went.
6 I thought he *'d changed* a lot when I *saw* him again.
7 It *'s been* difficult until now but I think it will get easier.
8 When I *got* to the theatre all the tickets *had gone.*
9 He *'s spent* too much money this month. He will have to be more careful.
10 When they *'d finished*/they *finished* their homework they *went* to the cinema.

WB 26.2
In the second exercise, students have a reading passage and have to answer questions on it. Tell them to read the passage and ask you if there is any vocabulary they don't understand.

Key
1 He walked along the road.
2 He fell asleep.
3 When they had almost arrived.
4 Because he realised he had almost arrived.
5 Because he had worked in a theatre as a boy.
6 There were a lot of houses where the park had been, and the front door, which had been green, was now yellow.
7 Probably because he had often played there as a boy.
8 She'd lived there for twenty years.
9 (There is no set answer for this. Accept any reasonable suggestions from your students.)

UNIT 26 *page 88*

> **New structures**
> Reported speech (present)
>
> **New functions**
> Reporting what people say
>
> **Vocabulary**
> go out with – promise – not feel very well – interrupt – candidate –
> apply – despatch rider – own – move – to get to know

Leave this to me!

- Ask students if they ever don't turn up when they have arranged to go out with a friend. What do they do when they have arranged to meet someone and they don't want to go? Do they invent excuses? What sort of excuses?
- Tell students to look at the cartoons while they listen to the cassette. Play the cassette once or twice. Check students have no difficulties with the vocabulary.
- Tell students to do the *true* or *false* exercise after the dialogue. They can do this individually then compare their answers in pairs.

Key
1 False   2 True   3 True   4 False   5 False   6 True   7 True
8 True

Supplementary Exercise 37 *(SB page 123)*
This is a more difficult exercise which you can give to the whole class as homework or use in class if you have more advanced students. They have to imagine the other side of Jo's conversation with Dave's mum.
- If you do the exercise in class, you can write the conversation on the board and invite students to come and fill in the missing parts. Discuss them with the whole class and modify them where necessary.

Key
JO	Hello, can I speak to Dave, please? This is Mrs Plane.
DAVE'S MUM	*Oh, hello, Mrs Plane. I'm sorry, but Dave's not at home at the moment.*
JO	Can I leave a message?
DAVE'S MUM	*Yes, of course.*
JO	Thank you. My daughter, Sue, was meeting Dave this evening.
DAVE'S MUM	*Yes, I know. What's the matter?*
JO	Well, I'm afraid Sue says she can't come.
DAVE'S MUM	*Oh dear! What's the matter with her?*
JO	She says she's got too much homework and she says she's not feeling very well either – she says she had a very hard day at school today.
DAVE'S MUM	*Mmm … I quite understand.*
JO	And she says she'll speak to him tomorrow. Have you got that?
DAVE'S MUM	*Yes, she'll speak to him tomorrow. I'll give him the message.*
JO	Thank you.
DAVE'S MUM	*Goodbye, Mrs Plane.*
JO	Bye.

 See Student's Book for tapescript 84.

4 *Language Focus*

- Explain that the words in brackets are direct speech and the words underneath are reported speech.
- Play the first part of the cassette while students look at the sentences. Point out what changes occur in the sentences when they are reported. (The verbs change person and pronouns change, depending on who is reporting the speech.)
- Play the next part of the cassette and tell students to listen and repeat. Tell students to practise in pairs. One student reads the direct speech, the other puts the sentence into reported speech. When students are confident, they can repeat the exercise with one student keeping the book closed.

PRESENTER	Tapescript 85. Unit 26. Listen.
SUE	I can't come.
JO	Sue says she can't come.
SUE	I've got too much homework.
JO	She says that she's got too much homework.
SUE	I had a very hard day at school today.
JO	She says she had a very hard day at school today.
SUE	I'll speak to him tomorrow.
JO	She says she'll speak to him tomorrow.
PRESENTER	Now listen and repeat.

- When you are happy that students understand how the change works, ask them to look at the second part and fill in the reported speech.
- Play the cassette while students check their answers.
- Tell students to repeat after the cassette and repeat the procedure described above.

PRESENTER	Tapescript 86. Unit 26. Listen.
DAVE	I'm fed up with Sue.
JOHN	He says *he's fed up with Sue.*
DAVE	She promised to go out with me.
JOHN	He says that *she promised to go out with him.*
DAVE	I'm not going to go out with her again.
JOHN	He says *he's not going to go out with her again.*
DAVE	I'll speak to her tomorrow.
JOHN	He says *he'll speak to her tomorrow.*
PRESENTER	Now listen and repeat.

UNIT 26 *page 89*

5 *Despatch riders*

1 In this exercise students work in pairs. They imagine they are looking for a new despatch rider for their company.

● Tell them to look at the advertisement and discuss what qualities they would look for. E.g. People with experience, not too young, people with their own machine, people who know London well.

● Divide the class into pairs. Explain that Student A has the application letters of Mike Lees and Susan Watson, while Student B has those of Peter Bull and Arthur Eastment.

2 Both Student A and Student B read their letters and fill in the information in their charts.

3 Student B now gives Student A the information about his first candidate reporting everything as in the model exchange. Student A notes the information in the chart. Then Student A gives B the information about his first candidate and so on until both students have a completed chart.

Key

Name	Age	Owns bike?	Experience	Knows London?
Peter Bull	17	yes	no	yes
Mike Lees	20	no (accident)	yes, 3 years	yes
Arthur Eastment	16	no	no	yes
Susan Watson	19	yes	yes, 2 years	quite well

4 Now they must look at the complete information and discuss who is the most suitable candidate for the job. There is no fixed answer to this exercise.

● When all the students have finished, compare the choice of candidate with the whole class and elicit why they chose that particular candidate.

6 *Old and young*

1 In this exercise students work in an even number of groups. Half the groups have to write four sentences about how old people view young people, while the other groups have to write four sentences saying how young people view old people.

● When you have divided the class into the groups you will find it useful to have a vocabulary brain-storming session as your students may not have sufficient vocabulary to complete the exercise.

● Draw students' attention to the model sentences and explain that their sentences must be similar, in reported speech.

● When they have finished, divide the board into two sections and ask a representative from each group to come up and write their sentences on the board.

● Discuss the sentences with the whole class.

2 During the listening, tell students to note what the old man and the young girl say.

● Allow students to pool their answers in groups before supplying the correct answers. Play the cassette as many times as your students find necessary.

3 Give them time to make comments on how the views of the two people on the recording differ from theirs.

 See Appendix for tapescript 87.

Key

1 Robert says he often goes swimming at the weekend and sometimes he goes running.
2 Sarah says she saw a good film at the Odeon last night.
3 Peter says he's going to spend the weekend in London.
4 Cathy says Arthur never comes to see her and he never phones her either.
5 David says he's been a despatch rider for three years now.
6 Joan says she's worked in Saffron Walden for three years but she's fed up with it now.
7 Roger says he'll go and see him about the job tomorrow morning.
8 Cindy says she's having a bath at the moment but she'll phone back later.
9 Kevin says he can do the shopping when he goes to town this afternoon.
10 Jan says she's never met Arthur, but she knows his wife.

WB 26.4

This exercise is more challenging. Students have to interview a member of their family or a friend about the topics listed. They then have to write a sentence for each topic. There is no fixed answer to this exercise.

Fair play for women's football

1 Skills Focus: Reading

1 The first activity in this lesson is a discussion activity which you may do in a number of ways. With books closed you can write the questions on the board and discuss them with the whole class. This eliminates the temptation that students may have to read the text when they should be discussing! Otherwise you may ask students to open their books and discuss the questions in pairs or groups. Tell them not to read the text yet.

● You may wish to go beyond the questions for discussion and talk about other ways in which women are discriminated against. Before you begin the study of the text try to establish that there are no logical reasons for women to be excluded from predominantly male sports.

2 In the second exercise students have to read the text quickly and make notes about the identity of the various people in the list. Emphasise that they must not stop and ponder over the meanings of words that they do not know. The object of this reading is just to get specific information and get a general idea of the content of the text.

Key
1 Sallie Jackson – played for Fulham.
2 Shauna Williams – played for Millwall.
3 Flo Bilton – is a Women's Football league official.
4 Ted Croker – is the secretary of the Football Association.
5 Linda Whitehead – is the secretary of the Women's Football Association.

3 This exercise deals with the most difficult vocabulary in the text.
● Students locate the words in the text before they try to translate them. They will have a better chance of guessing the meanings in this way. You may like to check that they are doing this by requiring students to give you the number of the paragraph or the line number for each word.
● Allow students to work in pairs to guess the meanings of the words and write down a translation.
● When they have finished, tell them to exchange translations with another pair of students and adjust their list if they think that the other pair has any better answers. There can also be cross-pair discussion.
● When students have had enough time to discuss their translations, supply the correct answers. (Be careful with the translation of *foul* which is used as a noun (and verb) to describe an improper action in a football match and as an adjective with the meaning of *bad* and *dirty*.)

4 Students have to find more specific information from the text. They work individually then compare their answers in pairs.

Key
1 Paragraph 5
2 Paragraph 3
3 Paragraph 1
4 Paragraph 6
5 Paragraph 2
6 Paragraph 4

5 Again students work individually then compare their answers in groups.
● Allow them plenty of time to discuss their answers and explain that if their answer differs from that of the rest of the group, then they must be prepared to give reasons for their choice. In this way weaker students will have help if they have misread the text. It is better for students to be corrected by their peers as they will accept this more readily and their errors will be less public.

Key
1 False   2 False   3 True   4 True   5 True   6 False   7 False
8 True

Students are required to write a history of women's football in England using the dates from the text as guidelines. They can pitch the level of this exercise themselves: they can either just write a sentence containing each date or they can be more ambitious and write a proper summary of the text.

2 Skills Focus: Listening

● Tell students that they are going to hear an interview with a member of the English international team.
● Tell students to close their books and ask them the sort of questions they would ask if they had to interview an English national player. Write their questions on the board.
● Tell students to open their books and compare their list of questions with the list in the book. Tell them to tick the ones they mentioned and tick any others in the list that they would also ask.
● Play the cassette two or three times to give your students a chance to listen for the questions. Tell them to tick the second column indicating the questions the interviewer actually asked.

Key
The interviewer asked questions 2, 3, 5, 7, 8, 9.

● Elicit the numbers of the questions, then play the cassette again and ask students to note the answers. If you think that this is rather a difficult exercise for your class, divide the class into six groups and make each group responsible for the answer to just one question. When students have finished, compare their answers with the whole class.

Key
Question	Answer
2	She's hoping to play for Napoli next season.
3	She can play on the right wing, but prefers centre mid-field.
5	Yes. On one occasion she attended some training sessions, but couldn't play·in the match at the end because she was a woman.
7	She started at a really early age; from four upwards.
8	Yes, she's played in Italy.
9	She doesn't know. She herself always gives everything she's got which may be aggressive in a way, but she doesn't feel aggressive.

Key
1 False   2 True   3 False   4 False   5 False   6 False
7 True

PRESENTER Tapescript 88. Unit 27. Listen.
PAUL Well, Michelle, first thing, when did you start playing football?
MICHELLE Well, I think I started playing football at a really early age, from about four upwards. So I've been told, apparently I used to pull my dolls' heads off and kick them around.
PAUL That's interesting. Good and erm, which position do you play in now?
MICHELLE Er . . . well, I can play out on the wing, on the right but I prefer centre mid-field.
PAUL Uhuh. Centre or mid-field. And erm have you ever played abroad yourself?
MICHELLE Yes, I've played in Italy.
PAUL Any other countries?
MICHELLE Er, no . . .

PAUL	Just Italy ...
MICHELLE	Yup.
PAUL	And which team do you usually play for now?
MICHELLE	Erm ... well, I'm hoping to be playing for Napoli next season. We're negotiating a contract at the moment.
PAUL	I see, so that's Napoli women's team ...
MICHELLE	Yeah ...
PAUL	Were you ever excluded from playing in teams because you were a woman?
MICHELLE	Er ... there was one occasion, when erm a friend and I, she's a lady footballer also, erm attended some training matches, er some training sessions, erm with the intention of playing in a match at the end of it. We were the only two girls on the course, and erm we were told to come along to the match, erm, but when we arrived we were told that we wouldn't be allowed to play because we were women.
PAUL	I see. Finally ... are women more aggressive than men when they play football, do you think?
MICHELLE	Erm ... I don't know whether they're more aggressive ... er ... I can't really say, I can't answer for all women. I know personally I give it everything I've got when I'm playing, so whether you call that aggressive or not. I suppose in a way it is. It's getting rid of some aggression, but because I enjoy the game, you know what I mean I don't feel that I'm being aggressive, really.
PAUL	It's just part of the game.
MICHELLE	Yeah.
PAUL	OK. Thank you very much, Michelle.
MICHELLE	That's all right. You're welcome.

Extra Activity

If your students seem particularly interested in this topic a good way to end the session would be to organise a class debate.

- Suggested title: *Football is not a suitable sport for women.*
- Set up the debate by getting two students to prepare a talk agreeing with the motion and two against the motion. They should have time to do this at home.
- The rest of the class should also put down ideas so that when the debate is on they will have something to add.

3 *Vocabulary Development*

- Bring a couple of dictionaries into the classroom to give students the chance to compare them and get used to using them. Give them plenty of practice looking for information in the dictionaries.
- Tell them to look at examples of entries and find specific information so that they will soon get used to doing this.

1 Give them time to read the entry for *foul* from the *Collins Cobuild English Language Dictionary*. Give them help with the vocabulary of the examples if they need it.

2
Key

Foul (N)	meaning 10	
Foul (ADJ)	meaning 4	(language)
Foul (ADJ)	meaning 1	(pitch)

3
Key

1 infringement   2 bad   3 filthy

4
Key

1 /faʊl/
2 fouler, foulest
3 fouls
4 fouling, fouled
5 bad (weather)

Key

short tennis, five-a-side football, mini-rugby, mini-cricket, netball, hockey, basketball, badminton, mini-volleyball.

WB 27.2
Key

everywhere in the country	*nationwide*
intended for	*aimed at*
soft rubber	*foam*
attractive	*appealing*
outshine / overshadow	*eclipse*
sudden increase	*upsurge*
completely	*universally*
hurt	*sting*

WB 27.3
Key

1 Foam balls, shortened racquets, 2 ft 7 in (0.867 m), simplified points system, badminton-sized court.
2 1982.
3 Because it's fun and realistic.
4 Not enough young people have been playing tennis.
5 Mini-rugby.
6 Because too much competition at an early age is not good.

WB 27.4
Students' own answers.

UNIT 28 *page 92*

> **New structures**
> Reported speech (past)
>
> **New functions**
> Reporting what people said
>
> **Vocabulary**
> hard – attitudes – hardworking – awful – symbol – ambassador – rule – especially – lazy – naturalness – friendliness – admire – charity – sense of humour – taxes – channel – national health – advert – documentary
>
> **Revision**
> Reported speech (present)

Revise reported speech using an introductory verb in the present. Write some phrases from the previous lesson on the board in direct speech and ask students to identify the speakers and put them into indirect speech.

The Royal Family

- Ask students what names of the members of the British royal family they know and the relationship of one to the other.
- Discuss with them their opinion of the royal family. Ask them if they like the royal family (have a show of hands). Ask them what they think the function of the royal family is. Ask which members of the royal family they like the most and which they like the least. Ask them which members have come to their country recently. Ask if they would like to be a member of the royal family and what the advantages and disadvantages of such a life would be.
- Ask your students to predict which members of the royal family are popular with British young people. Write the names on the board.
- Tell students to open their books now and read the text to check their guesses. When they have finished reading tell them to look at the chart with the list of engagements and number of days abroad.
- Clear up any problems that your students may have with vocabulary in the text.
- Tell students to do the *true* or *false* exercise.

Key
1 True   2 False   3 False   4 True   5 False   6 True   7 True

Supplementary Exercise 40 *(SB page 123)*
Key
52% Girls interested in the royal family.
29% People who thought that Prince Charles was hardworking.
 5% People who thought the royal family were ambassadors for Britain.
 9% People who thought the royal family were national symbols.
24% People who wanted the royal family to change.
22% People who thought that Princess Margaret was lazy.
34% Boys interested in the royal family.

UNIT 28 *page 93*

1 *Language Focus*

- Play the cassette while students look at the model sentences. Write the sentences on the board with a space underneath each one. Elicit the direct speech for each sentence and write it under the sentences.
- Point out the changes of tense. (You may like to point out to your students at this stage that it is in fact possible to keep the present after introductory verbs in the past if what is in the indirect speech is still true.) It is probably less confusing at this stage, however, not to mention keeping the tense the same if it doesn't crop up. Leave it until they reach the grammar section.
- Play the cassette and ask students to listen and repeat the model sentences.

PRESENTER	Tapescript 89. Unit 28. Listen.
	Many people thought that the members of the royal family were hardworking.
WOMAN	One girl said that Princess Diana wore awful clothes.
MAN	Over half the girls said that they were interested in the royal family.
WOMAN	Half the people thought the Queen worked very hard.
MAN	Some people said that Prince Edward was the laziest.
PRESENTER	Now listen and repeat.

- Tell your students to look at the photographs and listen to the next tapescript. Play this section once or twice.
- Tell your students to work individually and convert the direct speech into reported speech. When they have finished, supply the correct answers by playing the next section of the tapescript.
- Finally, ask them to listen to and repeat the reported speech.

PRESENTER	Tapescript 90. Unit 28. Listen.
DAWN	I like the Queen and the Queen Mother but I don't like Princess Anne.
GEOFF	I like Prince Charles because he has done a lot of good work with young people.
TERESA	I don't like the royal family very much. They cost the country too much money!
CLIVE	I'm not really interested in the royal family. I think they are quite boring people.
PRESENTER	Now listen and check your answers.
	Dawn said that she *liked* the Queen but she *didn't like* Princess Anne.
WOMAN	Geoff said that he *liked* Prince Charles because he *had done* a lot of good work with young people.
MAN	Teresa said that she *didn't like* the royal family very much. They *cost* the country too much money.
WOMAN	Clive said that he *wasn't* really interested in the royal family. He said he *thought* they *were* quite boring people.
PRESENTER	Now listen and repeat.

2 TV *survey*

- Ask students to tell you what they know about British TV. (Some may have watched TV while visiting Britain.) Ask them if they know anything about the sort of programmes shown on each channel. (BBC 1 is the lighter of the two BBC channels with quizzes, popular comedy shows as well as news broadcasts, while BBC 2 is more serious and shows art films, documentaries and more in depth news programmes. There are no advertisements on these two channels. ITV is the most commercial channel with many quiz programmes, chat shows, American imported programmes and soap operas, while Channel 4 is commercial television's answer to BBC 2, showing high quality films, news programmes and documentaries. Both of these channels are financed by advertising.)

- Tell students that they are going to hear a woman asking questions as part of a survey about people's TV viewing habits. Tell them to look at the questions she asks.
- Divide the class into groups of three students. Each member of each group is responsible for *one* of the people in the chart.
- Play the cassette two or three times while students fill in the information on the chart. Tell them not to write anything the first time they listen. (Do not supply the correct answer yet.)
- Students now report what their person said on the cassette to the others in the group. They use reported speech as in the example. The other members of the group fill in the rest of the chart.
- When all students have completed charts, write the correct version of the chart on the board. Play the cassette again while students look at the completed chart.

Key

| | TV CHANNEL | PROGRAMMES | | ADVERTISING |
		LIKES	DOESN'T LIKE	
Anita	BBC 1	films	quiz shows	indifferent
Paul	Channel 4	documentaries	soaps	likes them
Linda	BBC 2	news	films	indifferent

91

PRESENTER Tapescript 91. Unit 28. Listen.
WOMAN Excuse me! Can I ask you a few questions about your TV viewing habits, please?
ANITA Mmm ... how long will it take?
WOMAN Just a couple of minutes.
ANITA Yes, all right then.
WOMAN Which channel do you watch most?
ANITA BBC 1.
WOMAN BBC 1 ... And what are your favourite programmes?
ANITA My favourite programmes?
WOMAN Yes, which programmes do you watch most?
ANITA Films, I suppose ... I like films and there are some good ones on these days.
WOMAN Yes, there are. Now, are there any programmes which you never watch ... programmes that you really don't like?
ANITA Oh yes! Quiz shows ... I detest quiz shows and I never watch them.
WOMAN Thanks. Last of all ... What do you think of advertising on TV?
ANITA Well I only watch BBC 1 as I said and there are no ads on BBC 1 ... Is that all? I really must go now.
WOMAN Yes, that's fine. Thanks very much.

WOMAN Excuse me!
PAUL Who me?
WOMAN Yes. I'm doing a survey of TV viewing habits. Would you mind answering a few questions?
PAUL Not at all ... Fire away!
WOMAN Which TV channel do you watch most?
PAUL I watch all of them, but I suppose I watch Channel 4 more than the others. Yes ... Channel 4.
WOMAN And which programmes do you like the best?
PAUL Well ... there are lots of programmes that I like, but I think I like documentaries the best ... like that Attenborough thing, *The Living Planet* ... that was really good!
WOMAN What about programmes that you don't like?
PAUL Hate soaps! *Eastenders, Coronation Street, Crossroads.* I can't stand soaps, not one of them. And there are lots now.
WOMAN What about advertising? Do you mind adverts on TV?
PAUL Mind them? No, I like them. Besides they give you time to make a cup of coffee, that sort of thing.
WOMAN Thanks very much. That's all.
PAUL Oh ... right ... bye!

WOMAN Good morning. I'm trying to find out about people's TV viewing habits. Could you answer a few questions, please?
LINDA Yes, of course.
WOMAN First of all ... which channel do you watch?
LINDA I sometimes watch BBC 1 ... but most of the time I watch BBC 2. I like watching the news on BBC 2 – it's the most complete.
WOMAN What other programmes do you like?
LINDA Well, I don't watch much TV at all really. I'm a nurse and I work a lot of nights. I really only like news programmes.
WOMAN I see ... What programmes don't you like?
LINDA I don't like watching films on TV. I prefer to see them at the cinema. There are too many interruptions if you watch films on TV and the screen's a bit small.
WOMAN What about advertising? Do you watch TV adverts?
LINDA I don't mind them ... I'm indifferent really ... some are all right ... some are awful.
WOMAN Thank you very much. That's all.
LINDA My pleasure. Bye.

3 *Your own survey*

Students practise reported speech in this activity by reporting back answers to a series of questions on a theme chosen by their group.

1 Divide students into groups of four or five. Tell each group to choose a topic from those listed or to choose another which appeals to them more. Make sure that the groups choose a variety of topics – if necessary you may have to change the topic of certain groups to ensure that the ensuing pair practice will work.
- Tell students to prepare a list of five questions on their topic. Each student has to note all five questions.
2 The groups separate, and each member of the group talks to a member of another group who has a list of questions on a different theme.
- Each person makes notes of the other person's answers.
- The original groups re-form and each member of the group reports back the answers to the questions. One member of the group records the answers.
3 When they have finished reporting back, all members of the group help the group leader prepare a report which they can read to the rest of the class.

WB 28.1

Students read the comments about a fictitious film *Exterminating Cop**. They then rewrite the comments in indirect speech.
**Cop* is slang for *policeman*.

Key

Michael Wise said that it was an extremely boring film.
Jan Walters said it was the most exciting film of the year.
Ted Davis said he liked the film and that it was well-made and well-acted.
Ann White said she didn't like the film and she thought it was very dangerous.
Jo Dumfries said that *Exterminating Cop* was a load of rubbish. He said that the characters were unbelievable and the plot was incredibly banal.
Ed Bell said that he thought he had never seen such a bad film.
Les O'Sullivan said that it was a really good thriller and that he could recommend it for the whole family.
Sue Murphy said she really enjoyed a good thriller and that this (*or that*) one was excellent.

WB 28.2

In the second workbook exercise students write a report on the survey about British schools. No key is provided as there will be some variation in students' answers.

UNIT 28 *page 94*

New structures
Second conditional

New functions
Talking about future possibilities (2)

Vocabulary
emergency – faint – wound – bandage – choking – pinch

Revision
First conditional

Ask students to give you some examples of the first conditional. Put one or two examples on the board and compare them with the second conditional after they have done the first section below.

First aid

- Ask students if they have ever done any first aid courses. Ask them if the Red Cross operates in their country. Explain that there is also the St John's Ambulance in England which is a similar organisation to the Red Cross.
- Ask students the first three questions at the beginning of the text to see if they know anything about first aid. Then tell them to read the article. Give them any help they may need with vocabulary.
- Ask them how they would answer the question the participants on the course had to answer. Give them the chance to discuss their answers. (The best thing to do is to pour cold water on the burn to reduce the heat in the skin, but it is important to do it for about ten minutes. Then take the person to hospital. It is not wise to put anything greasy on the burn as this aggravates it and has to be cleaned before medical treatment can begin.)

Key

First Aid	is the first help given in an emergency.
Knowing what to do	can save someone's life.
The British Red Cross Society	runs courses in Britain.
First aid courses	help you know what to do in an emergency.
Enrol on one of these courses	before it's too late.

Supplementary Exercise 41 *(SB page 123)*
Key

First aid is the *help* given to people suffering from *accidents* or sudden *illness*. It is often given by people with no medical *training*. If you know what to do you might save someone's *life*. The British Red Cross Society runs *courses* in many parts of Britain to help *people* learn what to do in an *emergency*.

4 *Language Focus*

- Tell students to look at the model sentences taken from the text. Play the cassette while students read them.
- Ask students which verb tense they see in the *if* clause and which tense they see in the main clause. Explain that in English we don't use the conditional (*would*) after *if*. Ask them what other tense they never use after an *if* clause (the *will* future). Ask them what they notice about the first sentence (*I were*). What would they normally use instead of *were*? You may like to point out that this is one of the rare occasions when English uses the subjunctive.
- Students listen and repeat after the cassette.

PRESENTER   Tapescript 92. Unit 28. Listen.
If I were you, I'd enrol on one of these courses.
What would you do if there was an accident?
What would you do if your sister burnt herself badly?
If my sister burnt herself, I'd put butter on the wound.

Now listen and repeat.

- Tell students to look at the series of illustrations and choose the most suitable second half of the sentence.
- Play the next part of the cassette while students check their answers.
- Tell students to listen and repeat after the cassette.

PRESENTER   Tapescript 93. Unit 28. Listen.
If I were you, I'd go to bed.
What would you do if you saw a ghost?
If you went to America, you'd see the Statue of Liberty.
If I had a lot of money, I'd go to America.

UNIT 28 *page 95*

5 *What would you do in an emergency?*

The first part of this section tests students' knowledge of first aid.

- In pairs, students decide which of the suggestions of what to do in an emergency they think is best. They can put more than one suggestion for each thing and add another if they wish. Give them help if they need it.
- Students change pairs. In turn, they read out what they would do while their partners agree or disagree.
- Give them time to discuss their opinions before doing the listening exercise where they listen to English people talking about the same subject. They can then check if their suggestions were right.

 94 See Appendix for tapescript 94.

6 *Unique model competition*

Ask a couple of warm-up questions to find out if your students have in fact ever entered a competition and if they have, ask if they, or anyone they know has ever won a competition and what the prizes were.

1 Tell them to read the advertisement quickly to be able to answer the questions about it.

Key
1 One year (twelve months).
2 No, from Ravel, C&A Avanti and others (*such as* indicates a number of companies, but that the list is limited).
3 Unique's Chelsea office (in London).
4 Two photographs.
5 It's the closing date for entries to the competition.

2 There is now a listening exercise. They have to write down the things the people would spend their money on and the clothes they would buy.

Key
COLIN Buy a Giorgio Armani suit.
       Go to Italy.
JANE   Buy a new suit and boots from Ravel.
       Buy make-up, get hair done, go out.
MIRANDA Buy a lot of fashionable clothes.
         Pay off credit card.

 95

PRESENTER Tapescript 95. Unit 28. Listen.
JANE   Colin, how would you feel if you won the competition?
COLIN Well, I'd like the modelling contract.
JANE   Would you?
COLIN Mmm.
JANE   And what about the £250 worth of clothes?
COLIN Ah well, I'd buy erm a Giorgio Armani suit.
JANE   Ha-ha, yeah, good idea. And the £125 cash?
COLIN I'd go to Italy with £125.
JANE   Oh yes, I'd like to go to Italy.
MIRANDA What would you do, Jane?
JANE   Well... erm...
MIRANDA With the £125?
JANE   With the £125, oh, I'd buy some make-up or something um, get my hair done er, and swig back that that vodka that they're offering as well, and go out the town, you know, and blow it, you know.
MIRANDA Yeah. Do you think you'd enjoy the modelling?
JANE   No, I don't think I would, actually, I don't fancy kind of you know traipsing up and down and all that posing.
MIRANDA Oh! Really!
JANE   No, no. But the £250 worth of clothes, yes, I think, I think I'd

probably buy a new suit and er well a pair of boots from Ravel, perhaps.
MIRANDA Mmm, mmm.
JANE   And what about you, Miranda? What would you do if you won the competition?
COLIN Yeah.
MIRANDA Oh, well, I hope to start a career from this.
JANE   Really?
MIRANDA Yes, I mean, you know, sort of taking it up seriously. Erm, and therefore with the £250, I'd have to go and, you know, buy a whole new wardrobe of very fashionable clothes, because models have to have that.
COLIN Yes, yes, I would.
JANE   Yes, yes they do. They've got to look presentable, don't they?
MIRANDA Yes.
COLIN Yes, that's right.
JANE   And what about er the cash, the £125 cash?
MIRANDA Oh well, that would just go towards my credit card, which, you know, indirectly would actually be going towards clothes again, I suppose.
COLIN That's right, yes.
MIRANDA Yeah, that's where all my money goes.

3 For the last part of the section, put the students into groups and tell them to imagine they have entered for the competition. Encourage them to talk about what they would do with the money if they won and to use the expressions they have learnt in this unit.

WB 28.3
In this exercise the students have to give advice as in the example. When possible, they should be encouraged to give a reason for their comment.

WB 28.4
- Point out the examples of first and second conditional. Ask students if they can remember other examples from this unit and Unit 23.
- In this exercise the students must first decide which conditional to use and then make sentences. It is a good idea to leave the students to get on with this on their own although a weak class may need some initial help. They must decide whether the hypothesis is a likely one or not.

Key
1 Either (depends on current weather).
2 Unlikely; 2nd conditional.
3 Likely; 1st conditional (could be 2nd, depending on circumstances).
4 Unlikely; 2nd conditional.
5 Either (depends on the date).
6 Either (depends on their timetable).
7 Unlikely; 2nd conditional.
8 Either (depends on students' plans).

WB 28.5
This exercise follows on from section 6. Revise with them, if you think it necessary, the layout of an informal letter in English (Unit 5) before they do the exercise.

Moondown: Episode 6

Skills Focus: Reading and Listening

As with other episodes of *Moondown*, there is a certain amount of preparatory work to be done before students open their books and start reading the episode. First ask your students what happened in the last episode. Ask questions like: Where did Pete go? Did he find Cathy? Who was Cathy with?

1 Write the two pre-reading discussion questions on the board. Discuss them either with the whole class or with your students in groups.
2 Write the 12 key words from the story, which are listed in the Student's Book, on the board. You can use the book if you like, but there is a temptation for students to look at the text.

● Ask questions focusing on the words and encouraging students to guess their significance in the story. You will find that they are able to guess most of the action in this episode just by looking at these words. This serves to increase their motivation to read the episode.

● At this point tell students to open their books and read the episode while they listen to the cassette to check their theories.

96 See Student's Book for tapescript 96.

UNIT 29 *page 97*

3 The first comprehension exercise concentrates on the newspaper article. These are the central questions in journalism; if an article has this information, it has served its purpose.
- The questions which students produce should all be more or less the same.

Key
What happened?
When did the accident happen?
Where did the accident happen?
Who was involved in the accident? Who was in the car?
Why did the accident happen?

- When students have written their questions they can exchange them with another student and answer that student's questions.

4 Students prepare answers to the questions individually or in pairs.

Key
1 She's Cathy's friend who works in London.
2 He says 'Who is it?' when he hears the newspaper arrive. He is afraid that someone has come into the flat.
3 Graham Brooke.
4 He thinks she has been killed in the car with Jack Sims.
5 Because he wants her to help him.
6 No, he doesn't. (He introduces himself on the phone.)
7 Yes, she has. (We can tell this from Pete's words.)
8 No, she hasn't. (She asks him for the address.)

Supplementary Exercise 42 *(SB page 123)*
If you have a very mixed ability class, it is best to allow students to work through the exercises at their own pace and give the Supplementary Exercise to those who finish before the others.
- The exercise gives students practice in dialogue writing. Students have to imagine Linda Markham's side of her conversation with Pete and write out the whole conversation.

5 To prepare for the second part of the episode, ask them some questions about what they think will happen next or what they would do if they were in Pete's position. Then look at the *true* or *false* exercise but allow students to make guesses before they listen.
- Play the cassette at this point and allow students to check their answers. Play the cassette again if students get any of their answers wrong; it is better for them to discover their own mistakes than for you to correct them. Of course with a *true* or *false* exercise you can't draw attention to the specific items they have got wrong but you can tell them how many they got wrong. When you are satisfied, supply the correct answers.

Key
1 True   2 False   3 True   4 False   5 False   6 False   7 False

Supplementary Exercise 43 *(SB page 123)*
Students imagine that they are Pete and tell the story of his investigations so far. They have the beginning of his account. This is a very useful but rather demanding exercise as they have to use most of the tenses they have learned, and also practise their summary-writing skills.
- This exercise will work better set for homework. You can ask students to read their version at the beginning of the next *Moondown* lesson (Unit 35).

- If you have time at the end of the lesson, invite students to guess what will happen in the final episode of the story.

PRESENTER   Tapescript 97. Unit 29. Listen.
LINDA   Hello. I'm Linda.
PETE   Hi, I'm Pete, come in.

LINDA   Thanks. Now, tell me what happened.
PETE   Well … someone from Moondown power station phoned Cathy one day and told her that they were dumping nuclear waste in the sea at Star Point, a few miles away from Westfield.
LINDA   Star Point? That's where the accident happened, isn't it?
PETE   Accident? Yes, I suppose you could call it that. Yes, Star Point is also about two kilometres from Moondown. Anyway, when we started to investigate, our editor, Mr Eastwood, got very angry and told us to stop.
LINDA   Why did he get angry?
PETE   Well, I'm coming to that, but I didn't realise why at the time. Anyway, our informer at Moondown phoned again and told us when the next dumping was, so we went there. That was last Saturday.
LINDA   That's when you took the photos …
PETE   Yes, that's right. Unfortunately someone saw us … Jack Sims, the man who died in the car accident.
LINDA   I see. And I suppose he told the people at Moondown.
PETE   No, I don't think so … At least he said he didn't. I saw him yesterday. But Eastwood found out and suspended us for a month.
LINDA   I wonder how he found out.
PETE   I don't know, but I've got an idea.
LINDA   What's that?
PETE   Well … when I was reading the article about the accident I saw the name of the director of Moondown, Graham Brooke. Suddenly I remembered that Brooke was Eastwood's wife's name before she was married.
LINDA   So there's a connection between Eastwood and this Brooke, the director of Moondown.
PETE   Mmm … I think so. … Who's that, I wonder. Hello … Cathy! … Oh, thank God! You're alive!

WB 29.1
Key
1 Guy Fawkes' Night.
2 Shrove Tuesday.
3 Hallowe'en.

WB 29.2
Key
1 False   2 True   3 True   4 False   5 True   6 False
7 False   8 True   9 False   10 True

UNIT 30 *page 98*

Skills Focus: Writing

Formal Letters (2)

Refer the students back to Unit 10 where they learnt how to set out a
formal letter. The same rules about layout apply when writing any kind of
formal letter.
1   When the students read the advertisement they have to look for specific
information.

Key
1   Scottish Borders.
2   No, they guarantee individual tuition.
3   No. It's £89 for tuition and £16 per day for accommodation.
4   Yes, (*full board* means sleeping accommodation and meals).

2   Tell them to read the letter. Test their knowledge of the rules for writing
formal letters by giving them the exercise which follows the
reading.

Key

1 The address from the advertisement on the left hand side of the page.
  The formal language (particularly the third paragraph).
  The ending 'Yours sincerely'.
  The name typewritten under the signature.
2 Do you think you could ...?
  Could you ...?
3 Because he has recently bought an Amstrad word processor.
4 The first.
  The second
5 No.
6 It is polite to do this if you want to receive information.

3 Go through the advertisements, make sure they understand them, and then tell them to write a letter similar to the model one asking for information.

WB 30

This is a straightforward formal letter asking for information. The students will do well provided they organise their ideas and go through the activity carefully. To this end, it would be worth preparing the letter in class by discussing the four points to be included. Also, remind students of the correct layout. In marking their letters, insist on neat, professional presentation, preferably on writing paper.

REVISION FOCUS
Units 26–30 *page 100*

1 *Talking about an earlier past*

Students work with another student and make comments on things that happened as in the example.

- Good students can be encouraged to extend the dialogues beyond one exchange each. Make sure, however, that they are keeping to the constructions to be practised.
- No key is included for this exercise as answers will vary from student to student.

2 *Reporting what people say*

Students use reported speech with the introductory verb in the present in a game. They also revise the language of descriptions at the same time.

- Tell students to write descriptions of themselves on a piece of paper taken from an exercise book. The description can include physical characteristics, character, and hobbies. They must not show their descriptions to other students.
- When they have finished writing their descriptions, collect them in. Jumble the descriptions and give them out again. If a student gets his or her own piece of paper back, take it back and give him or her another one.
- When every student has a description, select students to report the descriptions, while the others listen. Students should use reported speech when they report what's on the piece of paper.
- The other students have to guess the name of the student from the description. When they have guessed, ask another student to report a description and so on.
- An alternative procedure is to give out the slips of paper and tell students to work in groups rather than as a whole class. This works best in large classes where it would be boring for everyone to wait for their turn to read a description.
- Another idea would be to get everybody to write a description of somebody else in the group for the others in the group to identify.

3 *Reporting what people said*

Students practise reported speech with an introductory verb in the past by doing a memory game.

- Tell students to read all three paragraphs by Neil, Melanie and Heather about their tastes in music. Tell them they can look at the paragraphs for two minutes, after which time they must close their books.
- Students now compete with each other in pairs. They take it in turns to report something that was written in the paragraphs. They must use reported speech as in the example.
- Students write down each fact that their partner remembers.
- When they can no longer remember any more facts they open their books and check their answers. The person who has remembered the most facts accurately is the winner.
- If you think that your students need extra practice in reporting, tell them to write out the paragraphs in reported speech for homework.

4 *Talking about future possibilities* (2)

Students write down what they would do in each of the situations. A couple of them may provoke some discussion of moral issues.

- When they have finished, tell the students to ask some more questions of a similar kind.

5 *Vocabulary*

Students' own answers.
Refer to the teacher's notes for Exercise 6, page 36.

6 *Pronunciation*

This exercise practises the different ways of pronouncing the letters *ou*. Students are sometimes not aware that there are three distinct pronunciations. Tell the students to classify the words in the list and then play the cassette for them to check their answers. They can listen and repeat the words as a final stage.

 *Key*

1 /aʊ/ out   2 /ə/ serious   3 /ɔː/ four

hour 1	course 3
bought 3	colour 2
found 1	your 3
unconscious 2	house 1
court 3	curious 2
loud 1	mouth 1

GRAMMAR FOCUS
Units 26–30 *page 101*

1 *Past perfect*

a Ask the students to tell you in each of the examples which action came first and so is in the past perfect tense.

b At the station I realised I *had left* my wallet at home.
I gave the book to my brother but he *had read/bought* it already.
By the time I arrived at his office, the meeting *had finished/started*.

c The past perfect comes before the simple past in a time sequence.
If we want to show that an action was completed before another action began, then we must use the past perfect.

2 *Reported speech (1)*

a Students look at the model sentences noting the word *says* and the tense of the sentence.

b She *says* that she *hasn't got* any money so she can't go to the cinema this evening.
He *says* he's *watching* a football match on TV, so he doesn't want to talk to you now.

c 'I can't come to the phone because I'm having a bath.'
'I'm doing my homework.'
Simple present: *says*.
No, the verb in the main clause doesn't change when the introductory verb is in the present. This is probably the same in your students' own language and therefore should present no problems.
Students may have realised that the pronoun *that* is optional in reported speech. We usually put it in when there is a series of main clauses that depend on the introductory verb. E.g. *He says he's very happy and that he'll write soon.*

3 *Reported speech (2)*

a Let students study the example sentences.

b She *said* that she *wanted/hoped/needed* to buy a car.
They *said* that they *were going/had been invited* to a party that evening.

c Michael: 'I like the royal family, especially the Queen.'   .
Rachel's parents: 'We don't enjoy going to the theatre very much.'
Simple past: *said*.
Yes, the verb tense in the main clause usually goes one tense further back in time, but not always. If the statement is still true then you can also leave the verb in the present tense. E.g. *He said that he doesn't like classical music.*
Where you have *will* in direct speech this becomes *would* in reported speech. E.g. 'I will probably go to London at the weekend.' *She said she would probably go to London at the weekend.*

4 *Second conditional*

a The difficulties that were encountered when studying the second conditional may well have been overcome by now. Go through the model sentences pointing out the structure.
Encourage students to talk about the use of the two types of conditional and to look critically at the reasons for using one rather than the other. It is important that they realise that the second conditional is used when the hypothesis is more unlikely.

b If I *had* a lot of money, I'*d go* to the States.
If someone *were/was* unconscious, I'*d give* artificial respiration.
If I *were* you, I'*d go* to the doctor.

c Simple past (the past continuous is also possible).
Conditional (i.e. *would* + infinitive).
First conditional.
Second conditional.

New structures
Present perfect continuous with *for* and *since*

New functions
Talking about unfinished activities

Vocabulary
back streets – suburb – talent – suffer – illness –
several – injury – together – victory

Revision
Present perfect with *for* and *since*

Diego Armando Maradona

- As a warm-up exercise, ask students to give you the names of some
  famous footballers. They are quite likely to mention Maradona. Ask them
  what they know about him. Some keen footballers may be able to give
  more information than is in the presentation text! You can take
  advantage of their knowledge and build up a more detailed biographical
  text about him.
- Go through the pre-reading questions with the class.
- Students read the text and discuss with another student any vocabulary
  difficulties they may encounter. If they cannot resolve their problems
  together, refer them to a dictionary or give them the words they need.

Key
Buenos Aires.
Since he was a very small boy.
Since 1984.

- They should be able to find the statements to justify the comments at
  the bottom of the page fairly quickly.

Key
1 Diego Armando Maradona is one of a family of eight children . . .
2 . . . a poor suburb of Buenos Aires.
3 He's been playing football since he was a very small boy . . . His
   outstanding talent was soon recognised . . .
4 . . . suffered from injury and illness.
5 He was with Barcelona for two seasons . . .
6 . . . leading them to victory.

Supplementary Exercise 44 *(SB page 124)*
- Let them read the text again but then tell them to try not to refer back
  to the text while they are doing the exercise. There is no key to this
  exercise as answers will vary from student to student. Make it clear to
  them that they are not required to memorise the text.

UNIT 31 *page 103*

1 *Language Focus*

- While students read the model sentences, play the cassette and discuss any comprehension problems relating to vocabulary or the meaning of the target structure.
- Play the next part of the cassette and allow students to listen and repeat. Point out that in spoken language they would be more likely to abbreviate *have* and *has* to *'ve* and *'s*.
- Go through the sentences with the students and get them to give you the complete forms.

PRESENTER   Tapescript 99. Unit 31. Listen.
How long has he been playing football?
He's been playing football since he was a very small boy.
How long has he been living in Italy?
He's been living in Italy since 1984.

I've been living here for several years now.
I've been working with a good team.
They've been working well.
He's been playing for Naples since 1984.

Now listen and repeat.

- Tell students to read the dialogue for completion and fill in the missing parts. Students should work on their own when they do the completion exercise but may well need help in understanding what they have to do. Explain that they answer from their own experience. Elicit some answers orally before they begin to write.
- When they have finished, tell them to check their work with another student by practising the dialogue together. Tell students to refer to you if they are in doubt.

2 *What have you been doing?*

- Students write sentences in the form *I've been + A + B.*
- When they have finished, put them into groups of three and tell them to play the game. Explain that Student A only gives the first part of his sentence in the first instance and Student B has to guess what the second part will be. Student C checks by asking Student A for the second part of the sentence. The game goes on until all three students have read their sentences. The winner is the one with most points.

3 *Group stories*

1 Students should try to be as imaginative as possible when doing this activity. They should get some ideas from the pictures but should feel free to insert whatever other information they need to get a good story.
- Give students as much time as they need to do the activity and go round monitoring their work as they are doing it.
- When they are ready, get one person from each group to tell their story to the class or to another group if the class is too big to allow all groups time to do it.
2 As a final activity tell them to write out the story they liked best.

WB 31.1
Key
1 She's been doing her homework since 2.30.
2 He's been waiting for the bus for half an hour.
3 He's been driving a car for three years.
4 They've been playing football since 5.00.
5 It's been snowing since 6.00 a.m.
6 They've been living in Venice for many years.
7 She's been writing letters all day.

WB 31.2
Key
A Mary's still *reading* that French novel. She*'s been reading* it for three months and she still *hasn't finished* it!
B But why? It isn't that difficult is it?
A No, but she*'s had* a lot of other things to do. She*'s been learning* to drive recently and so she*'s been going* for lessons every day. But she*'s taking* her test next week so then she'll have more time.
B Is she a good driver?
A Well, I *went* out with her last week and she almost *had* an accident but her instructor says she*'s getting* better.

UNIT 31 *page 104*

New structures
Verb + object + infinitive *(want, let, make)*

New functions
Talking about what you want, are allowed, have, to do

Vocabulary
let – persuade – change her mind – reasonable – lay

Revision
Using *can* to express permission

Plans for the end-of-term party

- It should be near the end of the school year when you are doing this lesson. As a warm-up activity ask students to tell you about any plans they have made for an end-of-term celebration.
- Let students look at the pictures in their books and ask what they think these people may be planning to do.
- Play the cassette and tell students to look at the exercise. This will focus their attention while they listen. Play the cassette a second time and tell them to do the exercise.

Key

The students in Karen, Julie and Stuart's class are having a *party* at the *weekend* because it is the *end* of term. *Julie* says she can't go. The party is starting at *8.30* and she usually has to be *home* at ten o'clock. They are going to phone *Dave*'s mum. She is a *friend* of Julie's mum, and they hope she can make Julie's mum change her mind.

Supplementary Exercise 45 *(page 124)*

- Students take one item from each column in order to form each sentence or sentences. They should check their answers with another student when they have finished. Go over the answers with them.

Key

Karen says:
  'We can ask David's mum to speak to her.'
  'I hope you can come. It'll be fun.'
Stuart says:
  'Can't you persuade her as it's the end of term?'
  'Why not? Everybody's going.'
Julie says:
  'She wants me to look after my brother.'
  'I'll give her a ring this evening.'

◖100◗ See Student's Book for tapescript 100.

UNIT 31 *page 105*

4 Language Focus

- Tell students to look at the sentences taken from the dialogue. Play the cassette while students read them.
- Ask students if they notice anything about the formation of these expressions. They should notice that they all follow the pattern *verb + object + infinitive*, but that *want* takes the infinitive with *to*.
- Students listen and repeat after the cassette.

PRESENTER	Tapescript 101. Unit 31. Listen.
JULIE	She always makes me come home by ten o'clock. She says she wants me to look after my brother on Saturday.
STUART	She doesn't let you do anything!
KAREN	Do your parents let you do everything you want to?
PRESENTER	Now listen and repeat.

- Tell students to look at the statements about Julie's mum. They should guess what happened when David's mum spoke to her on the phone.
- Play the cassette while students check their answers.

Key

Julie's mum let her go to the party.
Julie's mum wanted her to look after her brother.
Julie's mum wanted her to stay with Karen.

PRESENTER	Tapescript 102. Unit 31. Listen.
JULIE'S MUM	662 6754.
DAVID'S MUM	Hello Mary. How are things?
JULIE'S MUM	OK, but we've got a bit of trouble with Julie at the moment.
DAVID'S MUM	With Julie? Why? What's the matter?
JULIE'S MUM	Oh, it's this party they want to organise. She says she wants to go.
DAVID'S MUM	Isn't she going?
JULIE'S MUM	Well, no. I don't like her staying out after ten and anyway I want her to look after James.
DAVID'S MUM	Poor Julie.
JULIE'S MUM	What do you mean? Poor Julie?
DAVID'S MUM	Well they're all going. It is the end of term you know.
JULIE'S MUM	Why can't they have the party in the afternoon?
DAVID'S MUM	Oh, come on. They *are* growing up you know. You can't treat them like children all the time. Let her go.
JULIE'S MUM	Is David going?
DAVID'S MUM	Of course he is.
JULIE'S MUM	I don't like her coming home late on her own.
DAVID'S MUM	Yes, I can understand that. Why don't you let her stay with Karen? She's a nice girl and I'm sure they'd let her stay there.
JULIE'S MUM	Oh, I don't know. And what about James? I've got to go out on Saturday and I won't be back until seven or seven thirty.
DAVID'S MUM	I'm sure Julie can look after him until then.
JULIE'S MUM	That's true. The party starts at half past eight, doesn't it?
DAVID'S MUM	Yes. You see . . . There's no problem.
JULIE'S MUM	I suppose you're right. Well, all right. She can go if she can stay with Karen.
JULIE	Hey, Mum. What's that? Can I go to the party?

5 Parent power

- Give students time to look through the questionnaire and make sure they have no comprehension problems. Then tell them to fill in their answers in the column *YOU*.
- Now tell them to ask another student the questions and record the answers. Make sure they ask the questions in complete sentences.

- You may like to follow on from the pairwork activity with a class discussion. Ask the class to look at the first group of questions, then get one student to make a comment on one of them. Other students can then intervene with their own comments. For example, if a student says he can stay out late, another may ask what time he must come home. This can then lead to the students making statements like: 'My parents let me stay out till 11 o'clock.' Do not be tempted to let them go slowly through all the points. Limit it to one or two in each group.

6 *Teenagers*

1 Divide the class into groups of three and tell them that they are going to hear four students from other countries talk about what their parents let them do, make them do, and want them to do.
- Looking at the chart, they will see that the four students talk about coming home late at night and their future careers.
- Students listen to the cassette at least twice and fill in the chart with the information each is listening out for. They should write short notes.

Key

	Coming home late at night	Career
Jesus	• 8.00 – father tells him. (B) • Has to telephone if later. (B)	• Has to study. (C) • Can choose degree. (A)
Miwa	• Has to telephone and say what she is doing. (B) • 7–8.00. (B)	• Father wants her to be a pharmacist. (C)
Dominic	• No restriction. (A)	• Work for father. (C)
Maria Paula	• No restriction – Brasil. (A) • Weekends until 2.30. (A/B) • Friends stay out until 3–4.00. (A)	• Father doesn't say anything. (A) • He wants her to be successful. (C)

(A), (B), (C) indicates which student should have noted the information.

2 Students A, B and C now tell each other the information they have written down. They must use the structures, beginning each sentence:
'Jesus's parents let him ...'
         make him ...'
         want him to ...' etc.
- Go round the class, giving help where necessary.
- If your class is confident using this structure, this part of the activity could be done using reported speech. Students can use either the *says* or *said* form, as long as they understand the difference.

3 Finally, ask the students to write about teenagers in other countries.

PRESENTER	Tapescript 103. Unit 31. Listen.
PAUL	Jesus, what do your parents make you do at home?
JESUS	Well, I have to, I have to be at home, to, to get home at the time my father tells me ...
PAUL	What time is that?
JESUS	At eight o'clock.
PAUL	Uhuh. I see.
JESUS	So I have to get back before eight o'clock, or if I'm going to arrive later than this, in that case I have to phone home, I had to say I'm going arrive late.
PAUL	Uhuh ... Anything else, any other rules?
JESUS	Yes, study until I finish my homework.
PAUL	What about you Miwa?
MIWA	Yes, me too. When I want to go somewhere I have to call or say to my mother I'm going to the cinema with somebody, I have to say my friend's name, er ... things like that.
PAUL	Do you have to come home at a certain time every evening?
MIWA	Yes, about seven or eight o'clock.
PAUL	Seven or eight o'clock.
MIWA	Yes ...
PAUL	Do you ever stay out later?
MIWA	Erm ... no ...

PAUL	What about you Dominic? Erm, do your parents let you stay out?
DOMINIC	Yes, for me, there is no restriction, and erm, but I never want to go, to stay out longer than ten o'clock in the evening. But from my parents no restriction.
PAUL	Uhuh ... Erm, what about you Maria Paula?
M/PAULA	For me it's really different because in Brasil you go out really late and I can, er I can't go out every night but at the weekends I can go out and come back at half past two ...
PAUL	So that's very different ...
M/PAULA	Yeah ... And it's, it seems unfair to me, because all my friends can stay out until three or four o'clock and I have to go home at half past two.
PAUL	And what do your parents want you to do? Do they have any ambition for you at sixteen? Jesus?
JESUS	No, yes, to study er, I have no ... I can choose the degree and the programme at school it is my choice.
PAUL	Yes, what about you Miwa?
MIWA	My father is a doctor, so he always says to me I should be a pharmacist ...
PAUL	A pharmacist ...
MIWA	Yes ...
PAUL	Uhuh ...
MIWA	So now I am studying to be a pharmacist.
PAUL	What about you Dominic?
DOMINIC	Yes, my father erm he never says to me er you have to go to study business for his company er he has a company and but er for me there is no doubt, there is no doubt, that I won't do it ... erm ...
PAUL	So you're going to work for your father.
DOMINIC	I think so, yes.
PAUL	What about you Maria Paula?
M/PAULA	Well about my career? Yeah, he doesn't say anything. I'll choose my career and er he just erm wants me to be successful to study very hard to be successful ...

WB 31.3
Key
1 My mother wants me to work hard.
2 Mary lets her daughter go to the cinema every week.
3 I want you to come with me.
4 Does your sister let you wear her clothes?
5 Do you want me to go to the shops?
6 She makes me do my homework every evening.
7 Do they want you to go to university?
8 You made me love you.

WB 31.4
Key
1 She made me go to the supermarket.
2 I wanted her to swim better.
3 He let him go but he had to be home at ten o'clock.
4 My mother made me do my homework.
5 She wanted me to go to her house this afternoon.
6 She let me watch television in the evenings.
7 She wanted me to go and buy some bread.
8 She let me go to Bob's house.

WB 31.5
- Discuss with the students what sort of freedom they would give teenagers if they were parents. Get them to give some ideas and then set the exercise as a written exercise.
- In marking their work, look for correct use of the 2nd conditional and *let/make/want to*.

Playing with fire in the north frontier

1 *Skills Focus: Reading*

1 With Student's Books closed, write the headline *Playing with fire in the north frontier* on the board. Ask your students what they think the newspaper article is going to be about.

2,3 You can also deal with Exercises 2 and 3 with books closed if you like. Divide the class into groups, write the questions on the board and ask students to discuss them. When they have finished have a class check of students' answers.

4 Students open their books now and read the instructions. When you are satisfied that students know what they have to do, ask them to read the text and find the three alternatives. Allow students to check their answers in pairs before a class check.

Key
Join one of two sides in the conflict (be a hero), be a victim, or leave.

5 Ask students to find in the text the words listed and underline them. They now work in pairs and try to translate the words into their language. When they have a complete list of translations they hand the list to another pair of students or make new pairs and discuss each other's translations and adjust their lists where necessary.

6 Here students have to find the paragraphs which correspond to the phrases. Check that students understand the vocabulary in the statements before they begin.

● Allow students to check their answers in pairs before a class check.

Key
1 paragraphs 6, 7 and 8   2 paragraph 7   3 paragraph 4
4 paragraph 1   5 paragraph 3   6 paragraph 5
7 paragraph 5

Supplementary Exercise 46 *(SB page 124)*
● Students have to answer a series of questions on the text. Set the exercise in class or for homework if you think that your class will be able to do it successfully.

Key
1 Because he wants to give the reader the impression that the town is as peaceful as any other.
2 Calm, peaceful or similar.
3 Violent, horrific, etc.
4 They were excited at first then indifferent.
5 Presumably no.
6 From their address, school, games they play.
7 They are the colours of the flags of the two sides in the conflict.
8 No, they miss it.
9 Because he was involved in a bomb incident himself.

2 *Skills Focus: Listening*

This is an authentic unscripted conversation about the history of Ireland focusing more specifically on the problems in Northern Ireland (known as *the troubles*). Before you start the listening discuss with students their knowledge of Ireland and Irish history. They will probably know very little about it but discussion will serve to raise their interest in the listening.

1 There are two approaches to the first listening exercise. Either, ask students to look at the map and the names of the towns and predict where they are, (tell them to use pencil) and listen to check their answers. Or, simply tell them to look at the map and listen to Denis, noting down the towns as they listen. (They can use the initial letter of each town and fill in the full name afterwards.)

● Tell them to mark the border between the Republic and Northern Ireland after they have listened. Play only the first part of the cassette for this question.

Key

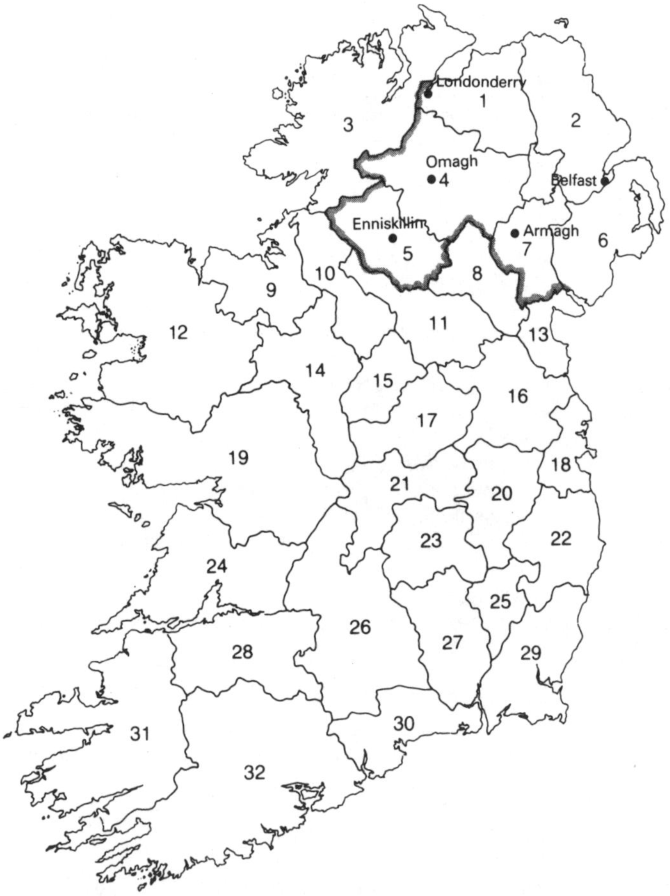

NB *Londonderry* is the official name of the city and county in north-west Northern Ireland, however, many people say *Derry* and *County Derry* in ordinary speech.

2   Move on to the next part of the listening now. Ask students to look at the list of dates and events in Irish history. If your students have some knowledge of Irish affairs, you may like to ask them to try to match the two before they listen, but avoid this procedure if they haven't as they will find it discouraging. Play the cassette one or two times and check students' answers.

Key

1608	Battle of the Boyne
17th Century	Plantation of Ulster
1801	Act of Union
1848	Feinian Rising
1916	Easter Rising
1916–1921	War of Independence
1921–1922	Civil War
1922	Partition of Ireland
1968	Civil Rights marches
1969	British Army sent to Northern Ireland
1985	Anglo-Irish Agreement

NB In fact the Battle of the Boyne was in 1690, the Plantation of Ulster began in 1609 (i.e. before the Battle of the Boyne), the War of Independence was 1919–1922 and the Civil War 1922–1923.

Supplementary Exercise 47 *(SB page 124)*
The third part of the listening goes into greater detail about the situation now and Denis talks about himself and his own feelings about the British presence in Northern Ireland.
● This is quite difficult and you should only attempt this if your students have had little trouble with the first and second part of the listening.

Key
1   Cork, in the Republic of Ireland.
2   About seven years ago.
3   He was living with his family and wanted something more adventurous, and it's difficult for young people to get a job there.
4   The British presence is contributing to the problem. He feels that the British should withdraw from Northern Ireland.
5   Sinn Fein, (Ourselves Alone), Ulster Defence Association.
6   He does not know what is going to happen, but he hopes that the British will leave Northern Ireland and that there will be a unified Ireland.

 See Appendix for tapescript 104.

3 *Vocabulary Development*

One of the best ways of learning vocabulary and recording it is in lexical sets. This exercise explains how to do this by pre-teaching vocabulary for Unit 35 and revising vocabulary from Unit 7 and the *Moondown* story.
● Check that students know all the words in the Camping holiday lexical set.
● Tell them to write out the table for Nuclear power in their vocabulary books and to fill it in, working in groups.

WB 32.1–4
These exercises concentrate on an article about an unusual school in Northern Ireland. Each exercise focuses on a different aspect of reading comprehension.

WB 32.1
Key
1   Belfast.
2   It was the first school to take both Catholics and Protestants.
3   1981.

WB 32.2
Key

	paragraph	
fully-integrated	1	open to all races and religions
daring	2	courageous
alarmed	3	worried
unknowns	3	strangers
mistrust	3	suspicion
bitterly	5	intensely
paved the way	5	made it easier
expenses	6	costs
dismisses	6	rejects
unemployed	6	without a job
concealed	7	hidden
guinea pigs	10	animals/people used in experiments

WB 32.3
Key

LAGAN COLLEGE (information true in 1987)	
Number of pupils	455
Proportion of Catholics and Protestants	50/50
Number of teachers	28
Geographical position	on hills overlooking Belfast
Similar schools which have opened	one secondary and three primary schools
Amount of Government aid given	85%
History syllabus	Irish and British Commonwealth

WB 32.4
Key
1   Some have free school meals, some parents are unemployed, some are from so-called ghettoes.
2   They are recognised, respected and discussed.
3   It stresses what the two communities have in common.
4   Because they were among the first pupils and therefore part of an experiment.

UNIT 33 *page 108*

<table>
<tr><td>

New structures
wish + past tense

New functions
Wishing

Vocabulary
wish – ugly – look like – spots

</td></tr>
</table>

I *wish I looked like* Tom Cruise

- Before students open their books discuss with them ways in which they think they would like to improve themselves. Ask them to name one feature, characteristic, or ability which they would like to improve.
- Students open their books. Tell them to look at the cartoon and listen while you play the cassette.
- Play the cassette once or twice, then ask students to do the exercise. Students can discuss the questions in pairs.

Key
1 Sue probably said she did not want to go out with him.
2 No, probably not.
3 Because he looks ugly.
4 Yes.
5 They are going to go out.
6 No, he feels happy and confident at the end.

Supplementary Exercise 48 *(SB page 124)*
Key

DAVE	Hello, Dave here.
SYLVIA	*Hello, Dave, this is Sylvia.*
DAVE	Oh, hello Sylvia. How are you?
SYLVIA	*I'm very well. What about you?*
DAVE	Yes, I'm fine.
SYLVIA	*Are you doing anything this evening?*
DAVE	This evening? No, I'm not.
SYLVIA	*Would you like to go to the cinema?*
DAVE	Yes, great, I'd love to.
SYLVIA	*Oh, good!*
DAVE	What time shall we meet?
SYLVIA	*Let's meet at eight o'clock outside the cinema.*
DAVE	OK, eight o'clock outside the cinema.
SYLVIA	*Fine! See you later!*
DAVE	Bye!

◄[105]► See Student's Book for tapescript 105.

UNIT 33 *page 109*

1 Language Focus

● Tell students to look at the six model sentences. Play the cassette.
● Play the cassette again, then play the next part of the cassette and tell students to listen and repeat. Check that students understand the concept involved in wishes.

PRESENTER   Tapescript 106. Unit 33. Listen.
DAVE   I wish I wasn't so ugly.
   I wish I looked like Tom Cruise.
   I wish I didn't have so many spots.
   I wish I didn't have such a big nose.
   I wish I was tall and slim.
   I wish I could play the guitar.

PRESENTER   Now listen and repeat.

● Tell students to look at the pictures and try to predict what the people are wishing. Students can check their answers in twos before you play the cassette so that they can confirm their hypotheses.
● Point out to the students that we can either say 'I wish I *was* ...' or 'I wish I *were* ...' Both are correct.
● Finally, ask them to listen and repeat.

PRESENTER   Tapescript 107. Unit 33. Listen.
MAN   I wish my ears weren't so big.
WOMAN   I wish I didn't have such a big nose.
MAN   I wish I was taller.
MAN   I wish I was more intelligent.
WOMAN   I wish I could ski.
WOMAN   I wish I looked like Madonna.

PRESENTER   Now listen and repeat.

2 'I wish ...'

● Tell students to look at the picture cues. Check that they have the necessary vocabulary to be able to do the exercise.
● Ask them to choose six things that they wish about themselves. They write the sentences then read them to another student and compare their wishes.
● To encourage interesting and varied sentences, elicit alternatives to the examples, e.g. *I wish I lived nearer the sea. I wish the sea was less polluted. I wish I wasn't such a poor swimmer.*

3 Wishing

1 Students listen to the conversation and try to identify the speakers and match them to the photos.
● Discuss the features of the faces of the people in the photos and ask students before you play the cassette what they think the people are going to say.
● Play the cassette two or three times. Allow students to check their answers in pairs before you supply the correct answers.

Key
From left to right:
Marcella   Isabel   Veronica   Catherine

PRESENTER   Tapescript 108. Unit 33. Listen.
   Four girls, Isabel, Marcella, Veronica and Catherine, are talking in a café.
ISABEL   Hi! Veronica! Catherine!
VERONICA   Hi!
CATHERINE   Hi!
ISABEL   Hi Marcella!
MARCELLA   Hi Isabel! Why are you so late?
ISABEL   Oh, I'm sorry. I've been trying to dry my hair. I wish I didn't have long hair.
MARCELLA   Oh, me too! My hair's impossible! I wish it wasn't so thick.
VERONICA   Oh, Marcella, you're only saying that because you've got lovely hair. I wish *I* had long hair. And I wish I didn't wear glasses.
CATHERINE   You could always get contact lenses. Veronica, like I do.
ISABEL   You wear contact lenses. Catherine? Oh, I never knew. I do envy you your straight hair. I wish I had straight hair.
MARCELLA   Well, I wish I had good skin. Nothing I do will get rid of these spots. Do you have any ideas Catherine?
CATHERINE   Maybe it's an allergy, Marcella. I'm allergic to strawberries.
MARCELLA   Oh!

2 Students discuss their wishes about themselves in a freer context here.
● Divide the class into groups of four or five students.
All the students in each group write four wishes about themselves on four strips of paper. Tell them to write their wishes in capital letters so that the others in the group will not be able to recognise their handwriting. It is best if all members of the group all write in pen or all write in ball-point pen. Tell them not to show their strips of paper to the others in the group.
● Students now fold their strips of paper and put them on the desk in the middle of the group. One student mixes up the pieces.
● Each student now takes four pieces of paper at random. It doesn't matter if he or she takes one or two of his or her own pieces.
● Students take it in turns to read the wishes on the paper. The other students have to say whether they would wish the same thing and why or why not. The person who wrote the sentence doesn't admit to having written it.

WB 33.1
Key
1 I was *so* tired that I went to bed at eight o'clock yesterday evening.
2 It was *such* a beautiful day that we had lunch in the garden.
3 The maths homework was *so* difficult that nobody could do it.
4 People in Ethiopia have *so* little food that many die of starvation.
5 She speaks French *so* well that people often think she's French.
6 There are *such* wonderful shops in Italy that it's almost impossible not to spend a lot of money there.
7 There were *so* many people in the pool that it was impossible to swim.
8 She ran *so* fast that she won every race last season.
9 She has *so* much to do that she has very little free time.
10 It was *such* a good film that I went to see it three times.

WB 33.2
Key
1 I wish I had a new bicycle.
2 I wish I had/lived in a nicer/new/better house.
3 I wish I wasn't so short and fat.
4 I wish I had a computer.
5 I wish I wasn't so tall and thin.
6 I wish I didn't have such big ears and such a long nose.
7 I wish I could play tennis better.

UNIT 33 *page 110*

> **Revision**
> Present continuous for present and future
> Simple present
> Simple past
> Past continuous
> *going to* future
> *will* future
> *used to*
> Present perfect
> Present perfect continuous

Mistaken identity

- Tell students to look at the pictures. Ask them what sort of people they think the people in the pictures are. Do they think they know each other? What do they think they are talking about? What do they think happens at the end?
- Play the cassette one or two times while students compare what they said with what actually happened. (The two people said *hello* because they thought they recognised each other whereas in fact they didn't know each other at all!)
- Tell students to do the *true* or *false* exercise. Allow them to work in pairs and when they have finished, supply the correct answers.

Key
1 True   2 True   3 True   4 True   5 False   6 False
7 True   8 False

Supplementary Exercise 49 *(SB page 124)*
Students have to write a series of questions about Jacky and Henry using the list of tenses given. When they have written their questions they can give the list to another student after which they can answer each other's questions. There are no set answers to this exercise.

 See Student's Book for tapescript 109.

4 *Language Focus*

- Students look at the model sentences taken from the text and listen while you play the cassette. Ask students to identify the various tenses. With a weak class you may prefer to write a list of tenses in jumbled order on the blackboard as a prompt.
- Play the next part of the cassette and tell students to listen and repeat.

PRESENTER	Tapescript 110. Unit 33. Listen.
HENRY	You used to live in Richmond, didn't you?
JACKY	No, er, it was Kingston, actually.
JACKY	Where are you living now?
HENRY	I'm living in Twickenham.
JACKY	You went to London University when you left school, didn't you?
HENRY	No, I went to Leeds.
JACKY	Where have you been working recently?
HENRY	I've been working in central London for the last two years.
HENRY	I'm going to work in the States soon.
JACKY	That'll be nice.
JACKY	You're a computer engineer, aren't you?
HENRY	No, I'm not. I'm a doctor. I've always been a doctor.
JACKY	When are you getting married?
HENRY	I'm getting married next month.
PRESENTER	Now listen and repeat.

UNIT 33 *page 111*

- Tell students to look at the answers and to try to write the questions.

PRESENTER	Tapescript 111. Unit 33. Listen.
WOMAN	*What do you do?*
MAN	I'm a shop assistant.
WOMAN	*Where are you working?*
MAN	I'm working at Waitrose Supermarket at the moment.
WOMAN	*Where do you live?*
MAN	I live in London.
WOMAN	*How long have you been living in London?*
MAN	I've been living in London for ten years.
WOMAN	*Where did you use to live?*
MAN	I used to live in Bristol.
WOMAN	*Where are you going for your holidays this year?*
MAN	I'm going to Spain this year.

5 *The verb tense game*

(You will need a dice for each pair of students.) In the verb tense game students have a chance to find out the weak spots in their knowledge of English verb tenses. The rules are quite simple although you may check them by asking students to read them and explain to you in their own words what they think they have to do.

- If your students haven't got a dice, you can improvise by telling them to write the numbers 1 to 6 on small squares of paper. They can put the paper in a pencil case and shake it before taking out a piece of paper and looking at the number on it.
- While students are playing the game you should go round the class and monitor carefully to see that students are not allowing incorrect sentences. Also, this will give you the chance to write down any mistakes that students are consistently making so that you can do remedial work later on.
- Each partner decides if the other person's verb is correct. If there is a dispute they should ask you to be the arbitrator.

6 *English studies survey*

Students revise a range of tenses in a freer context here. They discuss in groups their attitudes to their study of English.

- Divide the class into groups of four or five and tell each person of the group to write down one question for each category.
- If you have a weak class, elicit the questions which they are going to ask and write them on the board before they begin.

Key

1. Number of years of study.
   How long have you been studying English?
2. Number of visits to English-speaking countries.
   Have you ever been to England?
   How many times have you been?
3. Number of hours of study at home per week.
   How often do you study English every week?
   How many hours do you study English every week?
4. Frequency of use of English for
   a reading. *How often do you read English?*
   b speaking. *How often do you speak English?*
   c writing. *How often do you write English?*
   d listening. *How often do you listen to English?*
5. Plans for using or improving English.
   a Visits to English-speaking countries.
      Are you going to England this summer?
   b Further study of English.
      Will you study English in the future?
   c Use of English in a job.
      Will you get a job in which you use English?

- When they have written their questions, in which there will be some variation, they can ask each other the questions in the group and compare their experience of and plans for, their English
- If you wish, you can follow up the activity by having a class discussion and write the results up on the board.

WB 33.3
Key

1. I often *go* to France with my family. We like it there.
2. She *is studying* in her room right now.
3. They *have been living/have lived* in Manchester for the last two years.
4. Next month we *are going to visit/are visiting* our uncle in Canada.
5. I think it *is going to rain/will rain* tomorrow.
6. She *was crossing* the road when the accident happened.
7. He *stayed* at home last week because he was ill.
8. I*'m studying/'m going to study* political science at university next year.
9. They *are staying* at home this evening because they want to watch the tennis on TV.
10. She *used to play* tennis but she doesn't any longer. She plays volleyball now.

WB 33.4
Key

INFINITIVE	PAST	PAST PARTICIPLE
be	*was/were*	been
buy	bought	*bought*
come	*came*	*come*
cost	*cost*	cost
drink	drank	*drunk*
go	*went*	gone
leave	*left*	*left*
make	*made*	*made*
meet	mct	*met*
see	*saw*	*seen*
sell	*sold*	sold
take	*took*	*taken*
think	*thought*	thought
understand	*understood*	*understood*
write	wrote	*written*

Moondown: Episode 7

Skills Focus: Reading and Listening

This is the final episode of the serial. The second part is a listening exercise which makes it impossible for your students to read ahead and find out the ending of the story.

1 If you feel that students may be tempted to look àt the text while they are doing the pre-reading discussion exercise, write the questions on the board with books shut.

● Discuss the questions with the whole class, in pairs or in groups. There will not be a lot of discussion as most students are optimists and will predict that the answer to the second question is *Yes*! Before they read you may discuss the pictures as a way of predicting the content of the episode.

● Students read the episode quickly and get the general meaning. They compare their answers to the discussion questions with what actually happens.

UNIT 34 *page 113*

2 Students find the words in the vocabulary exercise in the text, underline them, discuss the meanings of the words in pairs and try to write translations. They then form new pairs and compare their translations.

● Discuss the meanings of the words with the whole class and check the answers.

3 Tell students to read the text again now that they have overcome the main vocabulary difficulties. They can then do the exercise and put the key facts from the story in order.

Key

3 Brooke and Eastwood locked Cathy in a room in the basement.
6 Pete told Linda about his phone conversation with Cathy.
5 Cathy phoned Pete.
4 Cathy climbed through a ventilation shaft into the next room.
1 Eastwood met Cathy at the pub.
8 Pete and Linda explained to a policeman what had happened.
7 Pete and Linda went to the police station.
2 Eastwood took Cathy to Moondown.

Supplementary Exercise 50 *(SB page 125)*
Students reread previous episodes of *Moondown* and look at their answers to the various listening exercises, and write a summary of the story using the guidelines given. This is quite a difficult exercise and is best set for homework.

 See Student's Book for tapescript 112.

4 Students discuss what they think will happen at the end of the episode and the story.

● Encourage students to discuss in pairs, in groups or as a whole class. Write their answers on the board.

● Play the cassette of the news item while students listen and check their answers.

Supplementary Exercise 51 *(SB page 125)*
Key
1 True   2 False   3 True   4 False   5 False   6 True   7 True
8 True

PRESENTER Tapescript 113. Unit 34. Listen.

NEWSCASTER It's ten thirty and here is the news read by Tim Britten. Police investigating the death of a lorry driver and a telephonist employed by Moondown nuclear power station have arrested the director of the power station Mr Graham Brooke and his brother in law, the editor of the *Westfield Gazette*, Mr Clive Eastwood. Police also freed a journalist working for the *Westfield Gazette*, Cathy Edwards, who was being held prisoner in the administrative buildings of Moondown. According to Ms Edwards and her colleague, photographer Peter Chisman, Brooke had authorised the illegal dumping of nuclear waste in the sea at Star Point near Westfield-on-Sea. Edwards and Chisman started investigating when they received information about the dumping from the telephonist, Rita Cummings, later killed in the accident with the lorry driver, Jack Sims. Police have established that the accident was caused by damage to the brakes of the car. Police suspect that Brooke and Eastwood interfered with the car and have charged the two men with the murder of the two Moondown employees. There is to be a full government enquiry into the dumping of the nuclear waste.

The Prime Minister spoke out in the House of Commons today about the rising cost of ...

Key
1 Isle.
2 Dual carriageway.
3 Traffic jam.
4 Magical.
5 Maintains.
6 Attractive.

WB 34.2
Key
1 Because it's so green.
2 No. The roads are free of traffic.
3 It keeps Northern Ireland very green.
4 They like outdoor activities.
5 In Victorian and Edwardian times.

UNIT 35 *page 114*

Skills Focus: Writing

Compositions

Before students start working on this activity, ask them to tell you what a paragraph is. (It is a section of writing containing connected ideas; or, one or more sentences about the same idea.) A new paragraph always begins on a new line and can be either indented or not.

- Refer the students back to the Writing Skills units on letter writing where there are notes on paragraphing (pages 18, 34 and 98).
- Tell them the example is about the advantages and disadvantages of camping holidays and contains four paragraphs. Ask if they can tell you what the content of the paragraphs is likely to be.
- Students now open their books and look at the description of the four paragraphs.
- Point out that it is important:
  a to introduce the topic clearly and concisely and this forms paragraph one
  b to give all the arguments in favour of the topic in one paragraph
  c to give all the arguments against the topic in another paragraph
  d to sum up. This will also take a paragraph.
- Students look at the words and phrases used when discussing the advantages or giving the arguments for. Ask them for any more. Do the same for the other paragraphs.

UNIT 35   *page 115*

1 Give them an opportunity here to talk about camping holidays. See how many have been camping. Ask those who enjoy going camping to give you their reasons. List these on the blackboard. Then ask those who do not enjoy camping to give their reasons and list them. Get them to express their views clearly and avoid vague statements.

● They read the composition in their books. Give them any help they may need with vocabulary. Ask them to give you any more reasons for enjoying and not enjoying camping and list them with their own original suggestions.

Key

presenting arguments
First of all, then, . . .
To begin with, . . .
People often say . . .
Also, . . .
They also say that . . .
On the other hand, however, . . .
Another thing is that . . .
Also, . . .

summing up
To sum up, then, . . .
In my opinion, . . .
In the end, however, . . .

2 Discuss the themes they are going to write about with the whole class. Get as many ideas as possible from them before they start. List these on the blackboard under + and − columns so that the students can concentrate on producing a logically constructed composition rather than scratching round for ideas.

● If there is another topic which they would prefer to write about, let them do so. The point of the exercise is that they should learn to order their ideas coherently and so it is obviously better if they write about something they are interested in or feel strongly about.

WB 35

In checking students' compositions, look for good paragraphing and the correct use of words and phrases to present and sum up arguments.

REVISION FOCUS
Units 31–35 _page 116_

1 Questionnaire: School career

- Go through the questionnaire with them and make sure that they understand that they can fill in the gaps as they wish. Students do this individually.
- Then they ask their questions to two other students and record their answers. They can finish the exercise by writing a paragraph about their two friends.

2 make, want, let

This exercise asks them to think of things various people make them do, want them to do, or let them do. Encourage them to be honest but original!

3 Wishing

- In this exercise students revise and reinforce their knowledge of how to express wishes.
- Ask them to look at the five categories. Elicit examples of the type of wish they can make for each category.
- Give the students sufficient time to write two wishes for each category.
- Divide the class into groups and allow students to discuss their wishes or discuss them with the whole class. If you go for the whole class option, ask them to correct each other if any mistakes should be made. If students work in groups, monitor their work and discuss their mistakes with them afterwards.

4 Vocabulary

Students' own answers.
Refer to the teacher's notes for Exercise 6, page 36.

5 Pronunciation

This exercise practises the pronunciation of the letter _r_. The letter _r_ is only pronounced before a vowel and is never pronounced at the end of a word or before a consonant.

- Tell students to look at the four model words and pronounce them. Ask them how many separate groups they fall into. Then tell them to classify the words in the list into the two groups. Play the cassette and give them time to check their answers.

▣114▣ _Key_

1 /r/ red   2 – pear
                   first
                   where

answer	2	street	1
foreign	1	car	2
there	2	real	1
fire	2	tree	1
tired	2	here	2
scream	1	learn	2
near	2	door	2

GRAMMAR FOCUS
Units 31–35 *page 117*

1 *Present perfect continuous with* for *and* since

a Elicit from students the structure and use of this tense.
b How long *have* you *been knitting/making* that sweater.
I*'ve been knitting/making* this sweater since the end of last month.
She *has been playing* tennis for an hour, so she's very tired.
c The present perfect emphasises a completed action.
The present perfect continuous emphasises an activity which began in the past and is still continuing.
The present perfect continuous is preferred when either may be used.

2 *Verb + object + infinitive*

a Students should remember that *want* takes the *to*-infinitive.
b I let her borrow my bike.
I want you *to* go to the supermarket.
She makes her daughter stay at home in the evenings.
c In many European languages, one would say: 'I want *that* you …'
Sentences with *make* and *let* take the infinitive without *to*.

3 *'I wish …'*

a Draw students' attention to the tense (past) following *wish*.
b I wish I *was* more intelligent.
I wish I *didn't have* so many spots.
c The past tense.
that, inserted after *wish*, does not change the meaning.

APPENDIX

UNIT 6 *page 22*

PRESENTER Tapescript 13. Unit 6. Listen.
SINAN Oh no, it's my sister's birthday today! I haven't got her a present.
KADER Mmm . . . what are you going to buy her?
SINAN I don't know . . . Got any ideas?
KADER Why not buy her a record?
SINAN Yes . . . good idea! I haven't got any money though. Where's the bank in Saffron Walden?
KADER Sorry, I don't know. Oh, look there's Judy. Ask her!
SINAN Excuse me, Judy, where's the bank in Saffron Walden?
JUDY Which one?
SINAN Er . . . Barclays.
JUDY Well . . . you turn right outside the school, go straight to the bottom of South Road past the County Junior School. Cross over Audley Road, go to the bottom of Fairycroft and you'll see the Chinese restaurant, it's called the Mandarin. Turn left and take the first right. There's an off-licence on the corner. Go past Boots the chemist and you'll see Barclays Bank on the right in Market Square.
SINAN God, that sounds complicated! Can you say it all again, please?
JUDY Oh, Sinan! It's not really complicated . . . you just go down South Road and keep going until you get to the Chinese restaurant. Turn left, then first right and it's in the square. Look here . . . look at this map. See . . . it's the fourth left then the first right.
SINAN Sorry, Judy . . . I think I understand now. Oh, it's late. I've got to go. Thanks, Judy!

SINAN Right, that's the money. Now, where's the record shop? Excuse me, is there a record shop near here?
MAN Yes, there's one down there. Chew and Osborne's . . . it's called.
SINAN Where is it?
MAN Look, you go across the square . . . that's King Street. It's about 50 metres on your right, opposite the bicycle shop.
SINAN Opposite the bicycle shop. Thank you . . . Mmm. There's the bicycle shop . . . and here's the record shop.

WOMAN Can I help you, sir?
SINAN Yes, I'd like Eric Clapton's Greatest Hits, please.
WOMAN Cassette, record or CD?
SINAN CD, please.
WOMAN Here you are. That's £10, please.
SINAN Thanks . . . Erm . . . excuse me, where's the post office?
WOMAN You go right when you get out of the shop, go down King Street and it's opposite you, on the other side of the High Street.
SINAN Thanks very much . . . Here it is – 'Post Office' . . . Oh no it's shut . . . after all that!

UNIT 8 *page 29*

PRESENTER Tapescript 21. Unit 8. Listen.
JUDY Hello Nick. How was your holiday?
NICK Oh, terrific. I just had a fantastic trip.
JUDY Where have you been?
NICK Trans-Siberian train, Moscow to Peking. Wonderful. It was very, very long journey but it was terrific. To go through Russia and China . . . just breathtaking, the scenery and the . . . to meet these people just so different from what you see here. Terrific. Have you been to Russia, Jane?
JANE No, but I've been to China. Ah, it was brilliant. We went on a tour . . . and, we, well, we started off in Beijing, and we saw the Great Wall.
NICK Mmm.
JANE Ah, it was fantastic. You can't . . . you know, you can't describe it unless you go there. And the Forbidden City was . . . oh it's . . . you have to go. But it's freezing. It's very very very cold.
JUDY I'm sure.
JANE Er . . . er Paul, where where where did you go?
PAUL I went to Greece. Yeah, I went with a, with a good friend of mine.
JANE Where did you go?
PAUL Well, first of all we travel travelled to Athens . . . er . . . which is . . . the the capital and then you er you can take boats out to the islands, which is what we did. We took a hydrofoil out to an island called Spetses, and er a a great way to see the islands is is to travel round . . .
NICK It's that rock, isn't it, in the middle of the Med.
PAUL That's right.
NICK Really nothing on it . . .
PAUL It's a lovely island. It's not so nice it's nowadays but er . . . it's lovely. And er . . . we travelled around on mopeds on the island . . .
JUDY Oh they're dangerous, aren't they?
PAUL . . . cos it's a great way to see . . . They are very dangerous because you don't wear helmets out there.
JUDY Were you okay on on your moped?
PAUL Well, I fell off.
JUDY Oh, dear.
PAUL You know, it was bound to happen.
JUDY Badly?
PAUL Yes. I had er . . .
NICK I bet you left all your skin on the road, didn't you?
PAUL Yes. Almost. And erm . . . I had a broken collar bone and I, I had to spend three weeks in hospital so . . . that part of it wasn't much fun but I did have a great time. Have you been to Greece, er, Judy?
JUDY Oh, no no, no I haven't. I think I prefer cooler countries, but erm I've just come back from Sweden. Yeah, er I was there for six months in Upsala, and I was actually working I was an au pair . . . so it was great, you know, I was living with a family out there and I, I wasn't just a tourist.
JANE Do you speak Swedish?
JUDY Oh, I picked up a little bit, yes, yeah.
PAUL Upsala. Great. Lovely name.

UNIT 21 *page 71*

66

PRESENTER Tapescript 66. Unit 21. Listen.

A Hello er good afternoon er ...

B Hello.

A I bought this er this computer here ...

B Yes, yes.

A ... from you last week and I'm afraid it's not working properly.

B Ah ... well these things happen. What seems to be the problem?

A We ... Well ... do you think you could take a look at the disk drive as I'm afraid erm it sometimes makes a clicking noise and er well it just doesn't work properly.

B I see, well erm. Are you sure you're putting the disk in far enough? Erm, sometimes when people er use the disk they don't quite ...

A Well I think I am putting it in correctly, I mean, I've been working with computers for a long time but ...

B I see, I understand.

A ... look as well as that er the roller on the printer doesn't go round, so that it keeps er well it keeps printing on the same line.

B Ah well er ... er you could have possibly not assembled the printer correctly, some, that, sometimes, that is a problem or or maybe you're not using the right sort of paper, sometimes people use too much ...

A Well, I am using the right sort of paper. Look, I'm not very happy about keeping it.

B I see, I understand.

A Er could you change it or or give me a, a refund?

B I'm afraid it's company policy not to change anything or give refunds. I'm afraid there's very little we can do.

A Would you mind fetching the manager?

B Certainly, certainly, I can fetch the manager. Yes.

A Right. Thank you very much.

B All right.

C Good morning sir. How can I help you?

D All good morning. Er yes I, I bought this clock here just before Christmas, a present for my mother and er it's broken, it won't go.

C Ah well. Let's have a look at it, shall we? Oh, dear, yes, it is in a bit of a state.

D Yeah it is but er it's, it's, it's much too expensive er not to work properly so erm do you think you could er change it for me?

C Well, did you buy it in this condition, sir?

D Oh yes, yes, er ...

C Well I find that rather hard to believe, we wouldn't have sold it in this condition.

D Yeah, well it must have been like that before er, er, you know, before I bought it, because I would have noticed, I'm sure.

C Er well, it appears to me it's ... looks like it's been dropped from, quite a height.

D Well, I er I ... well I, I can't say about that but I, I, I ... would you mind if I had a refund?

C Well, I don't really think I can, I can do that for you sir, because it's it's been damaged outside of the shop and er ...

D Well, could you, could you get the manager?

C Well, I'm afraid the manager will probably say exactly what I'm saying to you now sir. There's nothing we can actually do because er ... the clock is, is damaged and er ...

D Oh.

E Hello madam. May I help you?

F Er yes, please. Erm now I wonder if you wouldn't mind taking back this sweater. It's far too small for me.

E Ah, er, do you have a receipt?

F Er no, I'm sorry I don't, it was a present from my grandmother. It doesn't actually fit and the colour doesn't suit me at all, so ...

E Ah, well erm, madam, we don't usually give erm a refund without a receipt, you see.

F Well I, I don't have the receipt you understand, it was the, the, it was a present, but ...

E Yes I realise that.

F Yes well, I, what I'd like you to do is either give me a refund or perhaps you could erm give me a replacement ...?

E Well ...

F ... another sweater, a little bit larger ...

E Yes.

F ... and erm another colour.

E Well that's, that's erm, that's fine. If you'd like to have a look around ...

F Oh thank you.

E ... and erm find, find whatever you like and then bring it back and er, we'll replace it.

F Oh thank you.

E OK. Thank you.

UNIT 22   *page 75*

69

PRESENTER	Tapescript 69. Unit 22. Listen.
PAUL	David, erm you're active in the field of environmental education, erm. Perhaps you'd like to tell us erm something about acid rain. First of all, what is acid rain, exactly?
DAVID	Well, Paul, rain is acid quite naturally because as rain passes through the air it picks up carbon dioxide to produce a very weak acid, but in industrial countries that acidity is increased by oxides of sulphur and oxides of nitrogen, that are released by burning fossil fuels for example, and that causes the rain to become more acid, and that's where the problem lies.
PAUL	Fossil fuels, you mean er coal and . . .
DAVID	Coal and oil, yes.
PAUL	Erm . . . I see . . . and what's the single most important cause of acid rain?
DAVID	Well, there are two main causes, er, on the one hand we have coal- and oil-fired power stations, which generate a fair amount of oxides of sulphur particularly, then also we have vehicle fumes, which are particularly rich in oxides of nitrogen, and that produces weak nitric acid in the rainfall.
PAUL	Mm. Tell me, what are the effects of acid rain in Great Britain?
DAVID	There are two main causes of concern: one is to do with the effects on rivers and lakes, and the other is perhaps more to do with the effects on vegetation. Taking rivers and lakes and streams first of all, increased acidity can have very harmful effects on animal life in fresh water, for example fish can be completely killed in rivers.
PAUL	Mmm.
DAVID	The other area that we need to be aware of, is the effect on vegetation, and there is very widespread recognition of the damage that has been caused to forests in Europe, erm. There are many causes, perhaps, of damage to trees, some of which may be due to disease, some of which may be due to acid rain, and environmental groups have been very ready to lay the blame on acid rain, whereas in some instances damage to forests may be caused by disease or other factors.
PAUL	I see. Erm . . . so this is quite a serious problem. But what is the government doing about it?
DAVID	Well, in Britain the government is doing very little at present. They are thinking about the possibility of cleaning up the emissions from coal-fired and oil-fired power stations. Technically it would be possible to reduce the sulphur oxide emission from power stations, but it would be expensive, and if the authorities who produce power in Britain were to adopt these methods, then the cost would probably be passed on to the consumer. I think we're a long way behind other EEC countries and also North America in producing legislation to clean up the exhaust fumes from cars.
PAUL	I see . . . And what else needs to be done urgently about this erm problem?
DAVID	I think the most important thing is to recognise the international nature of the problem because the movement of air from one country to another obviously doesn't recognise international boundaries, so any leglislation that's brought in needs to be done internationally and one country producing its own legislation in itself will not solve the problem.
PAUL	I see. Right, well, thank you very much. That's been very interesting talking to you.
DAVID	Thank you, Paul.

UNIT 23   *page 79*

76

PRESENTER	Tapescript 76. Unit 23. Listen.
A	OK, right, let's see how quickly we can do this.
B	You read out the answers.
A	OK, right: if you go to Quebec, you will hear people speak . . .
B	French.
A	French, easy. Right, if you go to Rio de Janeiro in December, the weather will be . . . hot.
B	It's got to be, 'hot'.
C	Yeah, put 'hot'.
A	OK, we'll put 'hot', right.
B	Hot, yeah, it's south of the Equator.
A	Right. If you go to the U.S.A., you will have to put your watch back . . .
B	Well, it depends where you live in the U.S.A.
C	Yeah, it depends. It could be five hours, it could be eight hours if it was Los Angeles.
B	Five . . . Eight hours, eight hours, eight hours on the west coast, isn't it?
A	Well anyway. Anyway, moving on, moving right along here. If you want to climb Mount Fuji, you will have to go to . . .
B	Japan! Easy!
A	Japan. If you want to see the Taj Mahal, you will have to visit . . .
A,B,C	India!
A	This is too easy. If you want to see the tallest building in the world, you'll have to go to . . .
B	The States, it must be the States.
D	Chicago?
C	Is it the Sears Building?
B	Is it the Sears? Yes, in . . . Chicago.
A	And that's in Chicago, right, OK, well that's what we'll put down then. Where are we? Right yes tallest building . . . Right, if you want to visit the Forbidden City, you will have to go to . . .
B,C	China.
A	Peking that was. If you want to go for a trip on the River Thames, you will have to visit . . .
D	Oh, God . . . London!
C,D	London!
A	London. Yes. Right, if you stay in Bangor, you will hear people speak . . .
D	Welsh.
A	I suppose you will, ah. Ha. Right, if you go to . . ., you will see the Golden Gate Bridge.
B	San Francisco.
A	Oh! San Francisco, right.
D	Is it?
B	Yeah, yeah.
A	Yeah, yeah. Right. Mmm. Yeah. Bristol? No, it is San Francisco. Right, if you visit Australia at Christmas, the weather will be . . .
C	Hot.
B	Hot.
A	Hot. Yes. All right, if you want to see Saint Mark's Square, you will have to visit . . .
B	Venice.
D	Venice.
B	Is it?
A	Yes.
D	Mmm.
A	Yes. Right. If you go to . . .
B	I thought Saint Mark's Square was somewhere like Russia, or . . .
D	No, no, no.
A	No, that's Peter's.
B	Oh.
D	It's Venice, it's Venice, a friend of mine went last year.
A	All right, if you go to . . ., you will be able to visit the Parco . . . 'Gardi', 'Gwardi', 'Gaudi'.

B How do you spell it? How do you spell it?
A G–A–U–D–I.
D 'Gaudi', isn't it?
A I've got no idea.
B Oh, wait a minute, that, that's in Barcelona, isn't it?
A Is it?
B Barcelona, yes, I don't know, I think I've seen it in a travel brochure or something.
A Well, I'll take your word for it. Right. OK. Barcelona. Mmm. Right. If you go to Jersey, you will hear people speak…
B French.
A Yes, I suppose so. And English.
D French? French.
B Well, French really, it's native.
A Mainly French.
D Is it? Is it? It is.
A Well anyway, we'll put French. Right. If you want to climb Mount Snowdon, you will have to go to…
D Wales.
A Mmm. I suppose so. And er that's, seven out of twenty. Not bad.
B Not bad…

UNIT 26 *page 87*

PRESENTER Tapescript 83. Unit 26. Listen.
MAN Are you going to the reunion this year or not?
WOMAN Oh, I don't think so, I didn't go to the last one.
MAN Oh… Oh… Look you should. You'd see all your old friends. At the last reunion, in 1985, I saw Jack Beecham. Now do you remember him?
WOMAN Oh, yeah. What's happened to him?
MAN He… He'd left school early… and or… well now, I think he had to, he'd worked in a supermarket and he'd got fed up with that and had been to Australia. He worked on a farm, something I'd love to do, he was hoping to farm in Australia, sheep farming.
WOMAN Really?
MAN Mmm.
WOMAN And what about his girl-friend, Anne something?
MAN Anne Smith.
WOMAN Yes, yes, yes.
MAN That's right. Erm, what did she do? Had done well at school, as everybody expected, yeah, had been to university. And I think had qualified at a, as a doctor. Was trying to get a job as a doctor in Ethiopia… Mmm… Mmm…
WOMAN Really? Well, that's pretty good, isn't it? Erm, who else was there?
MAN Er, there's Tim Brown. I remember him, he, he'd stayed on at school.
WOMAN Yes.
MAN Then, er, when he left, he'd been to university.
WOMAN That's right.
MAN And, erm, what did he do? I think he'd studied something boring like economics, er, had got a job in a bank, and was hoping to become you know, yawn, yawn, a bank manager.
WOMAN Oh, dear! Oh, dear. And what happened to, erm Tim Margam?
MAN Er, no. Tom Margam.
WOMAN Oh, Tom, yes.
MAN That's right, yeah. He'd left school early, and had gone and worked er, in his father's factory, I think.
WOMAN Oh… Oh dear.
MAN He wasn't enjoying it, and was hoping to open his own factory. Make loads of money and all that.
WOMAN Oh, I hope he manages. And, er, what about Margaret Green?
MAN She hadn't liked school. But had got loads of A levels. You know, you remember, she made you sick. She was the sort who'd just sit there, do nothing all the time, and then come out with a string of…
WOMAN That's right.
MAN Remember. Well, she'd been to the US for a year; had taken jobs while travelling around, you know. And had come back and I think had done a, yeah, a nursing course. Had just qualified in 1985 when we saw her.
WOMAN Oh!… Really? Do you know what she's doing now?
MAN Er, no. No, I don't. Er, nothing, I think.
WOMAN Oh, dear. That's a pity. And um, what about Ian Blythe? What happened to him?
MAN Oh, yeah? Ian Blythe, yeah, he'd gone to university. He'd been an excellent athlete.
WOMAN Mmm… That's right, yes. I remember.
MAN Yeah… Mmm… Had left university to train, that's right…
WOMAN Yeah…
MAN And er, what did he do after that? He'd er, he'd won loads of competitions, that's right, he was hoping to be selected for the British Olympic team.
WOMAN Oh! That's wonderful. Really? Do, do you know what happened?
MAN Er, no. No I don't actually.
WOMAN Oh, well maybe, maybe I will go to this year's reunion then and catch up on everything.
MAN Why? Why? Do you want to see Ian Blythe?
WOMAN Yeah… Well, I, I'd like to see everybody actually, I mean it'd be nice to see Ian Blythe, but er, you know… Margaret…
MAN Don't you want to go with me, then?
WOMAN Yes, that'd be lovely…

UNIT 26 *page 89*

PRESENTER	Tapescript 87. Unit 26. Listen.
MAN	Er, I, I think that er one of the basic problems with the differences between young, you young people today and us er people who really saw the war erm and all that happened after it, is that you er you don't get that sense of community anymore that er you used to get.
WOMAN	No, no. I think we have a lot more freedom, though, than you had.
MAN	Yeah, but freedom to do what, you, you . . .
WOMAN	Well, I mean there's more opportunity erm to travel. There's certainly a, a better standard of living. Wouldn't you say so?
MAN	There is a better material standard of living, yes, but, er, what . . . There was, there's more to life than that. I mean, I'm not, I don't want to be political at all, but er . . . in the old days, er, ha, you really could, people would help each other. People in the same street would help each other, er . . . and if, if, if it was, if someone was in trouble, then, then, you know . . .
WOMAN	You'd offer a hand . . .
MAN	. . . the friends would would rally round and help.
WOMAN	And, and you don't feel that's the same today?
MAN	I don't, no. Er . . .
WOMAN	What, I mean among amongst the young?
MAN	Amongst the young, the young of today, they er . . . you, you expect the state to do it. And that's a big . . .
WOMAN	Well, I think there's so much pressure on us, you know, to get on with our own lives and and and to make it, to achieve . . . I suppose that we . . .
MAN	Yeah . . . Yeah . . . There is a lot of pressure, there is a lot of pressure in life that that that there probably wasn't then. I, I think that er you know that those people that that survived the the war er after you'd done that, then well there wasn't much more to fear, really. I think you just thought: 'Well, I'm alive and I'm very pleased to be that way.' And, erm and you . . .
WOMAN	Do you, do you feel you don't fit in today?
MAN	I, I just feel as though I'm standing outside it and I'm watching it go by and I don't really get, I don't really get involved in it, I mean . . .
WOMAN	I mean, you've retired, yeah?
MAN	Oh blimey! Yeah, I retired a long time ago, dear! Erm . . .
WOMAN	And, what do you do? I mean, do you just . . .
MAN	I watch life go by a lot. And, I think I'm glad, I'm glad actually . . . I, I lived, you know then when I did really, you know.
WOMAN	You are glad?
MAN	I am glad, yeah. I don't . . . I mean, I watch you rushing around like bushey-tailed whatsits and I think well, blimey . . . Oh, I can see that, I can see that the cars and and, and and all the material goods being very, very fine, but, ah . . . they lose their shine after a while, don't they?

UNIT 28 *page 95*

PRESENTER	Tapescript 94. Unit 28. Listen.
A	OK, everybody ready for this?
B	Yup. Yup.
C	Mmm.
A	Right. Question 1. If you witnessed a road accident, would you (a) leave the victim where he or she was and try to keep him or her warm? (b) move him or her off the road? or (c) stay and talk to him or her?
B	Can I answer this one?
C	Yes. Go ahead.
B	Right, I would erm, move him or her, but, (b) off the road. I think I would.
C	Well, I, I'd do the first one. Keep him warm, Not move him.
B	Ah! Well.
A	OK. Well, (a) is the best answer, but if the victim, or you, are in danger on the road, then the victim must be moved; so possibly (b). And (c) is also a sensible thing to do. All right. Question 2. If your brother cut himself badly, would you (a) put a tight bandage on to stop the bleeding? (b) give him a warm drink? or (c) press on the cut until the bleeding stopped, then cover the wound?
B	Ah. I think, probably. I, I would imagine you should do (c). Wouldn't you? Would you?
C	Press on the cut until the bleeding stopped?
B	I know. I couldn't do it, I think (a).
C	(a) yeah (a).
A	Sorry, (c)'s the correct answer.
C	(c) Oh! You press on the cut until the bleeding's stopped?
B	Oh, I suppose, because, if you wrap the bandage round, it might be . . .
A	Also, if the cut is on an arm or leg, you should raise the limb. OK. Right, then. Question 3. If your nose was bleeding, would you (a) sit down and blow your nose? (b) lie down and pinch your nose firmly? or (c) sit down and pinch your nose firmly?
B	I, I would do (c). I think that's what you should do.
C	Sit down . . . But shouldn't you put your head back? And, that would be lying . . .
B	Yes, but, by sitting down, you could well . . . Ah . . .
C	You . . . They don't say . . . Well, I'll go for (b). Lie down and pinch your nose firmly.
A	All right.
B	(c).
A	(c) is the correct answer to that one. You should also lean forward a bit, so that you don't drink or breathe in any blood.
C	I never touch the stuff.
A	All right. Question 4. If your mother fainted, would you (a) sit her on a chair and put her head between her knees? (b) lie her down and lift her legs up? or (c) lie her down with her head to one side?
B	Erm, I think, I think, actually, you would lie her down and you'd put her head to one side. Is that right?
C	I don't know. I'll say (a), I'll go for (a) anyway.
A	Well, you're both wrong on that one. The answer to that one is (b) but the most important thing is to check to she see she is breathing. Raising her legs will send the blood to the brain.
C	Then she hasn't fainted, she's just died.
A	That's right. All right. Question 5. If your father received an electric shock, would you (a) move him from the electric current? (b) switch off the electricity and then move him? or (c) put on a pair of rubber boots and then move him?
B	Well, I'm going to go for (b). I, I would do that . . .
C	Yes, and rubber boots just aren't me. So, well, I'd, (b), yeah.
B	Switch off the electricity.
C	Switch off the electricity.
A	Very well done, both of you. (b) is the correct answer. However,

it is always wise to move the electrical appliance rather than the person. OK. Final question, number 6. If there was a small fire in your kitchen, would you (a) throw a blanket over it? (b) pour water on it? or (c) get away quickly and close the door?

B Has to be (a). That's what I would do. I'd throw a blanket over it.

C But it would have to be a wet blanket.

B No . . . would it?

C No? . . . Well, it would help. I think, because it might be a very inflammable blanket and just make it worse. I don't know. Well, I'll go for (a).

A All right, well, bit of a complicated answer. The answer to this one depends on the type of fire. If it is an oil fire, like a pan, place a damp cloth or a blanket over it, so (a), but with a wet blanket. If it is an electrically-caused fire, do not put any water near the fire, so (a). If the fire is at all serious, then (c), and of course warn the neighbours and call the fire brigade.

C Yes. But it did say a small fire, so er . . .

A That's right, it did indeed.

UNIT 32   *page 107*

69

PRESENTER Tapescript 104. Unit 32. Listen. Part 1.

JUDY Denis, I wonder if you could erm, if you could tell me a few things about Ireland.

DENIS Yes, there are two parts of Ireland. There's the Republic of Ireland and Northern Ireland, which is part of the United Kingdom.

JUDY Mmm . . . and er the North has got six counties, I believe.

DENIS Yes, the six counties in Northern Ireland are called Fermanagh, Tyrone, Armagh, County Down, erm Antrim, and Derry.

JUDY Right. And what about the principal cities in Ireland . . .

DENIS The principal cities . . .

JUDY In Northern Ireland, I'm sorry . . .

DENIS . . . in Northern Ireland is Belfast, which is in County Antrim, the second city is Derry, which is in County Derry, erm Armagh is in Armagh, erm Enniskillen, which is in Fermanagh, and Omagh, which is in County Tyrone.

PRESENTER Part 2.

JUDY Denis, I wonder if you could talk about some of the main events in Irish history?

DENIS Yes, erm, we really have to go back to the 17th century, I think, to get some of the main events. In 1608 there was the Battle of the Boyne.

JUDY The Battle of the Boyne, now who, who was fighting that?

DENIS Er . . . James the Second of England and William of Orange.

JUDY And he came from Holland.

DENIS That's right.

JUDY And why were they fighting in Ireland?

DENIS They were fighting really about who should be King of England, but James the Second had fled, had left England.

JUDY I see. Erm, and that was won by William of Orange.

DENIS Yes, by William of Orange, who represented mostly erm Protestants and had mostly Protestant troops, er James the Second had mostly Catholic troops.

JUDY I see. Erm, and after that what was the main event, the next main event?

DENIS Yes, then you had what's known as the Plantation of Ulster, erm in the seventeenth century.

JUDY Uhuh, and that involved . . .

DENIS That involved erm the er government erm . . . What happened was that the people who lived in Ulster, mostly Catholics, erm were expelled from their land and replaced by people who were brought from England and particularly from Scotland. And those people had a, many of them had a different religion, most of them were Protestants. We native Irish tend to be Catholics.

JUDY I see. Erm, and still Ireland had a separate parliament at that time.

DENIS Er, yes. Of sorts. Erm, in the eighteenth century it it did have a parliament, but in 1801, we had the Act of Union, which erm effectively joined Ireland to erm Britain.

JUDY Uhuh . . . and can you talk about what the Irish did to try and get their country back?

DENIS Well, there were many, there've been many rebellions in Irish history, in the er, for example in 1848 you had an important uprising called the Feinian Rising.

JUDY Mmm . . .

DENIS Erm . . . then in 1916 we had the Easter Rising . . .

JUDY Yes . . . yes, I've heard of that, erm and that led to something in 1922, didn't it?

DENIS Yes, from 1916 to, 19 er after the Easter Rising from 1916 to 1921 you had the War of Independence, which was a war which the Irish waged against the British forces in Ireland.

JUDY I see, erm . . . and the country was divided, when did Northern Ireland come into being?

DENIS Really in 1922, after erm, after the War of Independence the British signed a treaty with Ireland . . . both sides agreed to a partition of the country.

JUDY Yes...

DENIS And then er the six counties of Northern Ireland since then have been part of the United Kingdom.

JUDY Right... Erm, and since then, erm, there's been a lot of trouble in the North of Ireland, a lot of unhappiness...

DENIS Yes, many people have opposed this, indeed there was a civil war between 1921 and 1922, er many Irish people opposed the partitioning of the country.

JUDY Uhuh...

DENIS Erm... and this is true.

JUDY Uhuh... and what about the troubles in the North of Ireland since then?

DENIS Well, in 1968, you had the Civil Rights marches. This was really, these were mostly Catholic people who really were looking for basic rights like better housing, better jobs or equal employment opportunities, that kind of thing.

JUDY I see, I see. Erm... and more recently what's the present situation, erm?

DENIS Well, in 1969, the British government sent in the army to Northern Ireland, the British Army, because of erm there were widespread rioting and houses being burned and er, a lot of er problems between Catholics and Protestants. And... since then the British Army has been in Northern Ireland.

JUDY Uhuh... Uhuh.

DENIS And there's been continual unrest since then.

JUDY Mmm... uhuh. And the situation at the moment...

DENIS At the moment the situation... there is still unrest in Northern Ireland there is still violence, erm, er there is still erm, a lot of it happening, but the er Dublin government, the government in Dublin have tried to er sign a treaty with the British government, that, to agree that the British government should consult them about the running of affairs in Northern Ireland and this is called the Anglo-Irish Agreement, which was signed three years ago, in 1985.

PRESENTER Part 3.

JUDY Erm, could I ask you a few things about yourself, now Denis?

DENIS Yes.

JUDY Whereabouts do you come from, which part of Ireland?

DENIS I come from the Republic of Ireland, I come from a city called Cork, which is the second city in Ireland.

JUDY Right, erm, and how long have you been away from Ireland?

DENIS Erm... about seven years, now.

JUDY Uhuh... Why did you leave?

DENIS Erm... I left Ireland well, I suppose because I lived with my parents and er, I was looking for er a bit something a bit more adventurous. Erm, also the, there's a very bad situation with employment in Ireland, particulary in the Republic of Ireland, and it's very difficult for young people to find jobs in Ireland.

JUDY Yes... yes. And what are your feelings about what's happening in the North at the moment, about the British presence, the British Army?

DENIS Yes, erm, I feel that the British presence is really contributing to the problem and I feel that erm, in, in the long run I feel that the British should really withdraw from Northern Ireland. You know.

JUDY Mmm... Can you talk about the names of the er principal groups who are involved in fighting?

DENIS The groups involved in the fighting... Yes... erm... there are political groups, for example there is Sinn Fein, which means erm, Ourselves Alone, it's two Gaelic words which means Ourselves Alone.

JUDY Gaelic is the language...

DENIS Gaelic is the language of Ireland. Yes... erm... They represent the Catholics, if you like, erm. There's the Ulster Defence Association, which represents er the Protestant interests.

JUDY I see, I see. Erm, and what do you think's going to happen, er in the future?

DENIS Erm... it's hard to say what's going to happen in the future. Erm ... I can only say what I would like to see happening...

JUDY Yes...

DENIS Erm... I think I would like to see the British er withdrawing from Northern Ireland, and erm, but in a structured way. And ultimately I think I would like to see a unified Ireland, with guarantees for the rights of Protestants in the North. But I think as long as Ireland is partitioned there will be er trouble.

JUDY Uhuh... well, thank you very much, Denis, that was very interesting.

DENIS Right... thank you.